No
Apology

ALSO BY MITT ROMNEY

Turnaround:
Crisis, Leadership, and the Olympic Games

No Apology

BELIEVE IN

AMERICA

THE CASE FOR AMERICAN GREATNESS

Mitt Romney

ST. MARTIN'S GRIFFIN

NEW YORK

NO APOLOGY. Copyright 2010 by Mitt Romney. All rights reserved. Printed in the
United States of America. For information, address St. Martin's Press,
175 Fifth Avenue, New York, N.Y. 10010.

www.stmartins.com

Design by Kathryn Parise

The Library of Congress has catalogued the hardcover edition as follows:

Romney, Mitt.
No apology : the case for American greatness / Governor Mitt Romney. — 1st ed.
p.   cm.
Includes index.
ISBN 978-0-312-60980-1
1. United States—Politics and government—21st century.   2. United States—Economic
conditions—21st century.   3. United States—Social conditions—21st century.   I. Title.
JK275.R66 2010
320.60973—dc22
2009052940

ISBN 978-0-312-67173-0 (trade paperback)

10   9   8   7   6   5   4   3

To Allie, Joe, Thomas, Chloe, Nick, Mia,
Nate, Grace, Wyatt, Owen, Nash, Soleil, Parker, Miles, Jonathan,
and all of Ann's and my grandchildren yet unborn

We must be ready to dare all for our country.
For history does not long entrust the care of freedom to the weak or the timid.
—DWIGHT D. EISENHOWER

Contents

Believe in America

S am Walton was all around me.

 It was a few days before the Christmas of 2008. I was standing in the checkout line at a Walmart, waiting to purchase the Tonka trucks and Buzz Lightyear action figures I had selected for my grandsons. As I looked around the store, I had to chuckle to myself. Somehow, that Walmart reminded me of Sam Walton himself. I'd never met the founder of Walmart, but I had read and heard a good deal about him over the years. People who knew him noted his attention to detail, his near maniacal passion about low prices, his plan to carry every single item a customer might want, and that he tended to be a spur-of-the-moment—almost impetuous—manager. I saw these very traits reflected in his store: low prices blazed from signage, everything from tires to toothpaste were available for purchase, and, well, the store was not as organized and buttoned-down as those of other retailers I know. At Target, for example, aisles are wider and shelves are stocked and segregated like the Swiss might have done it. At Walmart, things look a bit more helter-skelter, more jumbled and maybe a little more entertaining. Yes, Walmart today is a reflection of its founder.

 I've found the same to be true of a number of other businesses I know. Microsoft reflects the character and manner of Bill Gates, whereas Apple manifests that of Steve Jobs.

When I was a boy, I met Walt Disney. He noticed the boy among the grown-ups, bent down, and asked me if I was having a good time at the wonderland he had built. Disney loved to entertain kids, to kindle their imagination, to spark their dreams. At the same time, he was a no-nonsense businessman—I'd seen that in the way he negotiated with my dad over a sponsorship for his television show. Today, the Disney theme parks are in some ways the living legacy of Walt Disney himself: they amuse and delight children—and they make a great deal of money. Walt Disney's ways continue to shape his company many years after he is gone.

From time to time, I fly on JetBlue. Its founder, David Neeleman, is the consummate family man, with nine children. And "cheerful" hardly begins to describe him—every time I see him, he is smiling or laughing, even as he scurries from task to task. His airline has more than a bit of David in it: Flight attendants act like family—even with an occasional tantrum as with Steven Slater who swore, grabbed two beers, and chuted to the ground. The airline is friendly and executes admirably fast turnarounds from one flight to the next. Virgin Atlantic is a different story; it's more edgy and irreverent, just like its founder, Richard Branson.

I've found that it's not just businesses that are shaped by their founders, it's true of institutions of all kinds—schools, universities, charities, churches, even religions.

And it is also true of nations. Nations are shaped by their founders, often for many generations and centuries after those founders are gone. *The culture and character of America reflects the nature and convictions of the men and women who founded it.*

I've often imagined what it must have been like for those very first people who left Europe to immigrate to America. They left behind home, family, security, and predictability in exchange for a life-threatening ocean passage, the possibility of hostile indigenous people, and uncertain shelter, food, and climate. In the late 1500s, colonies failed in Virginia—e.g., the 117-person Colony of Roanoke was mysteriously lost. But colonists were ultimately successful in Jamestown and Massachusetts. What manner of person willingly left everything behind in exchange for perils known and unknown?

Some who came here sought fortune. Others sought the right to practice their religion according to the dictates of their conscience. In almost every heart, it was a strain of liberty that drew them here—religious liberty, economic freedom, freedom to pioneer, or freedom from oppression. The thirst for freedom drove these American colonists. And it is very much a part of what we are as a people today—we love freedom.

The Founders who drafted and signed the Declaration of Independence and those who framed and ratified the Constitution made choices as difficult and perilous as those made by the first colonists. They could have chosen the predictable and secure path, following the commands of the Crown. Instead, they risked their lives, their liberty, and their sacred honor.

Later, after the American Revolutionary War had been won, the Founders could have established their own form of monarchy: a powerful, autocratic government that would tell people what to make, where to sell it, and how much they would earn. But again, they choose freedom. Just as the people would be free to choose their president and their representatives, they would be free to choose their occupation, their religion, and their life's course—to pursue happiness according to their own dreams.

That first choice of freedom by the Founders—incomplete and only perfected by Lincoln four score years later—has made all the difference. People from all over the world who prized freedom—the innovators, the pioneers, the dreamers—came to America. And so they continue today. This is who we are as a people—it is in our DNA. It is this love of liberty and the accompanying spirit of invention, creativity, derring-do, and pioneering that have propelled America to become the most powerful nation in the history of the world.

But today, Washington is smothering the American spirit. Freedom, opportunity, innovation, pioneering—the very foundations of our national strength—are under assault. Those who took the helm of the ship of state in the elections of 2006 and 2008 believe that a wise and powerful federal government can better guide our economy and our lives than can the people themselves. They fundamentally reject the choice made by the Founders. America is a nation *for* the people because it is *of and by* the people; under Washington's new management, government has become the agent of guidance.

Those who believe in such an ascendant role for government would restructure the fundamental character of the nation. They simply do not believe in America as it was shaped by the Founders. They do not believe that the principles and values that made America a great nation still apply. They don't really believe in free enterprise, free markets, and free trade. They favor government management over consumer choice. They delight when they can replace personal responsibility with government requirements. Like the monarch the revolutionaries rejected, they have no limit on the amount they would tax the people and their enterprises, believing that government can better spend the resources of business and the product of labor. They brush aside the founding principle of federalism, asserting instead that there are no bounds to federal power. Rather than admire the heritage of peaceful assembly and petition, they ridicule and demean assemblies of ordinary citizens who protest their grand health-care plans, takeovers, and bailouts. In these and many other ways, they do not believe in America as it has been understood since its beginning.

Perhaps that is why they have been so quick to apologize for America. I had to nod my head when I read what Sylvester Stallone had said: "I think America apologizes too much." He's right, of course. No nation has done more to promote world peace and liberty than America. No nation has done more to combat disease and to salve humanity when it is suffering than America. No nation has done more to promulgate economic principles that have lifted billions of people from poverty than America. Yes, we have made mistakes and of course we can do even more for others, but this nation has from the beginning done what it believed was right and good, and the ultimate sacrifice made for liberty by so many hundreds of thousands of our sons and daughters is unrivaled in human history. Do not apologize for America.

Other great nations believe in America. In *Time* magazine on September 13, 2010, Tony Blair wrote:

. . . America is great for a reason. It is looked up to, despite all the criticism, for a reason. There is a nobility in the American character that has been developed over the centuries, derived in part, no doubt, from the frontier spirit, from the waves of immigration that form the stock, from the circumstances of independence, from the Civil War, from the myriad of historical facts and coincidences. But it is there. That nobility isn't about being nicer, better or more successful than anyone else. It is a feeling about the country. It is a devotion to the American ideal that at a certain point transcends class, race, religion or upbringing. That ideal is about values: freedom, the rule of law, democracy. It is also about the way you achieve: on merit, by your own efforts and hard work. But it is most of all that in striving for and protecting that ideal, you as an individual take second place to the interests of the nation as a whole. It is what makes the country determined to overcome its challenges. It is what makes its soldiers give their lives in sacrifice. It is what brings every variety of American, from the lowest to the highest, to their feet when "The Star-Spangled Banner" is played.

Tony Blair may understand America better than some of our politicians in Washington.

As the nation has encountered new threats and new challenges, Washington's 2006 and 2008 elected elite have tried to convince us that what has worked for America in the past is no longer applicable and effective. They are wrong. The Founders were right. The values and principles promulgated by them, earned by our heroes "proved in liberating strife," and confirmed by the prosperity and strength of the nation compel us to *believe in America*.

Believing in America Means Believing in Freedom

Lady Liberty's call to those "yearning to breathe free" has beckoned people from across the world. One of those millions was my mother's physician. Mom inherited sometimes debilitating allergies, including a severe reaction to anything containing calcium. She was frail to begin with, but without calcium, she was headed toward osteoporosis. Her doctor diagnosed her condition and devised an intravenously applied regimen that kept her bones strong—she suffered only one broken bone during her eighty-nine years. Mom called him a miracle worker.

Mom's doctor was a Jew, born in Russia. When he was just a young man, he and his fiancée hid in the coal bin of a ship that made it to America. I never learned his original family name because when he reached America he chose a new one: Freeman. In America, he said, he was a free man.

Like millions of others who have immigrated to this "sweet land of Liberty," Dr. Freeman sought to escape the oppression of government. There was no guarantee of fortune or comfort, only the assurance of freedom to choose the course of his life rather than have an oppressive government choose it for him.

Freedom does not require the complete absence of government—government plays a critical role in protecting our lives and liberties from those who would endeavor to take them from us. But freedom does demand restraint in government's intrusion into our life, freedom, and livelihood.

Among liberals in Washington, there are those who regularly endeavor to substitute government choice for personal choice. Fearing that we might make a wrong choice in the selection of our health insurance plan, for example, they would require every health insurance policy to contain the coverages that they would choose for us. These might include, for example, eyeglass coverage, in vitro fertilization coverage, or dental coverage. Rather than let the citizen choose which of these benefits he wants in his insurance policy, the choice is to be made for him by the government. Not only is the individual's preference frustrated, but the benefits package becomes subject to special interest lobbyists who influence—and donate—to government politicians.

Then presidential candidate Barack Obama revealed a great deal when he confessed his belief to "Joe the Plumber" that government should take the money of one citizen to "spread the wealth around" to others. This is not a matter of caring for those who cannot care for themselves—conservatives may well exceed liberals in their commitment to such genuine charity. His was an expression instead of a type of government oppression—taking from one citizen to give to another, selected by government. This lottery of benefits is the opposite of freedom.

The framers of the Constitution foresaw the necessity of restricting the reach of government and thus established boundaries of federal power. The need for such boundaries was also understood by those who ratified it.

Massachusetts farmer Jonathan Smith was elected to his state's ratification convention for the federal Constitution. "I am a plain man," Smith began in his speech to the convention, "and get my living from the plow. I am not used to speak in public, but I beg your leave to say a few words to my brother plow joggers in this house."

Smith explained that he had read the proposed federal Constitution, "over and over." Then, he continued: "I had been a member of the Convention to form our own state Constitution, and had learnt something of the checks and balances of power, and I found them all there. I did not go to any lawyer, to ask his opinion. We have no lawyer in our town, and we do well enough without. I formed my own opinion, and was pleased with this Constitution."

Like farmer Smith, Americans today can read the Constitution and observe the painstaking care exercised by its framers to protect the powers of the states and to preserve the freedoms of the citizens. But liberals in office and on the bench are increasingly creative in fashioning tortuous arguments to breach the Constitution's protective barriers. The wisdom of America's first president, however, should continue to guide: "Government is not reason; it is not eloquent; it is force. Like fire, it is a dangerous servant and a fearful master."

Believing in America Means Believing in Free Enterprise.

The economic crisis that began in 2008 led a number of people to question whether free enterprise really is superior to a government-managed economy. Liberals seized on the crisis to promote their long-held belief in a government-centric economy as well as their disdain for free enterprise. Politicians of both parties exploited the appetite for populism by singularly blaming greedy Wall Street capitalists for the collapse. Without question, free economies have been subject to the cycle of boom and bust, and when the latter occurs, many families feel the pain of unemployment, the loss of a nest egg, or the loss of a home. But the awful toll of the economic cycle is far from proof that a government-led economy is a better choice.

Communist and socialist economies suffer from cycles as well, and when they do, starvation and death have sometimes been the result. Chinese and Russian populations have historically experienced shocking devastation. Even in relatively good years, North Korean citizens are nearly starved so that the government and the military can be amply fed.

Nor should the 2008 economic decline be laid solely at the feet of Wall Street and the private sector. The government's interference in the housing market was a proximate factor in the collapse. And government officials, committees, regulators, and watchdogs had the necessary data and preventative tools that could have averted it, but they were either lulled into inaction by special interests or were asleep in their bureaucracies. Their incompetence and its collision with a severe economic cycle is no reason to write off free enterprise.

The evidence in favor of free enterprise, on the other hand, is overwhelming. Government-managed economies such as those of Cuba, North Korea, and Venezuela are basket cases. American free enterprise has led us to enjoy an average per-person income that is about one third greater than that of Western Europeans, where government has a heavier hand in the economy.

Perhaps there is no more stark comparison of free enterprise versus government enterprise than that of North and South Korea: same ethnicity, same geography, same national start date. I stood at the border between the two Koreas in 2007. To the south were factories, super highways, high-rise apartments, and skyscrapers. To the north, I could make out a city as well, but with satellites that can look behind that city's front face, we now know that it is no city at all: The North Koreans have set up a giant facade—like a Hollywood set—for us to see from the border.

At night, lights from the homes in South Korea fill the sky; to the north, it's dark, literally and figuratively.

A similar story is true of Cuba and, tragically, it is now true in oil-rich Venezuela. Hugo Chavez is destroying the economy of his resource-rich country even as he threatens his neighbor and our democratic ally, Colombia. Government-dominated economies inevitably malfunction. To deflect attention from their failures, they excite fear in phantom foreign threats, shut down the press, and celebrate their citizens' misery as a triumph of equality.

Most liberals in America are smart enough not to call openly for replacing free enterprise with socialism—the politics of that are still not good. So instead, when they are in power, they take action that is consistent with socialism but call it by a more palatable name. In the two years following their 2008 ascendancy to power, the actions that demonstrate their distrust in free enterprise are numerous:

- funds voted by Congress to save and secure the financial system were used instead for bailouts
- agreements to promote trade were stalled

- health care was put on the road to federal government takeover
- government became the venture capitalist of first resort to the "green energy sector"
- the rule of law was ignored in order to reward the auto workers union at General Motors
- scores of unelected and unaccountable boards, commissions, and regulators were installed in government bureaucracies
- and businesspeople and professionals of all kinds—from insurance executives to doctors to financial managers to pharmaceutical managers to attendees at trade shows and to bondholders—were demonized from the bully pulpit.

The administration's response to the downturn also evidenced the elevated esteem it holds for government over the private sector. The stimulus bailed out state governments and grew government employment, not private sector employment. Rather than enact incentives for private sector growth and investment, the administration burdened private sector employers with new regulations, new mandates, and higher taxes. Even as the president chose his cabinet members and senior staff, he selected people with virtually no private sector experience—government and academic experience is clearly what he values and prefers. A friend emailed me that he and his wife were thinking of moving to France: "If we're going to live in a socialist country, it might as well be one with really good food."

Over the past several years, I have spoken with thousands of people across the country. Without question, the economy has been their greatest concern. The many without work are worried about finding a job and those who have a job are worried about losing it. Some have lost their homes. Most are worried about a future of lower pay and higher costs of living. And for the first time in history, the majority of Americans believe their children's future will not be as prosperous as their own. President Obama calculated that these fears would be translated into willingness to embrace a government-led economy. He was wrong.

Everywhere I have traveled, people have told me that they want less government, not more. They believe in small business, in entrepreneurs, in consumer choice—they believe in free enterprise.

Many thousands of these people have joined Tea Parties and 9/12 groups. Many millions more don't rally or march but nod their head in agreement.

We need a U-turn from the policies of the past few years. We need more private sector growth and we need to pare down the government, dramatically.

Yes, there are a number of people who have become so dependent on government that they think only of how much it will give them. They are in the minority, and they will ultimately realize that government's ability to care for them is limited by the private sector's ability to grow the economy. As Margaret Thatcher famously quipped: "The problem with socialism is that you eventually run out of other people's money."

Liberals and Democrats have long characterized conservatives and the Republican Party as being "for the rich"—by which they also mean to imply "indifferent to the poor." Because liberals advocate for a bigger government that can provide larger benefits, they argue that they are the party for the common man. Their intentions may be good, but their reasoning is not. The best way to help the poor—as well as the middle class and indeed everybody—is by growing the economy and employment, and the compelling evidence demonstrates that free enterprise is the most successful system to do just that. Accordingly, we must look to measures that foster free enterprise and encourage businesses to grow, invest, and hire—not because we have a special liking for rich people (in fact, Democrats raise a lot more money from the very wealthy than do Republicans), but because we know that is the best way to provide for the prosperity of all Americans.

Not every government-directed economy is an entire failure, of course. While the more socialistic approach of some Western European nations has not produced average incomes as high, nor average unemployment levels as low as those of the United States, many Europeans are satisfied with their countries' mix of benefits and taxes. These are societies shaped by much different historical experience than ours. Thus, what may work adequately in Europe—where government has played a key economic role for hundreds of years—would be unlikely to be even moderately successful here. Our economic culture was shaped by our founding parents long ago and is embedded in our educational systems, incentives, institutions, and expectations. And perhaps most tellingly, European nations are increasingly emulating American-style free enterprise principles—because they work so comparatively well. It turns out that a growing slice of Europe has seen the future and concluded that their old ways won't work for much longer.

I wrote this book in the months immediately after President Obama's inauguration. Since then, my worst fears about the president have come true. Rather than focusing his energy and political capital on solving the economic crisis, he exploited it to promote his extreme liberal agenda. The economy will, in time, right itself—every recession inevitably comes to an end. He and Vice President Biden will undoubtedly take credit, but they in fact have made the downturn deeper and longer. The credit instead will belong to the innovative and entrepreneurial spirit of the American people. It is free enterprise, not enterprising government, that grows the economy.

The Founders' American experiment was not solely a political one. It was also an economic experiment: Could a free people pursuing their individual dreams create a vibrant and robust economy? The answer was and remains a resounding yes—they created a political and economic system that is unrivaled in history and in the modern world. Like democracy based on federalism and the separation of powers, free enterprise is an integral part of our national character.

Beliveing in America Means Believing in Opportunity

We've heard it since we were kids: "Every American should have the opportunity to realize the American dream." Many assume that the "American dream" means owning your own home. Others might substitute instead a certain degree of financial success or a comfortable lifestyle.

The phrase was originally coined by historian James Truslow Adams in his 1931 book, *Epic of America*. His description then was very different from the popular definitions of today. "The American dream," Adams writes, "has not been a dream of material plenty." Rather, he continues, the American dream is a "social order in which each man and each woman shall be able to attain to the fullest stature of which they are innately capable, and be recognized by others for what they are, regardless of the fortuitous circumstances of birth or position."

This dream was envisioned by the Founders of the nation and its basis was provided in the Declaration and Constitution they crafted. The tragedy of the founding was that some of the most eloquent of these early patriots failed to extend the American dream to African slaves and Native Americans, even as some of their colleagues urged upon them the necessity of doing so. The principles of freedom enshrined in our founding documents eventually triumphed, though at a price of hundreds of thousands of lives in the Civil War and decades more of the pain and suffering of segregation.

The American dream inspired every person in the world who sought opportunity—every pioneer, every inventor, every person who wished to breach the circumstance of their birth looked to America, "the shining city on a hill." And they came here by the millions, seeking freedom and seeking opportunity.

The pioneering, innovating, and entrepreneurial spirit that infuses the national economy is what drove ours past that of the great nations of the world. It is a large part of what enables us to outperform the world today— and what makes possible our enviable standard of living. There are nations that are larger and older, but America is still the most creative and inventive. If that were to cease to be the case, America's economy would fall behind, and so would the wages and incomes of our citizens.

Government can promote opportunity or it can crush it. Laws and regulations that govern business practices are essential for markets to function efficiently, fostering economic opportunity. Conversely, if they become outmoded and needlessly burdensome, they can cripple commerce and industry, reducing the opportunity for citizens. Similarly, safety, environmental, and labor regulations can facilitate economic activity. But if they are crafted with bias and political agendas, they can stifle small business and entrepreneurs.

Nowhere are the stakes higher than with education. Government's original decision to mandate and provide for the education of the public has both enhanced opportunity for our citizens and strengthened the nation. But its resistance to school choice, accountability, and standards has irreparably harmed generations of young people, for which the nation will suffer.

To a point, even taxes can foster opportunity. Taxes are necessary to provide essential security and infrastructure. But when taxes take from the individual the very resources she or he needs to pursue their ambitions, and further, when these monies are used to finance government inefficiency, waste, and excess, they drain opportunity from the people of the nation.

Unfortunately, the political elite who took power in the election of 2008 have so grossly expanded the scale and intrusiveness of government that they are choking opportunity. They have raised taxes on small business and on investment even though small business and investment are two of the most significant means by which Americans pursue opportunity. They have laid a crushing array of regulations and mandates on financial service enterprises, not only depressing opportunity in that sector but also making it more difficult for businesses and entrepreneurs in other sectors to obtain necessary financing. They have enacted two thousand pages of health-care legislation, and while the politicians did not take the time to read it before they voted, small businesses will have no choice but to read and comply with every one of its new mandates and provisions. They have slanted the labor-management environment so steeply toward their large-donor labor unions that small businesspersons correctly wonder whether they can afford to hire new workers. And they have successfully raised taxes across the board that will be paid by the American people, and they earnestly endeavor to do so again.

These actions—and many more like them—have sharply reduced opportunity in America. And they are smothering the American dream.

They are also deepening and lengthening the economic downturn that began in 2008. Businesspeople are so unsure of the future under this regime and so uncertain of the impact these new laws and regulations will ultimately have on their enterprises that they have been reluctant to invest in new hires, new purchases, and new investments.

As a result, a record amount of capital is sitting idle on business balance sheets. If we do not move quickly, a large measure of that capital will leave our shores for other, friendlier regions of the world. The investment of that capital must be earned, and it is earned by stable policies that promote growth and that do not penalize success. Had the administration implemented policies that fostered opportunity and encouraged entrepreneurialism such as lower taxes on employment, immediate write-off for capital expenditures, and greater incentives for innovation, much of the capital that today is waiting on the sidelines would have been employed, growing the economy and jobs.

Reducing opportunity is one of the worst things a government can do in a period of economic distress. It is the entrepreneur, the risk taker, the small businessperson who lifts the economy out of recession. Stifle opportunity and you stifle the economy.

In this country, there is a nearly direct tradeoff between growing government and growing opportunity: grow government and opportunity shrinks. Intrusive excessive government is the *enemy* of the American dream. Believing in opportunity means believing in a smaller government, restricted by its constitutional boundaries.

Believing in America Means Providing for a Better Future

I know how John Adams felt. Being away from Abigail was a hardship— John and she were each other's best friend, confidant, and advisor. They loved one another. But in order to build a free and prosperous nation for those who followed them, John Adams spent long years away from home, separated from the love of his life. And all alone, she raised children and managed their farm in sometimes cold, rocky Massachusetts. His son John Quincy Adams addressed his posterity: "You will never know how much it has cost my generation to preserve your freedom."

Adams's sacrifice is mirrored in the sacrifice today of the men and women of our military who serve multiple deployments for years at a time in faraway places, often where danger is continually present.

There is no separation as devastating as a permanent one. No sacrifice compares with that of the hundreds of thousands of soldiers who have given their lives. Many more thousands walk in the shadow of death, preserving liberty and life for us and for those who will follow. It has been part of the American experience since our beginning—soldier-heroes pay an incalculable price to purchase a better future for all Americans.

There is a desire in the hearts of Americans to create a future for our children that is better than the life we have known. This hope isn't hard to find. Over the years, I have ridden in quite a few cabs. Often, there is a picture of the cabbie's family pinned to the visor or taped to the dashboard. In conversation, many tell me of long hours and late nights away from home, and they point with pride to the accomplishments of their children for whom they have worked so hard. In ways as different as our many occupations, we make sacrifices for our children, and for the generations of descendants that will follow.

This is another reason why there is such discomfort with Washington— the very real sense that our government is destroying the hope of a better future for our children. It has spent too much and borrowed too much, leaving huge debts in its wake. It has made generous promises to citizens in my generation, but rather than put aside the funds that are needed to pay for these promises, it intends to pass those obligations on to our children. It has won the votes and endorsements of government unions by creating unfunded pensions that far exceed those in the private sector. All totaled, the debts and unfunded liabilities that government has imposed on future Americans amount to nearly 75 trillion dollars—five times the size of the entire economy.

Just as destructive to America's future is the liberals' accommodation of the demands of the teachers unions. Our public schools are among the lowest performing in the developed world. One half of the youth that live in our cities do not graduate from high school. Yet the reforms that are almost universally acknowledged as essential to improve our schools are vigorously opposed by the most powerful of the Democratic Party's special interests. That party has traded our children's future for votes and campaign contributions.

I began this introduction by recalling a Christmas shopping trip for my grandchildren and with a recollection of business founders. My father's generation left Ann and me and our children an America of unlimited possibility, a land where individuals—Sam Walton, Walt Disney, Bill Gates, and Steve Jobs—starting with little other than an idea could build vast engines of employment, prosperity, and wealth, not only for themselves but for millions of their countrymen. Each generation hopes to leave a better future to those who follow. It isn't so much the presents under the tree that matter, but our children's freedom to achieve their potential in a land of opportunity. Americans have become increasingly aware of the government's failure to protect so basic and intrinsic an American value.

The Choice for America

Arthur Brooks of the American Enterprise Institute observes in his book *The Battle* that there are two very different views regarding the source of human happiness. One is that happiness is the result of individual achievement and "earned success in life"—a view like that expressed by James Truslow Adams in his definition of the American Dream. Accordingly, the extent of individual happiness is dependent on the degree to which a society will encourage and protect the freedom and opportunity necessary to individual achievement.

The alternative view is that happiness is the result of financial equality. This view holds that to increase human happiness, government has to remove the rewards of success from those who have created it in order to give it to those who have not.

The Founders believed the former—hence their recognition that happiness would be a matter of "pursuit" rather than entitlement. America would be a land of equal opportunity, not of equal outcomes. That, too, is the view held by the great majority of Americans today. The liberal elite, on the other hand, say a few kind words about freedom but move to enact laws and regulations that promote the second view. In their hearts, they are statists. They believe in government's ability to enforce happiness through "economic justice," as they define it.

The disparate perspectives regarding happiness lead to very different convictions regarding the mission of government. Liberals favor higher taxes and redistribution of income. Unfunded liabilities and borrowing are means to their ends: Ultimately, they know that these promises will necessitate massive tax increases.

They are also highly suspicious of free enterprise because it offers unparalleled opportunity for individual success and reward, and thus enables inequality. They endeavor to grow the scale and reach of government, to empower it to guide the economy and make better choices for the people. While few of the liberal elite would ever openly advocate for the diminution of freedom and opportunity, that is the inevitable product of their policies.

These fellow Americans fail to appreciate the power of the choice that was made by the Founders—theirs was the creed of the pioneer, the innovator, the striver who expects no guarantee of success, but asks only to live and work in freedom. This liberating, inventing, creating, independent current now runs from coast to coast. It has produced not only the renown, like Bill Gates. It also accounts for men and women of every occupation who strive, who explore, who go beyond what is expected of them to reach for breakthrough and accomplishment. It is the engineer who tries to get one more mile from a gallon of gasoline, the chef who creates new recipes, the salesperson who goes off-script to make the sale, the educator who works with a child after school, the programmer who can't rest until she has eliminated every excess line of code, the entrepreneur who starts his own business, the kid who launches a commercial site on the Internet, the person who edits an entry on Wikipedia, the farmer who plants a new variety—the list is endless. The pursuit of achievement, of discovery, of greatness, is what has made America the powerhouse of the world. And it has made us happy as well. Smother this spirit with the weight of government and America ceases to be America. That is what Washington is doing, and we must not allow it. Washington believes in itself. The American people believe in America.

1

The Pursuit of the Difficult

I hate to weed. I've hated it ever since my father put me to work weeding the garden at our home in Bloomfield Hills, Michigan. It was planted with zinnias, snapdragons, and petunias, none of which seemed to grow as heartily as the weeds. After what seemed like hours of work, I never could see much progress, and I'd complain to my dad. "Mitt," he would reply, "the pursuit of the difficult makes men strong." It seems now like an awfully grandiose response for such a pedestrian task. I complained about the weeding often enough that I heard his homily regularly. I'm sure that's why it sticks with me to this day.

My father knew what it meant to pursue the difficult. He was born in Mexico, where his Mormon grandparents had moved to escape religious persecution. At five years old, Dad and his family were finally living pretty well. They had a nice home and a small farm, and Dad even had his own pony, called Monty. But in 1911, Mexican revolutionaries threatened the expatriate community, so Dad's parents bundled up their five kids, got on a train, and headed back to the United States. Their furniture, their china, his mother's sewing machine—everything they had worked hard to accumulate—had to be left behind. Once back in the States, they struggled. They moved time and again, and work was always hard to find. My grandfather established a construction business, but he went bankrupt more than once. Dad used to regale us kids with claims that one year in Idaho his family lived on nothing but potatoes—for breakfast, lunch, and dinner.

Dad began to contribute to the family's income early on. During his high-school years he worked long hours as a lath-and-plaster man, finishing the interior walls of new houses. He never was able to put together enough time and money to graduate from college.

Three decades later, by the time I was weeding that Bloomfield Hills garden, my father had become a successful businessman. I know he worried that because my brother, sisters, and I had grown up in a prosperous family, we wouldn't understand the lessons of hard work. That's why he put us to work shoveling snow, raking leaves, mowing the lawn, planting the garden, and of course, weeding—always reminding us that work would make us strong.

About this time, Dad faced a difficult pursuit of his own. In 1955, only five months after he became vice president of the newly created American Motors Corporation (AMC), the company's president, George Mason, died and the board of directors selected my father to succeed him. With news of Mason's death and mounting losses, the company's stock collapsed from $14.50 a share to $5.25. The banks didn't have much more confidence in the company at that moment than its stockholders did. I remember hearing my parents discussing with certainty that if the banks pulled out, the company wouldn't survive.

My parents had sold our home; we were living in a rented house while they prepared to build a new one. With my mother's blessing, Dad took the money they had put aside from the sale of their house and used it to buy AMC stock. He even used the savings he had given me for Christmases and birthdays to buy stock. He believed in himself, and he believed in hard work and what it could achieve.

Dad spent long days at the office, and when he was home, the work continued. He met with the company's bankers, shareholders, and employees, explaining his vision for the company's future: dropping the venerable Nash and Hudson brands and focusing instead on the Rambler compact car. He would eventually close the company's Michigan plant to consolidate production in Wisconsin. He agonized over that decision, but concluded in the end that "to save a patient this sick, surgery is necessary."

In 1959, AMC's stock was selling for more than $95 a share. Dad made the covers of *Time* and *Newsweek*. He and Mom built their dream home, and we kids, now even more prosperous, were given still more chores.

What Dad accomplished at American Motors prepared him for the challenges that would follow. He served as leader of Michigan's Constitutional Convention, as three-term governor of Michigan, as secretary of housing and urban development in the Nixon administration, and as founder of the National Center for Voluntary Action. And I have to admit that the weeding and chores probably didn't hurt me, either—something I understood well by the time I took the reins of the 2002 Winter Olympics.

Over the years, I've come to believe that the value of "pursuing the difficult" applies much more broadly than only to individuals. When I met Tom Stemberg in 1985, he had come up with an idea for a new business, one he believed would revolutionize the retail industry, and in particular the business of selling and distributing office supplies. Tom's vision was to create the world's first big-box office products chain, one with hundreds of stores, tens of thousands of employees, and billions in revenues. Most people I spoke with thought it would never work, believing that businesspeople wouldn't leave their workplace to shop for office supplies, no matter how great the savings. But they were wrong, and today Staples is what Tom dreamed it would be.

Reaching Tom's goal was difficult. At first the manufacturers of supplies didn't want to sell to him because his idea threatened their traditional distributors. Stores were hard to locate in real-estate-cramped New England where he began. A warehouse with multistore capacity had to be built and financed, even though at first there were only a handful of stores to serve. Copycat competitors sprung up everywhere; at one point, we counted more than a dozen. And money was tight. In the end, because Tom and his team achieved success in the face of so many challenges, Staples and its management team became very strong indeed, and now lead the industry.

Today the United States faces daunting challenges, and I am similarly convinced that if we confront them and overcome them, we will remain a strong and leading nation. Just like individuals, companies, and human enterprises of every kind, nations that are undaunted by the challenges they face become stronger. Those that shrink from difficult tasks become weaker.

Consider our nation's history and the strength we developed as we faced our greatest threats. George Washington's army was in no way comparable to the British forces he faced: his troops were untrained, unpaid, and out-manned. The British navy boasted 270 vessels, while the Continental navy had only twenty-seven. In April 1775, British warships laid siege on Boston Harbor and successfully took command of the city. But under General Washington's direction, during the following winter, Colonel Henry Knox and his men hauled fifty-nine heavy cannons on ox-drawn sleds three hun-dred miles from Fort Ticonderoga, New York, where they recently had been captured. Finally positioned on Dorchester Heights, a hill overlooking the harbor, the cannons threatened the annihilation of the British armada. The British navy withdrew and Boston remained in American hands. The victory was emblematic of the entire conflict: American ingenuity, derring-do, and faith in providence helped win our improbable independence from the world's superpower.

I was born after the Second World War and can only imagine the confu-sion, incredulity, and fear that must have overwhelmed the nation when the Japanese attacked Pearl Harbor. Yet once again, the United States rose to the occasion. In Detroit, where my father was already working in the auto industry, factories that once made cars were quickly turned into assembly lines for military aircraft. Cars and planes aren't very similar, but in only a year, Detroit was making bombers and fighters. We ultimately lost 418,000 men and women in World War II. The financial costs were great as well. But we also became far stronger. Women joined the workforce—a trend that would wane, then wax again to our economic advantage. Our factories became the most productive in the world. Returning GIs went to college in what was the greatest expansion of higher education in history. And Amer-icans recognized that while we constitute much of a continent, we are not an island—alone and isolated from the rest of the world.

I was in grade school when Sputnik was launched by the Soviet Union in 1957. Mr. Garlick, my high-school science teacher, hung a model of the small satellite from the ceiling of our classroom as a reminder, he said, that America had fallen behind the Russians in science and technology. The future was up to us, he'd say, sounding a lot like my dad.

Three months after the Soviets' first successful satellite launch, we at-tempted to enter space. Our Vanguard rocket failed to develop enough power to lift off the launch pad. It toppled over on its side and exploded into flames. Over the next three years, NASA tried and failed to launch eleven more satellites. Despite our dismal record, President John F. Kennedy called for us to put a man on the moon. Young people all over the country grew enthusiastic about studying physics, engineering, and the space sciences. We became a more technically proficient people. And we became the first nation on earth to put a man on the moon.

Facing Our Challenges Head-on

I can remember only one time during my life when most Americans presumed that we didn't really have any great challenges. It was during the period that largely coincided with the Bill Clinton presidency. George H. W. Bush and Ronald Reagan had pushed the Soviet Union to the wall and won. The Berlin Wall had come down, the Soviet Union had dissolved, and here at home, there was talk of a "new economy" that sent the bulls running on Wall Street. Columnist Charles Krauthammer has called it our "holiday from history." We believed that peace and prosperity were here to stay— without threat, without sacrifice.

In some ways, we advanced as a nation during these years. The Internet boomed, and the pockets of millions of average Americans grew deeper. But did these years of ease make us a stronger, more free or secure nation? We shrunk our military by 400,000 troops during the 1990s, retired over one hundred ships from the navy, and decreased the size of our air force by more than a quarter. More ominously, we gutted our human intelligence capabilities, and never took any real steps to infiltrate the violent jihadist groups like al Qaeda that had declared war on America. At home, births to teenage mothers rose to their highest levels in decades, teenage drug use climbed, and pornography became the Internet's biggest business. Our dependence on foreign oil rose from 42 percent of our total consumption in 1990 to 58 percent today.

I don't wish challenges and hard times on this nation, even though I believe they have made us the country and people we are today. But neither do I fear them. My sole concern is that Americans will choose not to act, not to face our challenges head-on, not to overcome them.

In the first decade of the twenty-first century, our economy has suffered its worst crisis since the Great Depression. We have amassed an unprecedented amount of debt and liabilities, and added to that, the Obama administration plans trillion-dollar deficits every year. Russian belligerence is on the rise. China holds over $750 billion of U.S. obligations. Iran and North Korea threaten the world with unbridled nuclear ambition. Violent jihadists like those who attacked us on 9/11 plot our destruction. The consequence of failure to act in response to these perils is unthinkable.

America will remain the leading nation in the world only if we overcome our challenges. We will be strong, free, prosperous, and safe. But if we do not face them, I suspect the United States will become the France of the twenty-first century—still a great country, but no longer the world's leading nation. What's chilling to consider is that if America is *not* the superpower, others will take our place. What nation or nations would rise, and what would be the consequences for our safety, freedom, and prosperity?

The world is a safer place when America is strong. Ronald Reagan remarked that "of the four wars in my lifetime, none came about because the U.S. was too strong." America's strength destroyed Hitler's fascism. It stopped the North Koreans and Chinese at the 38th parallel and allowed South Koreans to claim their freedom and reach prosperity. American strength kicked Saddam Hussein out of Kuwait, and later pulled him out of his spider hole.

There are a number of thoughtful people around the world who don't welcome America's strength. In 2007, several reputable polls asked European citizens which nation they perceived as the greatest threat to international peace. Their answer was the United States. I was incredulous when I first read this, and presumed the respondents must have had the Iraq War on their minds when they answered. Surely they hadn't considered what Russia would do in Eastern Europe if America was weak; what China would do in Taiwan; what the Taliban would do in Afghanistan; what Fidel Castro, Hugo Chávez, Kim Jong-il, or Mahmoud Ahmadinejad would have in mind for their neighbors. The very existence of American power helps to hold tyrants in check and reduces the risk of precipitous war.

Does America make mistakes? Absolutely. We never fully understood the enormously complex political, economic, and military issues we faced in

Vietnam, and we were wrong in our assessment of Iraq's weapons of mass destruction programs. But in every case throughout modern history in which America has exercised military power, we have acted with good intention—not to colonize, not to subjugate, never to oppress.

During my tenure as governor of Massachusetts, I had the opportunity to join a small group of people in meeting Shimon Peres, Israel's former prime minister and current president. In casual conversation, someone asked him what he thought about the ongoing conflict in Iraq. Given his American audience, I expected him to respond diplomatically but with a degree of criticism. But what he said caught me very much by surprise.

"First, I must put something in context," he began. "America is unique in the history of the world. In the history of the world, whenever there has been war, the nation that is victorious has taken land from the nation that has been defeated—land has always been the basis of wealth on our planet. Only one nation in history, and this during the last century, was willing to lay down hundreds of thousands of lives and take no land in its victory—no land from Germany, no land from Japan. America. America is unique in the history of the world for its willingness to sacrifice so many lives of its precious sons and daughters for liberty, not solely for itself but also for its friends."

Everyone in the room was silent for a moment, and no one pressed him further on his opinion about Iraq. I was deeply moved. And I was reminded of former secretary of state Colin Powell's observation that the only land America took after World War II was what was needed to bury our dead.

Some argue that the world would be safer if America's strength were balanced by another superpower, or perhaps by two or three. And others believe that we should simply accept the notion that our power is limited. British Marxist historian Eric Hobsbawm in his book, *On Empire,* asserts, "It is also troubling that there is no historical precedent for the global superiority that the American government has been trying to establish and it is quite clear to any good historian and to all rational observers of the world scene that this project will almost certainly fail."

I take a different view. The United States is unique. American strength does not threaten world peace. American strength helps preserve world peace.

It is true that the emergence of other great powers is not entirely up to us—several other nations are building economic and military power and we will not stop them from doing so. But we *can* determine, entirely on our own, that we will not fall behind them. And the only way I know to stay even is to aim unabashedly at staying ahead.

Four Strategies to Achieve World Power

A number of nations and groups are intent on replacing America as the world's political, economic, and military leader. In fact, there are four major strategies that are currently being pursued to achieve world leadership. I use the word "strategy" advisedly. For nearly ten years, I worked as a management "strategy consultant," first with the Boston Consulting Group (BCG) and then with Bain & Company. BCG's founder, Bruce Henderson, observed that in order to become a success, a business doesn't just have to do well, it also has to do better than its competitors. Being number one isn't just about bragging rights. Often it means the difference between prospering and merely hanging on. Accordingly, a few hundred of us were hired to help companies develop strategies that would allow them to outperform their competition.

Most people can recognize strategy as it plays out in the world of business. Facing Microsoft's PCs, Apple's strategy was to appeal to a different segment of customers and win among those buyers. It focused on educational and creative users rather than typical business users. It targeted the young and the hip. From creating products like the iPod, the iPhone, and the Mac, to their design, advertising, and image, Apple tailored every dimension of its offering to its brand of customer. The strategy appears to be working: in 2008, it generated $9 billion in cash.

Countries, like businesses, need strategies to survive and prosper. A nation's strategy should be designed to propel it beyond its competitors and to increase the security and prosperity of its citizens. While there are as many national strategies as there are countries on the global map, there are four specific approaches to geopolitics that have been embraced by various major players on the world stage. We must recognize and understand these if we are to be fully aware of the challenges ahead.

Each of the four approaches is being pursued to achieve world leadership status—superpower status—and perhaps dominion of the global order.

Their adherents are fully convinced that they have chosen the strategy that will propel them beyond their geopolitical rivals.

The first of these strategies is represented by the United States. Ours is a strategy based on two fundamental principles: economic freedom and political freedom. The two are not only harmonious, they actually empower one another. Individual freedom stimulates a spirit of entrepreneurship that in turn leads to innovation and enterprise. And the freedom to walk away from a job and create one's own enterprise breeds a sense of independence in a culture that prizes individual freedoms. It's a strategy that has led America to become the most powerful nation in the history of the earth. It has also created powerhouses like Japan, Germany, and South Korea, nations that had been devastated by war. And it has helped the twenty-seven-member nations of the European Union create economies whose combined gross domestic product (GDP) is 30 percent of the world's total, roughly the same as the combined GDP of the United States and Canada.

While the nations that pursue this "American" strategy are collectively referred to as the West, not all of them do so in a uniform manner. Sweden and several other European nations, for example, place a far heavier governmental hand on free enterprise and on economic freedom than does the United States. Citizens are highly taxed to provide not only a very substantial social safety net but also a relatively comfortable lifestyle. Businesses and employment are highly regulated. Despite the differences among Western nations, economic freedom and political freedom are at the core.

A second strategy is pursued by China. As with the West, theirs is based on free enterprise. Unlike the West, it is also based on authoritarian rule. On its face, the strategy is contradictory: the oppression of an authoritarian regime that severely limits individual freedoms must surely stifle entrepreneurship and enterprise. The conflict is so apparent that many Western observers have predicted that as China's economy and trade develop, the country will trend toward democracy and freedom.

China's leaders see things quite differently. They believe that the economic vitality produced by free enterprise, combined with the stability and vision of wise leaders, unaffected by popular whim, creates the winning strategy. Autocracies of the twentieth century were often wedded to socialism; its abject economic failure doomed these governments. But China is banking that having embraced a form of free enterprise, their autocratic future will be very different than their past failures.

I had expected to find the Chinese people frustrated with Communist rule and to encounter many who were agitating for the basic freedoms enjoyed in the West. But when I met with Chinese students at Tsinghua University in Beijing in 2006, they seemed much more interested in pursuing the lessons of American-style free enterprise than they were in promoting American-style freedom. The Chinese I met during the 2008 Beijing Olympic Games likewise had little apparent discontent with Communist rule. Perhaps they were on their best behavior when I spoke with them, out of fear of government reprisal. But there was another, more open expression of support for the government during the Games. The Opening Ceremonies were attended by over 90,000 people, the vast majority of whom were Chinese. When President Hu Jintao was introduced over the National Stadium's loudspeakers, the audience erupted in cheers. I did not hear a single "boo." From months on the presidential campaign trail, I've learned that boos stand out, even in the midst of a much larger number of people who are clapping and cheering. I remember popular Massachusetts politicians being drowned out at Boston's Fenway Park by a small minority of Bronx cheers. But there were no boos for Hu Jintao; instead, there were loud and exuberant cheers.

What has happened in China to the spirit of Tiananmen Square? It may simply be hidden for now, at least from public view. Or it may be that brutal repression and incarceration of dissidents has pushed the democracy movement far below the surface. Every year, there are literally thousands of protests in China, although these are typically directed at the corruption of local bureaucrats and politicians. Perhaps the combination of nationalistic pride and the elixir of newfound economic opportunity have, at least for a time, quieted the clamor for political freedom. In the long term, however, I am convinced that as the Chinese study abroad, trade with free nations, build enterprises, and become increasingly exposed to people and cultures from around the world, they will demand freedom and genuine democratic reforms. But what is uncertain is when that pursuit will reach a critical level, and whether the Communist Party will accede to popular demand. For now, and perhaps for a very long time to come, China's strategy is deeply grounded in authoritarian rule.

It's surprising to some that China's strategy is also based on free enterprise. Communism is, in fact, the opposite of free enterprise—at its core is state-owned industry and public land. But Chinese leaders watched carefully as the economies of the Soviet Union and its fellow travelers like North Korea and Cuba collapsed. In a head-to-head economic contest, carried out over half a century, Communism was the undisputed loser. Free enterprise won, hands down, and so the Chinese Communist Party adopted free enterprise. The Chinese are an enormously practical and intelligent people; their leaders saw that Communism could not feed China, much less make it prosperous. Free enterprise could do both, and the modern tools of repression have allowed the Chinese leadership elites to reap its benefits . . . for the time being.

Chinese free enterprise is not like that of the West, as least not yet. Major industries continue to be state-owned and -operated. And absent from the Chinese system is the rule of law and regulation that shapes free enterprise elsewhere. It has failed to prevent widespread practices that have tainted products from dog food to infant formula, and it quite clearly welcomes the rampant theft of intellectual property from Western businesses. It is free enterprise on steroids—anything goes. China brazenly sells sensitive technologies to Iran and buys oil from genocidal Sudan, and it vigorously defends these nations against international sanction.

And there is another way in which Chinese enterprise is distinguished from other economic systems around the world: it is *winning*. China is fast becoming the world's factory, successfully capturing the lion's share of world manufacturing for a growing list of products. The country is no longer content to make only toys and trinkets. It is manufacturing cars, aircraft, televisions, and computers. Foreign companies that have invested in China have certainly smiled as their sales and profits have grown, but their smiles aren't as wide as they once were, now that their Chinese "partners" are opening facilities of their own and appropriating foreign know-how and technology. All this has led to breathtaking growth for China's economy, now predicted to be larger than ours within the next twenty years.

The numerous Chinese leaders with whom I have met have always been very gracious. Typically, these formal meetings are held with a large number of observers. The two principals are seated next to each other, separated by flowers and interpreters, rather than sitting face-to-face and eye-to-eye. As a result, what is said tends to feel more like a speech for the gathered assembly than like a direct and personal exchange of views. It can be difficult to discern just what the Chinese are thinking and planning within the boundaries of their relatively closed society. Uniformly, I have been assured by the leaders with whom I've met that China has no global ambition. They remind me that China is still a very poor country in comparison with nations like ours. That may well be true, but I am certain that China intends to become a very powerful nation, and ultimately to become even stronger than the United States. If and when that happens, who knows what intentions China will harbor?

Russia is pursuing a third global strategy. Like China, it favors authoritarian rule, but Russia's economic strategy is primarily based on energy. By controlling people and energy, Russia aims to reassert itself as a global superpower.

To many of us, it is inconceivable that Russia could ever again compete for world leadership. Didn't the Soviet Union completely collapse? Wasn't its economy a basket case? Russian products were the laughingstock of free economies around the world. Even its military was in shambles because its feeble economy didn't permit it to maintain its armaments, its bases, or even a large part of its personnel. Hadn't Russia thrown in the towel?

Yes and no. There was indeed a time when Russia sought aid from the West, and when democracy was energetically, even heroically, pursued. Free enterprise was unleashed, despite concerns. Russia appeared poised to join the family of responsible nations, free nations. But that has changed under Russia's former president and current prime minister, Vladimir Putin.

Russia's rediscovered ambition for superpower status is fueled by its massive energy reserves. Russia has the world's largest reserves of natural gas and the second largest reserves of coal. It is second in the production of oil, following only Saudi Arabia. In all forms of energy, Russia already is the largest exporter in the world, actually outpacing Saudi Arabia. In 2008, Russia reached $300 billion in energy sales, a figure about two-thirds the size of the entire United States defense budget that year. Had Russia enjoyed comparable energy revenues during the Cold War, we might not have been able to so dominate the arms race that drove them to capitulate. We won the Cold War at the right time.

Russia's energy strategy has not crowded out the rest of its economy. Despite rampant corruption, a frightening level of organized crime, and the loss of investment predictability due to Putin's confiscations of private property, Russia has enjoyed the most rapid recent growth of any of the G-8 nations. Under Putin, the country's GDP has nearly doubled, averaging growth of approximately 7 percent per year. Adjusted for purchasing power parity, the Russian economy is now the world's seventh largest.

Beyond energy and commodities, Russia also relies on the strength of its science and technology sectors. I remember a conversation I had with Jim Sims, founder and CEO of a company called GEN3 Partners. His business concept was to provide research for American companies that had closed down their own research efforts. In effect, his company would become their various laboratories, enjoying the benefits of scale and the cross-fertilization of ideas. But as he went about hiring American scientists, he found they were in short supply. Ultimately, he found the research scientists he needed in Russia. There, he explained, the scientists were well educated, hardworking, and abundant. Russian enterprises take advantage of the same talent pool to achieve success in such fields as information technology, software, space technology, nuclear engineering, and military weaponry. Combined with its massive energy resources, Russia's technology sectors bolster its prospects to someday regain superpower status.

Russia's energy strategy explains a good part of what Vladimir Putin is doing internationally. Georgia has several thousand ethnic Russians, which provided a pretext for Russian aggression in the summer of 2008. But it was really Georgian geography with its energy pipelines that motivated Putin. The Ukrainians can't help but look at Russia the way Little Red Riding Hood looked at the wolf—Russia is hungry for a direct energy route to the Black Sea. It is not just energy reserves that Russia is counting on to propel its return to power; it is also monopoly power over the gas pipelines that provide energy to Europe and the West. When Putin shut gas off to Ukraine and Europe during the winter of 2009, *The New York Times* reported that it "sent an unmistakable message about the Continent's reliance on Russian supplies—and Mr. Putin's willingness to wield energy as a political weapon."

On the surface, Russia's support for Iran doesn't seem to make sense; after all, if Iran goes nuclear, its missiles will be a lot closer to Russia than they will be to the United States. But a nuclear Iran would become a Middle East superpower, and if Russia could influence Iran, it could have even more power over world energy supplies. The same holds true with Russia's burgeoning relationship with Venezuela.

Of course, Putin's moves have purpose beyond energy: anything that diminishes America pleases him, both because it weakens a competing power and because it gratifies his personal animus for the United States. Russian presence in Venezuela and Russia's resistance to severe sanctioning of North Korea and Iran as they have pursued their nuclear programs are a stick in the eye for the United States. So, too, is Russia's insistence that the world replace the dollar as the reserve currency. Putin also bitterly opposes any development that would strengthen the United States such as missile defense, particularly in Eastern Europe, and admission of the former Soviet satellites into the North Atlantic Treaty Organization (NATO). President Barack Obama's decision to walk away from our missile defense program in Poland and in the Czech Republic was a huge concession to Putin, as is the stalling on admission of Georgia and the Ukraine into NATO. Russia welcomes concessions and these, like their predecessors, were not repaid in kind. Russia takes, President Obama gives, and Russia demands more.

There is a fourth global strategy. It, too, is calculated to overcome the West and ultimately lead the world. Though this strategy is formally embraced by only one country—Iran—it animates many foreign leaders and some of the most infamous names on the planet, among them Osama bin Laden, Ayman al-Zawahiri, and Mullah Omar. It is violent jihadism: the fanatical, terrorist, and always threatening branch of extreme fundamentalist Islam. Despite the theological differences between radical Sunni Wahhabism and radical Shia extremism, both endeavor to cause the collapse of all competing economies and systems of government, and thereby, in a last-man-standing approach, become the world's leading power—in fact, its sole power. In the minds of the jihadists, there is only one legitimate government and it is waiting to be unleashed: a caliphate with global reach and power.

Violent jihadist groups come in many stripes across a spectrum, from Hamas to Hezbollah, from the Muslim Brotherhood to al Qaeda, and from

Lashkar-e-Taiba to Jaish-e-Mohammed. Each espouses causes that are unique to its own branch of Islamism and to its own geographic region—independence for Chechnya, political dominance in the Sudan, hegemony over Kashmir, and so on. But without question, the jihadists also share a common overarching goal: violent holy war on America and the West, the destruction of Israel and the Jews, the recapture of all lands once held by Muslims, the elimination of "infidel" leaders in Muslim nations like Jordan, Egypt, and Saudi Arabia, and ultimately, the defeat of all non-Muslim nations.

Theirs is a strategy based on conquest and compulsion. Because it has no singular or coordinated leadership—and because its objectives are both grandiose and fragmented—attempts to execute this strategy are pursued by a number of tactical means. Some, like the Wahhabis, focus on the virtual brainwashing of young people to help spread radicalism throughout the world of Islam. Others, like Hamas, recruit and train suicide bombers. Some endeavor to mollify and pacify the West, lulling these nations into complacency and inaction. Lebanese American scholar and NBC commentator Dr. Walid Phares argues in his book, *Future Jihad*, that the massive Saudi investment in Islamic study centers in Western universities is designed to do precisely that. Al Qaeda itself continues to plan devastating attacks like those it carried out on September 11, 2001, and also targets unstable nations like Somalia and Yemen for takeover, with the hope of converting them into training and launching sites for an ongoing series of massive attacks.

Regardless of the choice of tactics, the overarching objectives of the various radical groups are linked by adherence to common fundamental goals. One of these was spoken by jihadist Maulana Fazlur Rehman Khalil: "Due to the blessings of jihad, America's countdown has begun. It will declare defeat soon."

These are the four strategies for world leadership that are in competition today. Only one is founded on freedom. Only one. Think of what that means. Only if America and the West succeed—if our economic and military strength endure—can we be confident that our children and grandchildren will be free. A strong America is good for peace, and it is essential for the spread of freedom. Our superpower status and our leadership in the world, however, are not inevitable. Three other global strategies, each pursued by at least one state or major actor, are aggressively being pursued to surpass us and, in some cases, to suppress us. The proponents of each are convinced they will succeed. And world history offers us no encouragement: Every superpower in history has eventually weakened and fallen behind—many have ultimately collapsed. Given what is at risk, I have come to believe that our primary objective as a nation must be to keep America strong. I am convinced that every policy, every political initiative, every new law or regulation should be evaluated in large measure by whether it makes us stronger or weaker. Our freedom, security, and prosperity are at stake.

Some of us take our many personal freedoms for granted. Others in the world who have never experienced them, and who have instead only heard their autocrats malign freedom, may not yet fully understand what it means. But for most Americans, the pulse of freedom beats in our very DNA. The New Hampshire license plate reads LIVE FREE OR DIE, reminiscent of patriot Patrick Henry's famous entreaty. There are those who insist that New Hampshire's motto isn't politically correct. But most Americans envy the Granite Staters their motto and believe, as I do, that this is *the* American resolve.

I have been inspired by the passion of those who have recently won freedom. In 2002, I sat near Afghanistan's President Hamid Karzai at a State of the Union address in our nation's capital. As we were filing out of the House chamber, he encountered a serviceman who had lost his arm in the fight to free Afghanistan. He said to the soldier, "I and my people want to thank you for your sacrifice for our freedom. Thank you, thank you so very much." And the young man responded, "It is an honor to serve the cause of freedom."

Afghanistan under the Taliban had assailed freedom. For jihadists, the very ideas of democracy and freedom are blasphemous; they believe law is given by God, not chosen by man, and that freedom and democracy substitute the rights of the individual and the collective will of the people for the demands of Allah. The result of their belief has been unimaginable oppression administered by religious mullahs.

The oppression inherent in a society without personal freedoms is not always as obvious as it was in Afghanistan. By almost all appearances, China is a very impressive nation, as the Beijing Olympics were designed to demonstrate. The Chinese government spent an estimated $40 billion to showcase their Games. In comparison, Atlanta's Games were produced for less than one tenth that amount, even adjusting for inflation. Modern, cosmopolitan Beijing now resembles a typical Western city—bustling commerce in stores and malls, daunting traffic, even plenty of McDonald's restaurants.

During the Games, the people seemed the same as those you'd encounter in any modern city—large crowds on the sidewalks, people laughing and talking and engaging in the work and play of the day. But a closer look revealed what it is like to live in a society without a Bill of Rights.

There is no First Amendment freedom of the press in China. The media is prohibited from criticizing certain Communist Party officials—those who do may lose their jobs or be imprisoned. My wife Ann and I wondered whether the censorship actually had the desired effect. We got our answer during the Olympic Opening Ceremonies. The audience warmly welcomed every national team as it was introduced into the stadium, but the Chinese gave some of their loudest cheers to the teams from North Korea and Cuba. We wondered how it was possible that nations ruled by tyrants who deprive their citizens not only of freedom but also of economic subsistence could be celebrated. The explanation, of course, is that the Chinese people don't see media reports of North Korea's population being starved to feed the maniacal military ambition of Kim Jong-il or of Castro jailing dissidents who advocate freedom and democracy. The Chinese people receive only glowing accounts of these tyrants; their information is shaped by a monolithic government rather than by the varied perspectives of a free press.

Nor do the Chinese citizens enjoy the equivalent of the First Amendment protection of religious freedom. According to the international organization Freedom House, "While officially sanctioned groups are tolerated, members of unauthorized religious groups are harassed and imprisoned." Americans celebrate our almost impossibly varied spectrum of religious beliefs and practices. Most of us would fight to defend this freedom for our fellow citizens, no matter how deep the theological disagreements. In China, the average citizen must carefully consider whether to voice even the faintest of religious opinions.

The First Amendment right to peaceable assembly is also absent. Christine Brennan of *USA Today* reported during the Games that she had observed a gathering of about one thousand Chinese in a train station, watching an Olympic event on a big-screen television. The Chinese authorities turned off the television and told the people to leave. Any group assembly, even a small, peaceful, and celebratory one, may be viewed as a potential threat.

The international media reported that in order to construct the Olympic venues, the government had ejected many thousands of Chinese from their homes. Protests followed, during which the displaced complained that they had received wholly inadequate compensation. Absent a free press, there was no effective media effort to investigate the fairness of the payments or to ensure that those who protested were not subsequently punished. And without the equivalent of our Fifth Amendment guarantee of "just compensation," a fair redress through an independent judiciary was far from certain.

We are well aware of China's abuse of dissidents, but the absence of basic freedoms impacts not only the prominent and the outspoken, but also the ordinary Chinese citizen. As the bleak oppression of Mao Zedong's Cultural Revolution has been largely eliminated, the Chinese have become increasingly prosperous. But personal freedom as we know it is still fiercely resisted by the Communist Party. Given the attitude toward political liberty of the other aspirants for world leadership as well, freedom for our grandchildren and for people everywhere can be guaranteed only by America—a strong America.

A Change in Foreign Policy

Throughout the 2008 campaign, Barack Obama repeatedly portrayed himself as the embodiment of "change." As has been noted by Robert Kagan, the prominent military and foreign policy scholar, President Obama *is* in fact a departure from the past, and it is much more than a departure from his predecessor, George W. Bush: it is a rupture with some of the key assumptions that have undergirded more than six decades of American foreign policy. Given the challenge for global leadership that confronts us, it is a break that is unnecessary and unwise.

At the end of World War II, the United States executed a dramatic and profoundly meaningful shift in our relationship with the rest of the world. After a long tradition of guarding our own hemisphere while deliberately attempting to stay isolated from the affairs of Europe and Asia, the United States found itself the greatest single power amidst a world in chaos and disrepair. Secretary of State Dean Acheson appropriately titled his memoirs from this time, *Present at the Creation*. President Harry Truman, his secretary of defense George C. Marshall, Acheson, and a few other visionary leaders set out to help create nothing less than a new international order with the United States in the permanent lead, not as a neutral actor in world affairs but as the protector and defender of a particular world order. "The enormity of the task . . . after the wars in Europe and Asia ended in 1945, only slowly revealed itself," Acheson wrote. "The wonder of it," he said, "is just how much was done." And Truman and his team believed, as Winston Churchill did, that the hope of the world depended on the strength and will of the United States.

This was not an expression of American jingoism. The United States has never wanted to impose itself on the world. As General Powell noted, we do not seek conquest or colonies. We seek our own safety and, insofar as possible, the chance for other people to live in freedom. President Truman vividly understood the mutual dependence of these two goals. The world had just suffered through two of the most destructive wars in history. America had tried to stand apart from those conflicts; we did not want to become involved, but in both cases we found that our vital interests could not be secure in the face of threats to the cause of freedom elsewhere. At the dawn of the nuclear age, a third world war was unthinkable; it would mean the destruction of humankind. So the president and the leaders of both parties shifted America's foreign policy. America took on the task of anticipating, containing, and eventually defeating threats to the progress of freedom in the belief that actively protecting others was the best way to protect ourselves.

Broadly construed, the new order had three pillars: active involvement and participation in world affairs; active promotion of American and Western values including democracy, free enterprise, and human rights; and a collective security umbrella for America and her allies. Along with these pillars came new institutions to fortify them and give them expression: the United Nations, the International Monetary Fund, the World Bank, the GATT (later WTO), and NATO, among others. And specific actions and initiatives gave them expression as well: the Marshall Plan, the Berlin Airlift, the Truman Doctrine (aid to Greece and Turkey to defeat communist insurgencies), and the intervention in Korea, among others. President Truman's administration "played a vital role in setting the main lines of American foreign policy for many years to come." What Acheson did not know – what he could not know – is how long and deep those "main lines" would go. Every one of Truman's successors—Republican and Democrat— from Dwight Eisenhower through George W. Bush continued in these broad traditions. There were modifications, adjustments, and occasional deviations to be sure. But these three pillars essentially defined the American posture in the world for the duration of and in the aftermath of the Cold War.

The Cold War began with Soviet aggression deep into Western Europe and Asia and with Harry Truman's declaration in response that the nations of the world were obliged to choose between alternative visions of how life was to supposed to be led—as free peoples or as subjects of communist states—and that it was the duty of the United States to support free peoples who were then resisting subjugation and to assist them in the working out their own destinies in their own way.

Dwight Eisenhower consolidated and reinforced the institutions founded by Truman and the principles he championed. The most stirring description of these principles was offered by John F. Kennedy in proclaiming America's determination to "pay any price, bear any burden, meet any hardship, support any friend, and oppose any foe, in order to assure the survival and the success of liberty." At the end of the Cold War there was Ronald Reagan citing the words of John Winthrop and Thomas Paine and promising to begin the world anew in vanquishing an evil empire and leading the world to a new era of freedom.

America's next three post–Cold War presidents—George H. W. Bush, Bill Clinton, and George W. Bush—continued in that tradition by championing free trade and freedom by using the American military to thwart the ambitions of evil regimes, to expand NATO, and to make Europe "whole and free." Each of our post–World War II presidents—with Jimmy Carter being the closest to the exception—believed the United States should lead the free world, stand with our allies, confront our adversaries, and speak out for democracy.

The course has not been easy. But the policy followed by presidents of both parties from 1945 until 2008 had an unparalleled impact for good. Under the shield of American power and leadership, hope and freedom expanded as never before. The United States has enjoyed three generations of prosperity and liberty while preventing a general war. Japan and Germany, which had been dictatorships, are now secure democracies. So are Taiwan, South Korea, the nations of Eastern Europe, and many other countries across the world. Billions of people today live in freedom, or have the hope of freedom, who otherwise would have lived in despair if not for the greatness of the United States. And thanks to America's promotion of free enterprise, capitalism, and economic freedom, billions of people have been lifted from poverty.

President Obama is well on his way toward engineering a dramatic shift in this American foreign policy, based on his own underlying attitudes.

The first of these envisions America as a nation whose purpose is to arbitrate disputes rather than to advocate ideals, a country consciously seeking equidistance between allies and adversaries. We have never seen anything quite like it, really. And in positioning the United States in the way he has, President Obama has positioned himself as a figure transcending America instead of defending America.

This sentiment manifests itself in several different ways, including President Obama's American Apology Tour. Never before in American history has its president gone before so many foreign audiences to apologize for so many American misdeeds, both real and imagined. It is his way of signaling to foreign countries and foreign leaders that their dislike for America is something he understands and that is, at least in part, understandable. There are anti-American fires burning all across the globe; President Obama's words are like kindling to them.

President Obama, always the skillful politician, will throw in compliments about America here and there. But what makes his speeches jump out at his audience are the steady stream of criticisms, put-downs, and jabs directed at the nation he was elected to represent and defend.

In his first nine months in office, President Obama has issued apologies and criticisms of America in speeches in France, England, Turkey, and Cairo; at the CIA headquarters in Langley, Virginia, the National Archives in Washington, D.C., and the United Nations in New York City. He has apologized for what he deems to be American arrogance, dismissiveness, and derision; for dictating solutions, for acting unilaterally, and for acting without regard for others; for treating other countries as mere proxies, for unjustly interfering in the internal affairs of other nations, and for feeding anti-Muslim sentiments; for committing torture, for dragging our feet on global warming, and for selectively promoting democracy. So critical was President Obama at his speech before the United Nations that dictator Fidel Castro complimented him for his "brave gesture" and "courage" in criticizing the United States. Hugo Chávez, the president of Venezuela, said that the "smell of sulfur" (meaning the presidency of George W. Bush) had been replaced by the "smell of hope" (meaning the presidency of Barack Obama). And Muammar Qaddafi, the dictator of Libya, declared that "we'd be content and happy if Obama can stay president forever."

Such lavish praise for Obama—by Messrs. Castro, Chávez, and Qaddafi—tells you much of what his approach to foreign policy is and the audience to which he is playing.

If President Obama has won the praise of America's enemies, he has too often turned his back on America's allies. This has happened in Eastern Europe, where he shelved President Bush's plan to build a missile defense shield in Poland and the Czech Republic in order to "reset" our relations with Russia, without even advance warning to our allies, and without receiving any concession in return. This was understandably seen as a betrayal by our allies in Eastern Europe. The result was, in the words of the syndicated columnist and commentator Charles Krauthammer:

> an earthquake in our relations with Eastern Europe and the beginning of their detachment from the American umbrella. . . . We have now declared that Eastern Europe—which had assumed that after the Cold War [it] had joined the West indissolubly and would enjoy its protection—is now in many ways on its own, subject to Russian hegemony and pressure.

Poles "need to review our view of America," said Lech Walesa, the hero of Solidarity who won the Nobel Peace Prize in 1983. "We must first of all take care of our business."

Something similar is happening with Israel, where President Obama has exerted substantial pressure on Israel to stop its settlements while putting almost no pressure on the Palestinians. He has done this despite the fact that Israel is among America's greatest allies, a true and faithful friend, one that has made real sacrifices for peace. To take just one example: In 2005, Israel evacuated its settlers and handed over the Gaza strip and part of the West Bank to the Palestinians. This unilateral concession on the part of Israel was met in return by thousands of rockets fired into the cities of Israel. The Palestinians, fully aware that President Obama is pressuring Israel to make even more unilateral concessions, are content to sit back and make no concessions of any kind.

In our own hemisphere, President Obama has insisted that Manuel Zelaya, the corrupt autocrat who has allied himself with Hugo Chávez and Fidel Castro and who was lawfully removed from office by the Honduran Supreme Court, must be returned to power. It is stunning to think that the president of the United States would force Honduras to act contrary to its own laws in order to restore a repressive, anti-American leader to power. Yet that is precisely what the Obama administration has demanded.

When it comes to Colombia—one of our best allies in the Western Hemisphere, a nation that has assisted us in fighting against both terrorists and the drug cartel, and an important counterweight to the ambitions of Hugo Chávez in Venezuela—President Obama has done nothing to promote a free trade agreement that is vital to Bogotá.

This is the very opposite of the multilateralism candidate Obama promised throughout 2008—and the effects of his actions on our allies will be to create incentives for them to cut deals with our adversaries.

If President Obama has too often undermined American allies, he has too often sought to placate America's adversaries, including Iran and North Korea. In doing so, the president has shown weakness and irresolution when he needs to demonstrate strength of will. President Obama sends a signal that he is eager to negotiate at any time, any place, without conditions; the effect of this is to cede all of the power and leverage to our enemies. Time and again, President Obama's open hand has been met with a clenched fist.

Compounding all this is the president's reluctance to speak out with confidence for American ideals abroad—to carry on the tradition begun by

Harry Truman with a rhetorical lineage extending all the way back to our Founding era: While he will occasionally say a good word on behalf of democracy and human rights, there is no passion in his words—and he has not made them a priority anywhere in the world. The president's support for liberty appears to be pro forma and mechanical, as if it is an afterthought. The impassioned appeals for democracy that were heard from Democrats like Franklin Roosevelt, Harry Truman, and John F. Kennedy have been replaced by rote words or by silence. It is an extraordinary moment we are in, when an American president is eager to note all of America's failings, real and perceived, and reluctant to speak out in defense of American values and America's contributions to the freedoms enjoyed around the globe.

Another of President Obama's presuppositions is that America is in a state of inevitable decline. He seems to believe that we have entered the "post-American world" predicted by Fareed Zakaria's best-selling book of that name. The perspective is shared by many in the foreign policy cognoscenti, and apparently by the president himself. He therefore sees his task as somehow managing that decline, making the transition to post-superpower status as smooth as possible, helping Americans understand and adjust to their new circumstances.

Among the dangers is that if a president believes this, it is likely to become a self-fulfilling prophecy. A commander in chief's defense budget and security commitments will be based on a set of assumptions that will eventually become reality. If the president accepts that America is in an irreversible state of decline relative to the rest of the world, it may well come to pass under his stewardship.

President Obama is far too gifted a politician to say in plain words that America is merely one nation among many. But his rhetoric offers clues into his thinking. For example, while in Europe, he dismissed FDR and Churchill's dominant role at Bretton Woods, saying, "If there's just Roosevelt and Churchill sitting in a room with a brandy, that's an easier negotiation. But that's not the world we live in, and it *shouldn't be* the world that we live in [emphasis added]."

It has expressed itself in President Obama's insistence that there is "no senior partner and no junior partner" in our relations with Europe—

meaning Luxembourg and Andorra carry the same weight and influence in world affairs as the United States and Great Britain (a claim even Andorrans and citizens of Luxembourg would probably reject).

And it has expressed itself when, in response to a question about whether he believed in "American exceptionalism"—a phrase that indicates America has a special place and role in the world—he replied, "I believe in American exceptionalism, just as I suspect the Brits believe in British exceptionalism and the Greeks believe in Greek exceptionalism." Which is another way of saying he doesn't believe it at all.

Nowhere has the president's radical reworking of American and Western leadership been more obviously on display than in his address to the United Nations in September 2009. The heart of his remarks came in this passage:

> In an era when our destiny is shared, power is no longer a zero-sum game. No one nation can or should try to dominate another nation. No world order that elevates one nation or group of people over another will succeed. No balance of power among nations will hold. The traditional division between nations of the south and north makes no sense in an interconnected world. Nor do alignments of nations rooted in the cleavages of a long gone Cold War.

If no nation that is elevated above another can succeed, that by necessity means America does not have the ability to maintain a dominant position in the world—something which President Obama seems to believe is a bad idea even if it were possible.

Indeed, a recurring theme in President Obama's rhetoric is that "more than at any point in human history, the interest of nations and peoples are shared" and that the "common interests of human beings"—ending global warming, stopping nuclear proliferation, achieving peace and prosperity—is stronger than the differences among nations. His job is to remind nations of the importance of "mutual respect" because of our "mutual interests." And only by "breaking old patterns" can we become more interconnected. President Obama envisions himself as the world's great bridge builder and synthesizer.

Beyond that, if a president engages the world—tyrannies and autocracies like Iran and North Korea, Syria and Russia, Darfur and Zimbabwe, and a dozen other nations—based on the conviction that we are always dealing with common interests more than we are dealing with competing interests and ideologies, it could lead to serious miscalculation, decline, and even disaster. Here again we can turn to Dean Acheson for wisdom. "Released from the acceptance of a dogma that builders and wreckers of a new world order could and should work happily and successfully together," he wrote, "[Truman] was free to combine our power and coordinate our action with those who did have a common purpose."

Between Harry Truman and Barack Obama, give me Truman every time.

In the face of Obama's approach and foreign policy agenda, we need to do several things.

The first is fairly elementary: We should treat our allies like the allies they are. That means, for starters, not being harder on them, or demanding more from them, than we do from our adversaries. It means treating them with respect rather than with offense. It means striving to make their lives easier rather than harder. It means consulting them on key decisions before they are made, and especially communicating with them if we must take a route they find troubling. And it means not stabbing them in the back.

We should honor the basic rules that govern state-to-state affairs. "Foreign policy commitments are not to be made and unmade at will," Margaret Thatcher has said. "We are bound by past commitments. We have a respect for past contracts, both as governments and as ordinary citizens. We cannot expect others to keep their word to us unless we keep our word to them."

Keeping our word to our allies is a matter of honor, then, but it is also a matter of self-interest. The United States needs allies for economic, political, and national security reasons. Good allies and strong alliances allow us to share the burdens we carry, complement and supplement our efforts, and present a united front against those who wish us harm.

When we treat allies in a desultory manner—and especially if we act in a way that causes them to question our reliability and resolve, our commitment and staying power—they will, out of their own self-interest, turn to others, including those wishing America ill. If Poland and the Czech Republic can't count on America to support them, they will have to bend to the will and wishes of Russia. If our friends in Latin America become convinced that we are turning our back on them, they will feel compelled to reach out to Hugo Chávez, who is seeking to lead a revolution on the continent that takes its inspiration from Castro's Cuba. If the Arab nations believe that America will allow Iran to dominate the Middle East and will acquiesce in its acquisition of nuclear weapons, they will inevitably move into Iran's sphere of influence, even though Iran is a Shia nation and the Arab Sunni states have hitherto resisted Iranian power projection. If Japan believes the United States is weakening its commitment on the Asian continent, it will distance itself from America and be forced to seek an alliance with China. By seeking to appease its enemies, the United States will only alienate its allies, and eventually America will have no friends at all.

We must also act to strengthen the American economy, which has been the cornerstone upon which America's international leadership has rested in part during the last half-century. As I will discuss at length in later chapters, our economy has been the wonder of the modern world. We can outwork and outproduce any nation on the planet. When we unlock the full talent and energy of individual Americans, it results not only in prosperity but in innovation, in the capacity to adapt to a rapidly changing world, and in stunning breakthroughs in technology and science. What I am describing is not Pollyannaish speculation; it is the record and achievement of modern free-market capitalism.

These things are now at risk because of the economic policies of President Obama. His effort to expand the size, reach, and role of government is without precedent in our history. His plans would leave us with a crushing deficit and debt, far beyond anything we have ever experienced. Confiscatory taxes will have to be imposed on future generations to make up for the shortfall. This in turn will undermine growth and the spirit of entrepreneurship that have characterized our nation at its best.

It is an often-remarked-upon irony that at a time when Europe is moving away from socialism and its many failures, President Obama is moving us toward that direction.

To ensure that America remains safe and maintains its role as a defender of freedom, we also need to increase our defense spending to at least 4 percent of our GDP per year, including substantial and increasing support for missile defense. Under President Obama, our defense spending will decline as a share of our economy and of the federal budget. And it will fall far below what is required to meet our global commitments. We are engaged in two hot wars in Iraq and Afghanistan, and facing growing threats in almost every region of the world. Weakness invites challenges, acts of intimidation, acts of aggression, and sometimes war. Right now America is, based on its defense spending, well on the road to weakness.

We also need to remind ourselves that the most attractive thing about America is our ideals: our commitment to democracy and free elections; to limited government and the consent of the governed; to unalienable rights and political equality; to freedom of the press and speech, assembly, and religion. We believe in championing democracy and human rights because they lead to human flourishing and to a more peaceful and prosperous world, one that more closely aligns with the values and interests of the United States. To again invoke the words of Margaret Thatcher:

> Democracies . . . have never been engaged against each other in warfare in any major way. To reduce the risk of war, therefore, we must work for steady progress towards more democracies. With the advancing tide of democracy, the risk of war recedes. If the tide of democracy recedes, the risk of war advances.

So we should encourage democracy where we can, give aid and comfort to those who want it, and not undermine those who already have it.

Undergirding all of these things must be the certain conception of the goodness and greatness of America. The United States is the birthplace of modern politics, the first nation to be founded on a transcendent set of political principles. America was not only founded on these principles, it has fought and died for them in wars across the globe. These were conflicts we participated in, not in order to claim new territory but to uphold certain human ideals; to free people from death camps, gulags, and killing fields; and to defeat malevolent ideologies, whether Nazism, fascism, communism, or violent jihadism.

That doesn't mean, of course, that America is a perfect country. We have made mistakes and committed grave offenses over the centuries. Too often we have failed to live up to our ideals. But to say that is to say that we live in this fallen world rather than a perfect one, a world composed not of angels but of flawed and imperfect beings. And, crucially, our past faults and errors have long been acknowledged and do not deserve the repetition that suggests either that we have been reluctant to remedy them or that we are inclined to repeat them. What we should say and repeat is this: No nation has shed more blood for more noble causes than the United States. Its beneficence and benevolence are unmatched by any nation on earth, and by any nation in history.

Abraham Lincoln understood that the destiny of the world was twined to the destiny of America. It is why he called the United States the "last, best hope of earth." It is still so. As citizens of America, we should be filled with love and gratitude for what this country has been, for what it is, and for what it can still be.

And of all people, we should expect our president to understand these things, to expect that his bonds of affection for our country would be obvious and unbreakable. In a world composed of nations that are filled with rage and hate for the United States, our president should proudly defend her rather than continually apologize for her.

America deserves that, and it deserves much more than that.

I reject the view that America must decline. I believe in American exceptionalism. I am convinced that we can act together to strengthen the nation, to preserve our global leadership, and to protect freedom where it exists and promote it where it does not. What is ahead of us now will not be easy. It will be difficult to overcome the challenges we face, to maintain our national strength and purpose even as China, Russia, and the jihadists pursue their own ambitions. It will be difficult to repair the damage from the economic panic of 2008 and the intemperate actions that have been justified as steps to remedy it. I don't worry about our ability to overcome any problem or threat. But I do wonder whether we will take action that is timely, and that we will act before the necessary correction is massively disruptive, or thrust upon us in the midst of agony and surprise even greater than 9/11 or Pearl Harbor.

We have been accustomed to being the world's leading nation for so long, enjoying the freedom, security, and prosperity that comes with that leadership, that we have tended to avoid the hard work that overcoming challenges requires. When I was about ten, I asked my dad how he thought his company's Rambler automobile could ever successfully compete with General Motors; they were so far ahead that catching up appeared impossible. He said something that has since been widely attributed to him: "There is nothing as vulnerable as entrenched success." I believe that our many years of success may, in fact, be the greatest obstacle we face. In election after election, candidates have told us that simple measures will solve our challenges, and that their election alone will guarantee a bright future. We have joined in the cheering for this heady prospect. But much more than cheering is going to be required in the years ahead.

It is time for America to pursue the difficult course ahead, to confront the looming problems, to strengthen the foundations of our prosperity, and to secure the sources of our liberty and safety. The sacrifice and hard work will not sap our national energy; they will restore it. I'm one of those who believe America is destined to remain as it been since the birth of the Republic—the brightest hope of the world. And for that belief, I do not apologize.

2

Why Nations Decline

It is inconceivable that America would ever be surpassed by another nation. As long as any of us can remember, America has been the power "of last resort"—the nation the world turns to when matters get completely out of hand. America stopped Adolf Hitler; we stopped Imperial Japan; we stopped Slobodan Milošević; we stopped Saddam Hussein. Our economy dominates as well: our currency is the world's standard; our GDP is the world's largest; America is where the Internet was born, the place where titans like Apple and Microsoft battle it out. Even our culture is on top: Our music, movies, books, and fashion are enormously influential in almost every nation. It is simply inconceivable to us that America could ever be eclipsed.

We're not the first people who believed that about themselves. The Ottomans, the Spanish, the Portuguese, the Chinese, the British, the Soviets—these and others were superpowers, and they were all surpassed. The advantages of leadership are so significant that it's hard to imagine how any nation could squander them. But that in fact has been the usual course of world history.

This kind of collapse is not unique to nations. We've witnessed business powerhouses lose their lead to upstarts. United Airlines was upstaged by Southwest. Sears and Kmart were passed by Wal-Mart. Western Union and AT&T watched Verizon speed by. And look at General Motors: it was once the undisputed automotive heavyweight, the champion here and around the world. No more.

The fall of leaders doesn't make sense in the private sector, either—the advantages of leadership should ensure invincibility. But they demonstrably do not. My first job following graduate school was working for Bruce Henderson at the Boston Consulting Group. Bruce had set out to determine the mathematical advantage of leadership. He discovered that in almost every industry, the enterprise that had the most "experience" doing or making something could enjoy a calculable economic advantage over an enterprise with less experience. His analysis demonstrated that a company with twice as much experience as another should enjoy a 20 to 30 percent cost advantage. That's why, he concluded at the time, IBM should be more profitable than Burroughs, GM more than Chrysler, Owens-Illinois more than Anchor Hocking, Sears more than JCPenney, Goodyear more than Firestone, and Xerox more than AB Dick. His predictions were borne out, at least for a time. But one by one, great leading companies, like leading nations, found that their potential for advantage was not a guarantee for success.

Why is it that the great fail? It's a question America must ask, not only because we are the world's leading nation, but because the continuation of our lead has been called into question.

The Ottomans

The improbability of decline by the great has long piqued my interest. I could observe the fall of businesses firsthand. Growing up with a father in the car business, I had a front-row seat to the decline of the Big Three automakers. When it came to nations and civilizations, however, I read. There's nothing approaching consensus when it comes to the reasons for the fall of empires, of course. But there are common causes, and in some respects they parallel what I had seen in the small backyard of the American business world.

In high school, history teachers made us draw maps of the world at different points in time. (It was mostly a tracing and coloring project; we evidently hadn't made much progress since kindergarten.) One of the most striking maps was one that delineated the Ottoman Empire. It was astonishingly large, including Turkey, Greece, Syria, Egypt, North Africa, and a large swath of southeastern Europe reaching all the way to the gates of Vienna.

The Ottoman achievements spanned seven hundred years. The empire's wealth was amassed from pillage and taxes. Culture flourished in poetry, ceramics, weaving, and architecture. The sultans managed it all with massive political and military bureaucracies. Then Christian Europeans won the Battle of Lepanto in 1571 and decimated the Ottoman navy. Rebellion and war ultimately were overwhelming. But why was the empire unable to rally to victory? What had so weakened the Ottomans?

Highly beneficial global trade routes that had traditionally passed through Ottoman territory had been abandoned for ocean passages, and the empire's revenues dropped accordingly. More important, while Europe embarked on the early stages of manufacturing, the Ottomans did not; they were confident that their pillaged wealth would sustain them indefinitely. The Ottomans' growing isolation from the dynamic world of manufacture and trade was reinforced by the conviction that their holy scriptures provided all the knowledge that was necessary; foreign technology was infidel technology. The empire banned the printing press for half a century.

Like the Ottomans, the Spanish and Portuguese achieved wealth through plunder, and their empires fell for remarkably similar reasons. Christopher Columbus didn't find a route for spice; he found a route for gold—Incan, Aztec, and Mayan gold. The Portuguese pioneered trade to the Indian subcontinent and the Orient. And they capitalized on their innovations in navigation with another: the cannon. Safely anchored offshore, they could lay waste to any mainland enemy they chose. Spain and Portugal became extraordinarily rich.

While the rest of Europe was learning how to make things people wanted to buy, Spain and Portugal stuck to the buying. They were the centers of wealth consumption; France, England, and Germany became the centers of wealth creation. And just as the Ottomans had done, the Spanish and Portuguese shut their borders—and their minds—to innovation, technology, and learning. The Protestant Reformation to the north had spawned not only dissent and skepticism but also literacy and innovation. Spain and Portugal isolated themselves from such heresy. Portugal placed strict controls on printing presses. The Spanish crown banned scientific works by Protestant authors. They banned study abroad in any non-Catholic country. Spain went so far as to impose the death penalty on anyone who imported an unauthorized foreign book. Like the Ottomans, Spanish and Portuguese isolation became complete: They eschewed the manufacture and trade of goods that was sweeping the rest of Europe, and they closed their borders to outside thought.

The Great Wall

For many centuries, the Chinese were the greatest power in the world. When Marco Polo reached China in the thirteenth century, he encountered technology that surpassed anything the rest of the world had achieved. Advances in astronomy, physics, chemistry, meteorology, seismology, engineering, and mathematics came to the West from China. In the first century, China was first to manufacture paper—a huge improvement over papyrus and parchment. They invented the first printing press, published the first newspaper and the first book, and they invented moveable type around 1041—*four hundred years* before a German named Johannes Gutenberg developed similar technology.

Some of China's innovations had important military implications. They invented the first compass and the first seismograph. They were the first to cast iron; they machined it into firearms as well as cooking pots. While Taoist monks were looking for an elixir for immortality in the ninth century, they stumbled on gunpowder, something far more suited to inducing mortality. Rockets, bombs, mines, cannons, and of course, fireworks soon followed.

Chinese ships were the envy of the world; some of them were as long as 400 feet, with multiple decks and masts. In one three-year span, they built more than 1,600 ships outfitted for trade, transport, or war. What the Chinese accomplished was nothing short of spectacular.

And then China declined.

As ships from foreign lands increasingly docked in their ports, the Chinese feared cultural contamination. Confucians claimed that commerce would corrupt the society, calling for a return to the primacy of agriculture.

The government moved the capital from Nanjing, at the mouth of the Yangtze River, to Beijing, hundreds of miles inland. And rather than build ships to trade with the world, it built the Great Wall to lock it out. By 1500, anyone who built a ship with more than two masts was put to death. Then the government charged coastal authorities with the task of destroying *all* oceangoing ships and arresting their owners.

The Chinese rejected not only all things foreign but even technology that they had devised themselves. For the Ottomans, the Qur'an contained everything that life required; for the Chinese, it was their ancient culture that was to be revered and sustained, even at the cost of abandoning innovations like the printing press.

China's cultural and economic isolation continued throughout the twentieth century. Mao Zedong sought to revitalize the country with his Cultural Revolution. But rather than viewing learning and innovation as paths to prosperity, he saw them as threats. Merchants, writers, researchers, and intellectuals were jailed and sometimes killed. Professors were removed from universities to become peasant farmers.

China's neighbor, Japan, shared a penchant for isolation, but the Japanese had a very different self-identity. Proud and confident, the Japanese sought to extend their self-perceived superiority over the rest of the world. And rather than reject foreign technology, they assiduously gathered it, improved on it—and thrived. As their economic and military prowess surpassed that of China and other neighbors, they pursued imperial ambitions in Asia and across the world. And China, long the world's leader, was eclipsed by a nation only a fraction of its size.

The Sun Sets on the British Empire

England is just a small island. Its roads and houses are small. With few exceptions, it doesn't make things that people in the rest of the world want to buy. And if it hadn't been separated from the continent by water, it almost certainly would have been lost to Hitler's ambitions. Yet only two lifetimes ago, Britain ruled the largest and wealthiest empire in the history of humankind. Britain controlled a quarter of the earth's land and a quarter of the earth's population.

Late in the eighteenth century, after the loss of their American colonies, the British set out to compensate for what had been lost, first by defeating Napoleonic France and then by expanding the reach of the crown in colonies from India to the tip of South America and from Africa to the islands of the Western Pacific.

Britain's might was military, having built the most powerful navy the world had ever seen. But what enabled their military superiority was their industrial might. The British had pioneered the Industrial Revolution, and they enthusiastically promoted free trade, understanding the huge export potential for their products. By 1860, the nation's economy was the biggest in the world.

But maintaining leadership proved more difficult than achieving it. Whereas other nations extended the manufacturing revolution by embracing new technology and innovation, the British reversed course and tried to contain it. The country's culture of class immobility stymied the entrepreneurialism and initiative that propel a competitive economy. From owner to laborer, the British were eager to protect the status quo. Industrialists secured subsidies for themselves and tariffs on foreigners rather than face foreign competition and technology head-on. When subsidies proved insufficient for the most unproductive businesses, the government took them over. The nation spent national resources to keep sick companies alive rather than inventing new ones and investing in those that were strong.

Britain's economic missteps were compounded when it was forced to fight and endure the cost of two world wars. By the end of World War II, its national debt had tripled. Massive loans were required to shore up the ailing economy; they came from its former colony.

Common Causes?

There are similarities between the different countries' paths of decline. Many turned toward isolation; most important, isolation from knowledge: the Ottomans, Spanish, Portuguese, and Chinese purposefully shut out foreign invention and learning. And they adopted economic isolation as well: China, Spain, Britain, and the Ottomans expressly or effectively retreated behind barriers to foreign trade, each convinced that competition had made them weaker. Their retreat from the marketplace of ideas and their retreat from the marketplace of goods inevitably led to their retreat from the pinnacle of leadership.

This is a lesson that shouldn't be lost on us. When we face challenge, there will always be cries for protection. They will be heartfelt and not entirely illogical. Foreign competition will seem unfair—after all, if foreign products and services are more desirable to consumers, it must be due to some form of advantage. And if one's competitor has an advantage, that doesn't feel fair. If the advantage persists, it will mean that jobs will be lost, well-connected people will be affected, and government will lose revenues.

The only successful way to overcome foreign advantage, however, is to create an advantage of one's own—to innovate. And if you conclude that your competitor's advantage is permanent and insurmountable, the best course is to choose new paths and new products. Over the centuries, the siren songs of protectionism and isolationism have taken down some very impressive empires.

Some of these failed powers were weakened as well by wealth and spending that exceeded their own production—in other words, by easy money. The spoils of the Ottoman pillage, the gold the Spanish stole from the Americas, and the tribute the Portuguese exacted from trade—all allowed each of these nations to live well in excess of their productivity. In the same way that inherited wealth can lead descendants to profligate spending and economic ruin, easy money weakened these nations' willingness to work and invest.

Harvard historian David Landes, in his book *The Wealth and Poverty of Nations*, sees an even more fundamental factor in the rise and fall of powers: "If we learn anything from the history of economic development," he writes, "it is that culture makes all the difference." Just as Islamic culture rejected foreign influence, so the Ottomans rejected foreign technology. The religious beliefs of the Spanish and Portuguese led them to deny foreign discovery and innovation. China's economic isolation was the logical extension of its rejection of cultural diversity. And the British culture of order, organization, and rigid structure—once assets in Britain's conquest of nations in the undeveloped world—may have prevented it from developing the risk-taking approach and entrepreneurialism critical in free markets. Culture did indeed make a difference.

Of course, America can learn from these historic causes of failure; in some ways, they are eerily familiar. We, too, have been lavishly spending the easy money we obtained through excessive borrowing; there are growing calls for protectionism; government is expending resources to preserve the failed practices of declining industries; and the culture that led us to become the world's greatest nation is under attack. Following the same path that has led the great to decline in the past is reckless and perilous.

The history of leading nations that have fallen has even more to teach us, however, perhaps at a more fundamental level. In the face of evident decline, why do nations fail to act? Are there cases where nations have instead acted to halt their decline? What accounts for the difference between the two? The answers to these questions may be the most instructive because they can suggest a course of vigilance in the modern world very different from that of the Ottomans, the Spanish, the Portuguese, or even the British.

Why Nations Fiddle as They Burn

I'm reminded of the words from Proverbs, "Where there is no vision, the people perish." If a nation simply doesn't *see* a threat, it is unlikely to do something about it. It's entirely understandable that the people of imperial Spain were blind to the downside of having too much money; when all seems to be going extremely well, it's hard to envision anything but blue sky. In 1675, one official even boasted that "Madrid is the queen of Parliaments, for all the world serves her and she serves nobody." But soon thereafter, the Spanish government was bankrupt.

The Dutch also suffered from unearned wealth. Their trade monopolies, underinvestment in productive industry, complacency, and cultural decay led this condition to be called "Dutch disease." Lack of vision, lack of awareness, is an integral part of the malady. Today, Dutch disease afflicts a number of oil-rich nations; people literally live like sheiks thanks to the wealth under their feet. Relying on foreign labor for even the most basic domestic tasks, they have failed to develop productive economies and populations. Their future depends on the flow of oil, just as the Ottomans depended on pillage, the Spanish on gold, and the Dutch on monopoly. They are not alone, however, in failing to see peril.

Our own lack of vision led to the collapse of our financial markets and our economy. It precipitated a global recession, triggered the loss of $12 trillion of our citizens' net worth, and dealt a sharp blow to world freedom. We simply did not see that so-called subprime home mortgages, liar loans, and nonqualified loans had the potential to cause such destruction. I know some believe that "the powers that be" saw it all along—that the greed of Wall Street tycoons, for example, was the root cause. But I believe lack of vision played every bit as big a role.

However, lack of vision is the exception when it comes to the decline of great powers. In most cases, there were warnings. Farsighted Ottomans warned that adherence to religious dogma and reliance on oversized bureaucracy would doom the empire. Portuguese diplomats returning home cautioned the crown that the inquisition against the Muslims, the redirection of the country's wealth to the church, and the failure to develop agriculture and industry would lead to ruin.

The warnings were discussed, debated, and then dismissed. Why?

One answer has to do with human nature. We tend to repress the possibility of catastrophic events. One day some years ago, I was in the office of my boss, Bill Bain. We were watching progress at a construction site across the street. Cranes were unloading and staging forty-foot steel-reinforced concrete piles that were about to be driven into the ground to form the foundation for a skyscraper. These piles were passing only a few feet above the heads of construction workers on the ground. It was astonishing to me that none of them looked up, ducked, or cowered—they simply went about their work. Bill's observation has remained with me. "If they allowed themselves to feel the fear that one of those piles might come crushing down on them, they'd go nuts," he said. "Their brains just simply have to shut that out."

When an authority on the subject tells us that gasoline is going to cost four dollars a gallon, or that the value of the stock market will be cut in half, or that excessive spending and borrowing will severely jeopardize our children's future, we're likely to minimize or even dismiss the warning, in part because it's so frightful. Or we seize on the opinion of someone who tells us what we would prefer to hear instead.

There is another human tendency that often comes into play. We find it difficult to accept the possibility of dramatic change, whether good or bad.

If we have been healthy all our lives, it's difficult to conceive that we may become unhealthy. If energy has been cheap as long as we can remember, we can't imagine it becoming expensive. If the economy is booming, it's difficult to internalize the fact that it will someday be in recession. And when we are in a recession, we feel like it will go on forever. It's a phenomenon that has led some investors to do quite well for themselves—investors who steel themselves against their emotions to buy in bad times and sell in good. At a time in the late 1980s when the state of Texas was an economic basket case, the partners in my private equity firm decided to buy Texas businesses— from retailers to oil-production equipment companies. We knew that Texas had to come back someday, but I admit that investing in Texas businesses at the time was frightening. The eventual reward, however, more than made up for the fright.

When it comes to our nation and its future, these human inclinations can blind us to the consequences of ignoring challenges and threats. We simply don't want to see it if, in fact, we are headed downhill. Warning voices among the Ottomans, Spanish, and British were raised, but leaders and citizens did their best not to hear, tuning their ears instead to the comforting voices that claimed continuity and comfort.

Reassuring voices are easy to find; there are always people who benefit from maintaining the status quo. If warnings are heeded and change occurs, they may lose their position, their power, and their wealth. These people and institutions work very hard to silence dire warnings or to diminish them. And because those at the top have the most to lose, they are typically the most vocal in dismissing—or silencing—the warning voices. The religious hierarchy in Spain and Portugal surely recognized the inevitable implications of shutting out science and learning that came from the rest of the world, but their own power and privilege was at stake. So, too, for the mullahs of the Ottoman Empire. In Britain, the owners of uncompetitive businesses had enormous self-interest in obtaining subsidies and protection from foreign imports, as did the employees and unions that relied on those businesses.

The self-interest in preserving the status quo on the part of those in power accounts for several otherwise inexplicable realities in the modern world. Kim Jong-il and the Castro brothers, for example, surely recognize the economic and human bankruptcy of their socialist regimes. Sudan's

Omar al-Bashir, Zimbabwe's Robert Mugabe, and Burma's General Than Shwe likewise must be aware of the dire implications for their citizenry of their policies. But when the people in power wish above all else to preserve their power—and when they have all the guns—the prospects for change are very limited.

There may be a dangerous strain of self-interest among the citizenry in democracies as well, one that draws a nation away from the risks and sacrifices that are involved in changing course. Ronald Reagan once referenced a statement that he and others attributed to a late-eighteenth-century Scottish-born English lawyer and writer named Alexander Fraser Tytler. "A democracy cannot exist as a permanent form of government," Tytler is said to have written. "It can only exist until the voters discover that they can vote themselves largesse from the public treasury. From that moment on, the majority only votes for candidates promising the most benefits from the public treasury, with the result that a democracy always collapses over loose fiscal policy, always followed by dictatorship."

Although I haven't found an original source for the above quote, I have come across a verifiable Tytler observation that expresses a similar thought: "It is not, perhaps, unreasonable to conclude that a pure and perfect democracy is a thing not attainable by man, constituted as he is of contending elements of vice and virtue, and ever mainly influenced by the predominant principle of self-interest."

Whether from Tytler or from Reagan, the observation remains: If citizens in a democracy foster short-term self-interest rather than promoting the long-term interests of the nation—placing themselves above their descendants—there is little likelihood that they will vote for visionary, transformative leaders who advocate difficult change and sacrifice. When popular opinion places self above nation and the present above the future, nations slide from power to weakness. The self-interest of the common citizen can be just as hazardous to national strength as that of the rich and powerful.

National declines also may be attributable in part to the failures of independent opinion leaders—educators, writers, scientists, and the media—to say what needed to be heard. In some cases, such independent voices were virtually nonexistent; the church and government strictly controlled what people heard in the Chinese, Spanish, Portuguese, and Ottoman empires.

Independent inquiry, investigation, or warnings often resulted in people being sent to the dungeon or worse; beheadings and burning at the stake tend to silence the outspoken. The absence of free expression and a free press made the recognition of challenges and action in response to them far less likely.

But where independent voices have been plentiful, they, too, have sometimes failed to arouse public awareness and commitment to a course of change. I admit to having been more than a little surprised that many of the serious challenges facing America today were not forcefully examined by the media during the 2008 primary and general election campaigns. It's well understood by those who have studied the federal budget, for example, that our entitlement programs will eventually swamp us. But neither party's candidates were pushed to explain what they would do about it. In one of our Republican primary debates, for example, we were asked, "Specifically, what would you do to fix Social Security?" Most responded by restating the problem—"Social Security is bankrupt"—rather than by addressing a solution; politicians have learned from experience that it is unwise to "touch the third rail of American politics." But why is that? Why is it that the media doesn't hold accountable those who duck this critical issue? Why isn't it instead that *failure* to address entitlement and Social Security reform is the "third rail"?

Neville Chamberlain's now infamous celebration of his agreement with Hitler was widely heralded at the time by the British and world media—few independent voices warned of its risk and peril. Winston Churchill had spoken repeatedly about the dangers posed by Hitler and Germany, but the British parliament and the British people were in no mood to listen. The many agreements the United States has reached with North Korea over the years—virtually all of which were subsequently and quite predictably violated by that country—have largely been welcomed by the press with only scant skepticism. The alarms sounded by the late senator Daniel Patrick Moynihan, actor Bill Cosby, NPR correspondent Juan Williams, and others about the disintegration of the family and the dire consequences of homes without fathers have been dutifully reported, but they have been given very little real attention. And other, similarly vital warnings are often simply ignored by the media. Why?

In some cases, of course, bias about the topic colors the coverage. But equally responsible, I believe, is group think. It's hard to think independently once you have heard the opinion of the institutional elite. Some members of the media decided early on that Ronald Reagan was not particularly intelligent. That bias colored a good deal of the reporting during his presidency. When the accounts of those who had worked most closely with him were written, and particularly when his diaries were published, the public finally got a very different picture of the man: He was brilliant.

The media elite similarly took the early view that Iraq was a hopeless quagmire. There was often thereafter a perceptible snickering in the coverage, especially when the surge initiative was unveiled. Then, when the surge actually worked, the media coverage of Iraq noticeably fell off.

Perhaps there are also cases of intellectual laziness. If academics, writers, and opinion leaders have never visited China or worked in the private sector, for example, how can they knowledgably assess the implications of China's developing industrial strategy? Examination and analysis that go beyond Google, Wikipedia, or a few selective interviews can be difficult and time-consuming, and not everyone is willing to go to the expense and to make the effort that in-depth reporting requires, particularly as media budgets are being slashed. Media outlets have been closing foreign bureaus: Many major newspapers and outlets no longer have Kabul or Baghdad bureaus.

The failure to see growing threats, the interests of the powerful in preserving the status quo, the short-term self-interest of common citizens, and the absence or forced silence of independent voices have combined to prevent world powers from correcting course. Interestingly, that has not always been the case.

Throughout history, there have been fortuitous reversals of national decline. Rome approached collapse in Nero's time, but later thrived under the "Five Good Emperors." The Ottomans overcame an eleven-year civil war, capturing Constantinople from the Christian Byzantines and then expanding their empire to the east. Great Britain, lulled into passivity by Chamberlain's appeasement, rallied under Churchill's stirring leadership. "You ask, 'What is our aim?'" he said in his first speech as prime minister. "I can answer with one word. Victory—victory at all costs, victory in spite of all terror, victory however long and hard the road may be." The British people responded with such fortitude and strength that their resolve continues to inspire us today.

In the 1990s, America was blind to the threat of violent jihad. Few of us had even heard of al Qaeda or Osama bin Laden, and our leaders failed to take aggressive action against them. Former president Bill Clinton rejected an opportunity to assassinate bin Laden, cut human intelligence resources by 25 percent, and countenanced a CIA with only a handful of agents who could speak Arabic. Opinion leaders and the media largely ignored the threat as well. But the attacks of September 11, 2001 changed all that. We removed the Taliban from power in Afghanistan and set out to find and expunge bin Laden and his cohorts. America changed course.

Why do some nations turn around while others do not? One or more of four conditions or catalysts have been present when corrective action was successfully undertaken. The first is the occurrence of a catastrophic event that is alarming enough to spur action but not so large that it dooms the nation. The launch of Sputnik set America on a course to match and exceed Soviet superiority in space. Pearl Harbor struck a severe blow, but in the words attributed in film to the commanding Japanese admiral, "We have awakened a sleeping giant and filled him with a terrible resolve." America's pacifists and isolationists were overwhelmed by stark reality.

The second catalyst is the presence of a great leader—a person of un-common vision, political courage, statesmanship, and persuasiveness. In nations with millions of citizens, it is remarkable that one person can have such a dramatic impact. During my lifetime alone, numerous singular fig-ures have changed the course of their nation's history. Consider Mahatma Gandhi, Winston Churchill, Golda Meir, Nelson Mandela, Lech Walesa, Mikhail Gorbachev, Boris Yeltsin, Konrad Adenauer, Václav Havel, Harry Truman, Dwight Eisenhower, and Ronald Reagan.

A third condition is national consensus. In most instances, the consen-sus is spurred by either crisis or national leaders, but there are occasions when citizen leaders, media voices, educators, or opinion leaders have moved a nation, sometimes in spite of its political leaders. Lech Walesa galvanized a movement that brought down the Iron Curtain, first in Poland, then across Eastern Europe. Scientists, concerned citizens and the world media have succeeded in convincing the public that global warming is a real and present danger.

The final conducive condition for turnaround is when a nation enjoys deep, broad-based national strength—a productive and inventive economy, an educated and entrepreneurial population, and an extensive bench of able leaders. America was able to successfully rebound from the attack on Pearl Harbor in part because of our ample national assets. Nations whose leadership is derived instead from a single asset or competence are less able to recover. When Spain and Portugal lost access to plundered riches, they were unable to fall back on other compensating capabilities. The stress that strengthens the strong is calamitous for the weak.

The lessons from past powers can inform our prospects for preserving America's place in the world. They give cause for concern as well as grounds for optimism. No great power in history has endured indefinitely; they have failed to see and failed to act, lulled into complacency by selfish stewards and by citizens too willing to turn a blind eye. Like them, we failed to see the threat from violent jihadists, we failed to envision the perils of our mortgage practices, and even today, we fail to see the danger from our excesses. The powerful, often wedded to the status quo, have front-row seats in Washington; virtually all are represented by well-placed lobbyists. Our citizens often prefer the politicians who promise them the most and who paper over the needs of future generations. The failing of some in the media to present unbiased and rigorous analysis is the subject of books and blogs. In fact, each of the conditions that existed in the failed great states of the past is present in America today. This alone is cause for concern. The apprehension is compounded by the number and severity of the threats we face.

The good news is that America also possesses the qualities that have allowed great nations in the past to reverse course and to overcome challenges. We have recently experienced near-catastrophic events that have stirred us to act—the attack of September 11, the meltdown of our financial sector, the near collapse of our economy. We are blessed with a number of strong leaders and statesmen among our elected and private-sector leaders. Our media voices have become as diverse as they are unfettered. And the foundations of America's strength are the most robust of any nation in history. Our economy is based on a wide spectrum of industries. Our agricultural and natural resources are abundant. The American people are educated, inventive, creative, risk-taking, entrepreneurial, patriotic, family-oriented, willing to sacrifice, and committed to freedom. Our history demonstrates that when we have faced challenges, Americans have always risen to the occasion. Blessed with these extraordinary strengths, America can overcome today's extraordinary challenges. But doing so will require uncommon truthfulness, candor, decisiveness, and sacrifice from citizens and leaders alike.

3

The Pursuit of Power

The best ally world peace has ever known is a strong America.

Historian Donald Kagan argues in his book *On the Origins of War: And the Preservation of Peace* that the most favorable political circumstance "is the possession by those states who wish to preserve the peace of the preponderant power and of the will to accept the burdens and responsibilities required to achieve that purpose." In simpler terms, it is a very good thing when those nations which desire good are strong.

Hypothetically, a situation in which no nation is more powerful than the others might seem preferable. After all, "power corrupts," and a good nation that holds disproportionate power may become less good, acting out of self-interest or a desire to appropriate the wealth of others. But in the real world, there will always be those with more power and those with less, and it's far better if those nations that hold power are "good."

The United States is good. And so today are a great many other nations. Even as vociferous U.S. critics like Putin, Chávez, and Ahmadinejad readily rehearse our faults in front of any audience that will listen, there can be no rational denial of the reality that America is a decidedly *good* nation. Therefore, it is good for America to be strong.

We should not underestimate the salutary benefits of robust national power. A powerful nation can stop or restrain a tyrant from executing his villainy. We can prevent them from threatening our homeland, as we did when we blocked Soviet missiles from Cuba and destroyed terrorist launching sites in Afghanistan, and when we "convinced" Muammar Qaddafi to abandon his calamitous pursuit of weapons of mass destruction. Power can promote freedom and human rights, and it can deter ethnic cleansing, genocide, and the abuse of women. Power provides the means to alleviate the devastation of natural disasters like the 2004 Indian Ocean tsunami. During my lifetime, I have seen again and again that American power has been good not only for America, but also for the world.

The Middle Kingdom Flexes Its Muscle

Each of the four competitors pursuing distinct strategies for twenty-first-century world leadership—represented by China, Russia, the jihadists, and the United States—recognizes that power is critical to its success. Today, the extent of their respective military power varies significantly. In this regard, perhaps no nation is gaining ground more rapidly than China. Throughout much of its history, the Chinese military was shaped by threats from the nomadic societies of Mongolia, Manchuria, and central Asia, as well as by invasions from Japan. At the dawn of the twentieth century, China had just endured a humiliating defeat at the hands of the Japanese, the result of which was the loss of Taiwan as well as of China's suzerain role in Korea. Only a few years later, the British successfully invaded Tibet, securing advantageous trade and political positions for themselves and weakening China's sovereign claim over the Tibetans.

Japan and China continued to engage in periodic skirmishes and battles, but despite China's huge advantage in population, it lagged well behind Japan industrially. Further, the Chinese did not share a comparable sense of nationalism. Even after the founding of the Republic of China in 1912, it was still no match for Japan's modern military.

Japan had long harbored a vision of dominating China and securing the use of its abundant natural resources. In 1937, Japan launched an invasion of the mainland, attacking Beijing and commencing a war that would last more than eight years. It may not figure prominently in our history text-books, but it should; it was a conflict of unbelievable horror. The Japanese used chemical and biological weapons against the Chinese, which China maintains included fleas infested with plague dropped from aircraft. Chinese women were forced to provide sex for Japanese soldiers. The anger over the forced servitude of these so-called comfort women continues to this day. By the time the Sino-Japanese war was finally brought to a close by Japan's 1945 surrender to the Allies, the Chinese had suffered at least fifteen million casualties. Japanese losses in the conflict totaled about two million.

China's war effort had been both helped and hurt during the conflict by the emergence of Mao Zedong and his Communist Party. Mao's soldiers proved to be motivated and effective in fighting the Japanese army. But the civil war Mao instigated against Chiang Kai-shek's Nationalist Chinese army required the Nationalists to fight two enemies at once.

In 1949, Mao defeated the Nationalists, driving Chiang and his followers to Taiwan. But Mao's military was not a modern war machine; it was simply a cadre of zealots who had become highly sophisticated in the battlefield tactics of ground warfare. When the United States came to the aid of South Korea in 1950, it was unimaginable to many of our commanders that China would enter the fray, as Mao had neither an air force nor a modern navy. But fearing that a new foreign invader was at their southern doorstep, China did indeed join the conflict, and the chairman's forces proved to be highly effective once more, eventually forcing the United Nations' troops, led by the United States, into a costly stalemate.

Yet Mao never really took to modernity and technology, and his military continued to reflect that prejudice, maintaining a massive four-million-soldier army as only a weak compensation for the nation's obsolete or non-existent weapons systems and logistical support. It wasn't until approximately twenty years ago that China decided to build a modern world-class military. Since the mid-1980s, the People's Liberation Army has been reduced by two million soldiers, cutting its size in half even as military spending was doubled time and again. The new funds went to programs designed to professionalize and train Chinese soldiers as well as toward the purchase of modern arms from Russia: fighter aircraft, helicopters, destroyers, submarines, and antiship missiles.

China also expanded its own defense industrial capacity, developing an

F-10 fighter aircraft that can challenge our F-16, as well as an extremely effective armada of ships and submarines, and advanced missile systems. China's military buildup over the last two decades has been nothing short of stunning. In 2009, China boasted approximately 1,900 combat aircraft, 200 more than Russia. And even with its armed forces cut in size, China still maintains nearly a million more armed troops than the United States.

The country's investment in submarines is particularly ominous for the United States, dependent as we have always been on our sea power. Since the mid-1990s, China has commissioned more than thirty new submarines and now has an estimated sixty-two subs, only a few of which are nuclear-powered. In comparison, the United States has seventy-one all-nuclear submarines. China clearly intends to catch up; it is on track to deploy five classes of subs, more than any other nation.

The threat posed by China's submarines was brought home in 2006, when one of its conventional submarines tailed the USS *Kitty Hawk* off the coast of Japan—completely undetected by our navy. U.S. commanders only became aware of its presence when it surfaced well within the firing range of its torpedoes, and our chagrined crew could do nothing but imagine the smiles on the faces of the Chinese crew.

China has completed a massive new naval base on Hainan Island, one capable of projecting power into the South China Sea and Indian Ocean. The facility includes underwater caves for docking submarines, making it much more difficult for us to know when those subs have been deployed.

Perhaps most sobering of all, Defense Secretary Robert Gates reported to Congress in 2008 that "China has the most active ballistic missile program in the world." China is developing new submarine-launched missiles and anti-ship missiles, modernizing its intercontinental missiles, purchasing state-of-the-art cruise missiles, and adding 150 ballistic missiles a year, approximately a thousand of which are currently deployed along the Taiwan Strait.

China's aggressive pursuit of space-warfare and cyber-warfare capabilities is part of this high-tech transformation of the People's Republic of China's military might. In 2007, China successfully shot down an orbiting satellite. Official Western computer systems are frequently attacked by China, whose government is the most active cyber-combatant in the world.

According to China's Colonel Yuan Zelu, these technologies "will shake the structure of the opponent's operational system of organization."

China has come a very long way since Mao, yet it remains far behind the United States in military power—in a head-to-head matchup, China is not in the same league. Despite reductions made under the Moscow Treaty Agreement, the United States still has 2,200 operationally deployed warheads while the Chinese have less than 200. We have twelve aircraft-carrier battle groups, they have none. We have more than twice as many combat-ready aircraft, and ours are more modern.

But note two important points.

First, China is catching up.

Second, they have not yet built their military to challenge us head-to-head around the globe. Instead, they have shaped it to deter us, to match us, or even to defeat us in the specific theaters and missions that are most important to them. China has very little interest today in constructing a military capable of fighting us in Africa, Europe, the Americas, or the Middle East. They don't yet have the aircraft carriers needed to launch fighters—although one is now under development. Nor do they have the airlift capacity required to deploy troops in distant lands. They lack the necessary combat helicopters: We outnumber them 5,700 to 160. But they build submarines capable of checkmating our carrier battle groups and they invest in cyber- and space-warfare that can blind or at least blinker our navy and air force. And if they become capable of declawing America's military in Asia, they will gain freedom of action to do whatever they choose in the Pacific and Indian Oceans.

There are those, of course, who take comfort in our overall military lead over China and the projections that we will retain that advantage for decades to come. The Council on Foreign Relations reports that at least until 2030, there is "no evidence to support the notion that China will become a peer military competitor of the United States." On the other hand, Afghanistan fighters were certainly not a peer military with the Soviet Union, yet they defeated the Soviets—not globally, of course, but certainly in Afghanistan. What is most relevant in China's case is its quest for the asymmetric capacity to neutralize the United States in specific potential conflicts involving Taiwan, North Korea, or even South Korea or Japan. China is fast developing the capability of doing precisely that.

Some see China's military buildup as being driven foremost by a desire to reunite parts of the country's ancestral homeland, territories that the Chinese people have long been taught were taken from them by foreign aggressors. In 2006, former U.S. ambassador to China Clark Randt, Jr.— someone who knows the Chinese people intimately after having lived in China for many years—reminded me of their belief that holistic energy flows throughout each person's body, and that when that energy is "blocked," illness is the result. In the minds of many Chinese, he explained, the nation itself possesses energy, and that energy is greatest when the territory and people of China are united, whole. When foreigners cut off Tibet, Hong Kong, and Taiwan, this theory holds, they weakened China, preventing it from regaining its past greatness. This, Ambassador Randt continued, explains in part the vigorous and almost hysterical reaction the Chinese bring to any discussion of an independent Taiwan. Given this cultural context, one may be tempted to ask whether it is really so bad if China wants to put itself back together. In my view, yes, it is.

Taiwan is not China. It is an independent democratic country of 23 million people—more than Australia and more than four times the population of Israel. Taiwan holds free and fair elections, guards its citizens' civil rights and political liberties, and is also a model of free enterprise, having the twentieth largest economy in the world. If the people of Taiwan were to choose to unite with China, that would be their right, but that has never been the choice of a modern, free Taiwan.

And can we be certain that China's interest is only in Taiwan? China once oversaw Korea. It could conceivably decide to end any possible future threat from Japan. And it is almost certainly intent on projecting power throughout Eastern Asia and beyond, despite the fact that the Chinese vigorously protest any suggestion of that inclination. Yet their protests may well simply follow the counsel of Deng Xiaoping, the visionary leader of China's military modernization: "Observe calmly; secure our position; cope with affairs calmly; hide our capacities and bide our time; be good maintaining a low profile; and never claim leadership."

Whenever I hear a Chinese demurrer of ambition, I am reminded of Deng's counsel.

In virtually every meeting I have held with Chinese officials, I've been assured that they intend to build a positive relationship with the United

States. In fact, there are good reasons for them to do so: Russia is becoming more militarily assertive and the Chinese economy depends heavily on trade with the West. Former president George W. Bush recounted a private conversation with Chinese president Hu Jintao during which Bush explained that his number one concern was a terrorist attack against American citizens. President Hu replied that *his* greatest concern was whether the 20 million rural Chinese who move to the cities each year will be able to find work. China desperately needs our trade and goodwill. The economic growth that the People's Republic of China needs for its domestic stability provides us with the opportunity to build a more collaborative relationship and to make China a lasting partner.

It is in our best interest to draw China into the circle of responsible nations and, at the same time, to strengthen our capacity to intervene in Asia, if necessary, to prevent China from imposing its will on independent nations. We must also reach out to the Chinese people through all the means that modern technology provides. With millions upon millions of Chinese connecting to the virtual world every year, we should greatly expand our nation's capacity to communicate in Chinese.

These steps are important for freedom, for humankind, and for America. As American Enterprise Institute scholar Dan Blumenthal wrote in *Newsweek,* "devoting more military resources to the region and strengthening U.S. allies in order to reassure them and send Beijing the message that the United States is committed to the regional status quo—which means the maintenance of free markets and free governments across the Pacific . . . would be in everyone's interests."

The Great Bear Roars Again

Russia has once again changed course. Twenty years ago, Soviet leader Mikhail Gorbachev did what President Reagan had asked him to do and let the East Germans tear down the Berlin Wall. Inside the Soviet Union, he inaugurated the perestroika and glasnost reforms that paved the way for the USSR's dissolution. His successor, Boris Yeltsin, delivered his courageous defense of democracy standing on the turret of a tank. Yeltsin went so far as to suggest that Russia should join NATO, and Vladimir Putin, his successor, appeared to agree that Russia now shared common interests with free nations. When he was once asked whether Russia might join, he replied, "Why not?"

That was then.

Today, Putin is taking Russia in a different and worrisome direction. According to Fyodor Lukyanov, editor of the journal *Russia in Global Affairs,* "Russia is now inclined not only to reject completely a path determined by Western values but actually to deny that such values even exist." Far from celebrating the liberty achieved by the former Soviet republics and the growth of the Russian people's prosperity and freedom, Putin— who as prime minister retains much of his former power as president— laments the dissolution of the former Soviet Union and Russia's consequent loss of power. He has opined that the dissolution of the Soviet Union was the "greatest political catastrophe of the twentieth century." He is taking steps to rebuild what was lost.

Lukyanov has written that Putin's dramatic change of course was driven by the failure of global financial institutions and by the go-it-alone approach taken by the United States in invading Iraq. He reasons that the West's recognition of Kosovo's independence and the encroachment of NATO forces toward Russia's border gave Putin no option but to increase Russia's might. I disagree.

Putin is doing a good deal more than strengthening his nation. He has embarked on the authoritarian path traveled by Russia's past tyrants— complete with the aggregation of personal power for himself, awards of wealth to cronies, suppression of free speech, attempted intimidation of the West, nationalization of key industries, and the invasion of Georgia, an independent nation. The moves are reminiscent of Russia's Cold War playbook, but this time, they are funded with the wealth generated from Russia's abundant energy and natural resources.

During Putin's presidency, the pro-democracy candidate in Ukraine's 2004 presidential election, Viktor Yushchenko, was poisoned with dioxin, a dissident former spy was murdered in London, and opposition voices in the media have been silenced by suspicious deaths. Joseph Stalin—father of the gulag and perpetrator of the murder, starvation, and deportation of tens of millions of his own people—is being systematically rehabilitated in state media, textbooks, and schools. Why? Because in Putin's view, Stalin was a leader who made possible the Soviet Union's "glorious and powerful past," while Gorbachev and Yeltsin were men of "weakness." Today, it is the personalities and power of the Soviet era that are celebrated: Thousands of Russian soldiers wear Soviet-era uniforms and wave Soviet flags parade through Red Square to the enthusiastic cheers of their countrymen.

Just as they were during the decades of the Cold War, Russians once again are subject to an avalanche of vitriolic anti-American propaganda. On a recent anniversary of the attacks of September 11, 2001, Russia's largest state-owned television station broadcast an utterly specious documentary arguing that the tragedy was actually planned and carried out by the CIA as a way to legitimize our invasion of Iraq.

The Russian people are exposed to a media barrage that characterizes Russia as a nation besieged on all sides by America and our friends. They were told that their 2008 invasion of Georgia was simply a humanitarian response to American-led genocide committed against ethnic Russians living there. A Russian general even produced the passport of an American that had been "found" during the Georgia assault. What the Russian people did not hear, however, was that the same passport had been reported missing years earlier, following a flight from Moscow to New York, and that at the time of the Georgia offensive, the holder of that passport was in Texas caring for his ailing father. Every new woe and long-latent fear is portrayed as the product of an American effort to threaten Russia.

Putin has taken personal control of companies in some of Russia's most important industries including oil and gas, broadcasting, and journalism. By doing so, he both appropriates their wealth for his geopolitical ambitions and secures his personal political power. Observers estimate that Putin's personal and political friends serve as board chairmen of companies that represent as much as 80 percent of Russia's economy. He now leads what is increasingly referred to as a "corporatist state."

Much of what is happening inside Russia is veiled to observers in the West, but Putin's foreign policy is in plain view for all to see. He seeks to extend his grip on the world's energy by blocking neighboring countries' construction of energy pipelines to Europe, and, apparently, no tactics are off limits in this effort. Intimidation and invasion are acceptable as means to his ends. He is rebuilding alliances among the world's repressive nations, particularly those that are energy-rich or energy-linked. As a case in point, his support for Serbia has strengthened his hand in preventing Europe from building the Nabucco energy pipeline—one that would be free from Russian control.

Putin is working tirelessly to recover the geostrategic assets that he believes Russia tragically lost in the dissolution of the Soviet Union. His invasion of Georgia not only advanced his control over energy but captured the nervous attention of political leaders throughout the former Soviet republics and sent them an unmistakable message. The NATO countries' unwillingness or inability to prevent or repel the invasion sobered those leaders who were moving toward greater cooperation with the West and independence from Russia. These concerns—plus a few billion dollars—were enough early in 2009 to convince Kyrgyzstan to initially retract its agreement to allow NATO aircraft landing rights as they ferried troops and supplies to Afghanistan.

Putin's intention to recapture key parts of the former empire is further evidenced by President Dmitry Medvedev's not-so-veiled threat to protect the "life and dignity" of Russian citizens throughout the former Soviet republics even as his agents reportedly pass out Russian passports to citizens in those very republics. In the then UN ambassador John Bolton's words, Russia has returned "not to the Cold War but to a thuggish, indeed czarist, approach to former dominions."

Russia no longer makes any pretense about finding common interest with the democratic world. After ten years of negotiations to prepare for entry into the World Trade Organization, Russia put that membership in jeopardy with its invasion of Georgia. When Putin was asked whether he was concerned about Russia's position among the G-8 nations, he responded, "Should we agree to be killed in order to remain . . . in the G-8? And who will remain in the G-8 if all of us are killed?" Killed? Just who is killing whom? Perhaps most chilling was President Medvedev's boast, "We are afraid of nothing, including another Cold War."

Of course, given the Russian leaders' new agenda, rebuilding the nation's military is a high priority. Under Yeltsin, it had suffered badly. Despite the fact that the military was responsible, in part, for his rise to power—and for saving his life—Yeltsin let the Russian military atrophy to the point that it barely resembled its former self. His official defense budget plummeted from $74 billion in 1993 to $42 billion just three years later.

Aircraft, ships, and tanks fell into such disrepair that many were unusable. Russia's defense minister shockingly concluded in 1998 that "two thirds of all aircraft are incapable of flying" and "about one-third of the armed forces' military hardware is not combat ready."

Troop strength had not only declined by more than half, the army that remained had become increasingly weakened by corruption, inadequate training, insufficient compensation, and lack of discipline. When Yeltsin ordered the invasion of Chechnya, the Russian army at his disposal was far from being a skilled fighting force. According to the U.S. Foreign Military Studies Office, "More than 50 percent of the men sent to war had never fired live shells with their tank cannons, and had no idea how to do so. Military cooks, signalers, and mechanics were appointed to shoot anti-tank guns and missiles as well as machine guns."

Not long after Putin came to power, the world got a glimpse of Russia's hobbled military when in 2000, the *Kursk,* one of its largest and most modern submarines, was lost at sea with all 118 of its crew. The Russian navy failed to execute a credible rescue effort, and it exacerbated the tragedy when it refused to allow rescue attempts by our navy. Twenty-four sailors had survived for an undetermined time in one of the sub's airtight chambers, but their lives—and the lives of others perhaps—were sacrificed to protect Russian military secrets. It wasn't surprising when the Russian media blamed a U.S. sub in the vicinity of the *Kursk* for the loss, but even with such scurrilous propaganda, the sinking of the *Kursk* became a symbol of Russia's military disarray.

Putin's effort to rebuild the Russian military began with the budget—he has increased annual defense spending by almost 600 percent. According to some accounts, however, unreported spending on classified projects is even larger than the official figures and has grown even more significantly.

Putin has done much more than spend rubles. He also went to work to transform the Russian army. He restructured the military draft by limiting deferments, attacked the practice of bribery within the draft office, increased soldier pay and housing allowances, and inaugurated an effort to build a professional volunteer army not unlike our own. At just over a million soldiers, Russia's active-duty force is only a third smaller than our own, and its two-million-soldier reserve force is nearly twice the size of ours.

When it comes to rebuilding its conventional military hardware, Russia has a long way to go. The country has just under 2,000 combat-capable aircraft—about half our number—but the Russian air force doesn't come close to matching our capabilities. The United States has nearly 100 fifth-generation fighters; Russia has none. We have 1,700 generation 4.5 fighters; Russia has 90. The United States's lead in airpower is enormous. A similar picture exists in battlefield support capabilities, where, for example, America has four times as many combat-capable helicopters as Russia.

With all that said, there are two things to remember.

First, Russia doesn't have to stand up to America on a neutral battlefield. Instead, it can choose to deploy its military power only where the geography compensates for our overwhelming advantages, such as in its backyard. The invasion of Georgia was certainly well planned and orchestrated, despite the Russians' lack of satellite reconnaissance systems and high-tech weaponry. According to an analysis by the Heritage Foundation, some 25,000 troops and 1,000 armored vehicles attacked on two fronts simultaneously. Air support came from fighters and long-range bombers. The Russian navy attacked Georgia's harbor, and ballistic missiles hit military and civilian targets. Even cyber-attacks were part of the coordinated assault. To countries such as Georgia, Ukraine, Moldova, and Belarus, Russia is still an overwhelming power. Even Western Europe's militaries, standing alone, compare unfavorably to Russia's reinvigorated conventional forces.

Second, Russia's global power is, of course, based on its nuclear arsenal. Russia has over 5,000 operational nuclear warheads, including its tactical weapons. The United States has less than 3,000 operational warheads. When one includes nonoperational but potentially useful warheads, Russia boasts a stockpile of 14,000—an almost threefold nuclear lead over the United States.

Russia remains an important regional power, and given its energy wealth, by mid-century it could again be a world superpower capable of an equal say in any major global controversy. Every indication is that Putin intends to keep Russia on precisely that track.

Yet, Russia's looming demographic crisis has the potential to prevent the realization of Putin's vision. The average Russian male's life expectancy is a shockingly low sixty-one years. Combined with low birth rates, that factor has produced a population decline of 7 million people in just fifteen years. The United Nations projects that the Russia population will fall by another

10 million by 2020. Some analysts predict that the Russian population will decline from a high of 148 million people in 1992 to approximately 110 million in 2050. The impact on the available population for economic growth and for military purposes is staggering. It's arguable that this demographic calamity will stop the Russian march toward renewed superpower status.

But Vladimir Putin is far from foolish. He is tailoring his economic and military strategies to meet demographic reality. Energy production is not workforce intensive, and the reaggregation of some of Russia's former republics would readily provide new citizens to meet its military and civilian needs.

There was a time when we simply and unwisely stopped worrying about Russia. The long Cold War had ended and we hoped the Russian people would join the ranks of those who live in freedom. There was every reason to believe that the majority of Russians wanted just that.

The chaos of freedom, the greed of elites, and the instability of the first generation of post–Soviet Russian leadership squandered that opportunity. Reactionaries have seized their own opportunity to take Russia backward even while rebuilding Russian military power. We are now obliged to be wary and vigilant once more, because by mid-century, our grandchildren may well view Russia with the same concern that we and our parents once did.

The "Holy" Warriors

Both China and Russia pose threats to the United States, but the likelihood of near-term head-to-head war with either is low. That is not the case with the radical, violent jihadists. They are at war with us at this very moment— not because we declared a war on terror, but because they have repeatedly attacked us and in 1998 even declared war on the United States. Their war planning continues even as their operational effectiveness waxes and wanes. Every IED that kills an American soldier or marine in Afghanistan or Iraq, every terror attack in London, Madrid, or Bali, is just another engagement in their war.

That war goes on whether or not the United States chooses to acknowledge it and no matter what our political leadership and media elite decide to call it. As the American Enterprise Institute's Michael Landon wrote in *The Wall Street Journal*, "The world is simmering in the familiar rhetoric and actions of movements and regimes—from Hezbollah and al Qaeda to the Iranian Khomeinists and the Saudi Wahhabis—who swear to destroy us and others like us. Like their twentieth-century predecessors, they openly proclaim their intentions, and carry them out whenever and wherever they can."

I refer to these terrorists as "jihadists" because it's the term they use to describe themselves—"the men of jihad"—and the word itself refers to what some call the sixth pillar of Islam. Classically, *jihad* was a call to action to serve the Islamic state or caliphate, either by defending it or conquering new lands and expanding its borders.

Contemporary Muslims look at militant jihad in different ways. Many millions of moderate Muslims reject it out of hand and work to keep their lands free of its scourge. Thousands of Muslims have been killed by the radical jihadists, and many of our allies in the Muslim world are working side by side with us to thwart their cause.

Other Muslims simply ignore the extremists as they attempt to lead productive lives. For some, this acquiescence is a choice of necessity, as it was for moderate Afghans when the Taliban ruled their country.

Radical, fundamentalist Muslims—Islamists—are estimated by Indonesia's former president to number about 200 million people. Some believe that this is a very low estimate—that Islamists may be a "substantial minority" of the Muslim population. While most Islamists do not condone the tactics of the violent jihadists, they share the same vision for the course of the Islamic world. Every non-Muslim state is to be removed from any land that was once under Muslim control—including part of Western Europe, all of northern Africa, and the Persian and Arab lands of the Middle East. Within those lands, they seek to eliminate all governments and national boundaries in order to unify them under a religious caliphate. And ultimately, they subscribe to an Islamic quest to conquer the entire world.

All violent jihadists are Islamists, but not all Islamists are terrorist jihadists. And while the number of jihadists—including both those who carry out terrorist attacks and those that finance and enable those attacks—is unknown, it is certainly a very significant number.

The jihadists view America as the world power that stands in the way of their achieving their goals, and as a nation bent on denying the divine will of Allah. The United States is the primary target of the jihadists—not to negotiate with, but to destroy.

Even after the attacks of September 11, some Americans cannot bring themselves to recognize the scope and reality of the jihadist threat. Others have simply chosen to forget the horrors of that day, or have concluded that the burden of preventing future attacks is too great. At President Obama's first press conference, then media grande dame Helen Thomas referred to the jihadists as "so-called terrorists." Her dismissive view is shared by millions of Americans, anxious to deny the reality of the jihadists' ambitions and abilities. That so rudimentary a military force could expect to conquer vast territory and defeat the United States seems so fanciful that many Americans feel that jihadist threats must be simply rhetorical or political.

But jihadists see the world in starkly different ways from most Americans. Saudi oil revenues continue to fund the spread of Wahhabi Islamic fundamentalism throughout the Islamic world. Through the proliferation of children's madrassas, mosques, and centers of higher learning, large segments of Islamic society have been indoctrinated with fundamentalist views—ideas that powerfully motivate their behavior, regardless of how illogical they may seem to us or how different they may be from our own. As the *National Review*'s Andrew McCarthy writes, "Fundamentalist strains of Islam, including Salafism, have been developed by extraordinary minds. It is not that these Muslims fail to comprehend our principles; they reject them. They have an entirely different conception of the good life."

There fundamental differences between our respective worldviews are both striking and numerous. For example, while Western nations take care to separate church from state, for the Islamists, religion and government are to be one. The founding fathers of Islam proclaimed that "Islam is a religion and a state." Rather than limiting itself to prescribing only spiritual laws, fundamentalist Islam seeks to dominate and control every aspect of society, from economic policies to social interactions, and from individual daily habits to the functioning of government. Thus, Islamists would replace secular systems of justice with *sharia*. From the viewpoint of the Islamist, the government of an Islamic nation that is not sufficiently fundamentalist is not just wrong, it is evil. According to Middle East authority Lawrence Wright, the Pulitzer Prize–winning author of the seminal work on the founding and spread of al Qaeda, *The Looming Tower*, the jihadists have adopted the concept of *takfir* to deal with these Muslim governments—in essence, it is a license to kill apostates. Jihadists believe that moderate Muslim officials and rulers have "excommunicated" themselves from the faith and that therefore the Qur'an sanctions the killing of these leaders. This doctrine motivates the plotters against moderate Muslim leaders today just as it emboldened the assassins of Anwar Sadat.

Another example of the difference in perspective between Islamists and the West: Rather than embracing discovery, the Islamic fundamentalists condemn it. For them, the Qur'an contains all information and learning that is needed, and everything that *should* be known. In this view, modernity itself is evil—contemporary law, business practices, social mores, tolerance, rationalism, and scientific inquiry are heresy. And as the world's epicenter of innovation and intellectual discovery, America is emblematic of the world's sinful pursuit of everything forbidden by Allah. When jihadists call America "the Great Satan," it is not only because they believe we are evil, it is also because they believe America is the great tempter, drawing people to sin.

For an American, freedom is one of our highest values. We consider it an inalienable right, bestowed by God. For an Islamist, freedom is evil and it is contrary to the will of God. Iranian Ayatollah Khomeini decried "freedom that will corrupt our youth, freedom that will pave the way for the Oppressor, freedom that will drag our nation to the bottom." For the jihadist, whether Sunni or Shia, there should be no freedom to disobey God's will.

To the Islamist, democracy is a form of blasphemy; in democracies, immutable law proscribed by God may be changed by man. In the eyes of the Islamic fundamentalists, America as the "author of liberty" and "champion of democracy" is the most immoral of nations.

While we in the West see great value in the wide diversity of the world's peoples, nations, regions, and continents, the Islamists see only a single dividing line, one between the state of Islam (dar al Islam) and the state without Islam (dar al Harb)—literally, the house of war. Once a territory has become part of the state of Islam, it must remain so forever, and all former Islamic lands are to be returned to Muslim control. Accordingly, Islamists have no interest in seeing an independent Palestinian state established alongside Israel—the so-called two-state solution. Their goal is to remove the Jews from land that they believe is an integral part of the state of Islam, land that will be claimed once more for Allah, land that once having been conquered for Allah belongs to Allah for all time. For jihadists, no peace is possible with the state of Israel, on any terms.

In America, we understand the concept of expanding the reach of one's religion through evangelism and persuasion. But as the Islamic fundamentalists see history, the state of Islam has primarily expanded by divinely mandated conquest. Under the lead of the caliph, early Muslims were given authorization to conquer non-Muslim lands and peoples, a conquest known as *fatah*. Once a people were conquered, they had three options: convert to Islam, accept second-class citizenship and onerous taxes, or be subject to ethnic cleansing. The rate of conversion was brisk. In the words of Hassan al-Banna, the 1928 founder of the Muslim Brotherhood, a branch of jihad in Egypt—and what many consider to be the root of al Qaeda—"It is the nature of Islam to dominate, not to be dominated, to impose its law on all nations, and to extend its power to the entire planet."

There is a saying among people of religious faith in the West, "Pray as if it's up to God, and act as if it's up to you." To an Islamic fundamentalist, however, when it comes to everything in life—and to a *fatah* war in particular—God calls the shots. Allah decides who will win a war and who will lose it. And most important, Allah will *always* grant victory to Muslims *if* they are sufficiently strict in their adherence to all aspects of Islamic law and custom. This conviction is deeply ingrained in indoctrinated Muslim youth, and it is promoted by reference to historical evidence. Fatah armies made up of inexperienced and poorly armed and clad Arab nomads defeated the Byzantine Roman army in the battle of Yarmuk in AD 636 and the Persian army in the battle of Qadisiya the following year. In a repeat performance in the eleventh century, Mameluk fatah armies defeated both the Mongols and the Crusaders. Modern history is also viewed as evidence that Allah will grant victory to fatah armies, even against seemingly insurmountable odds. This is how Ayatollah Khomeini's defeat of the U.S.-backed Shah of Iran is viewed by Shia Islamists. Jihadists also claim that they caused the collapse of the Soviet Union as its dissolution occurred shortly after their victory in expelling the Soviets from Afghanistan.

Americans may smile at the suggestion that jihadists are responsible for the demise of the Soviet Union, as we recall the decades of Cold War that preceded the fall of the Wall, but that only demonstrates again how differently we see the world. Jihadists are entirely convinced that Allah grants them victory against any foe if they are worthy. And to the jihadist, there is nothing at all irrational about aiming to win a war against the United States, causing the collapse of the West, and establishing a worldwide caliphate. If Allah is with them, they reason, no one can stand against them.

The intellectual roots of jihadism extend at least to the thirteenth century. Ibn Taymiya, a Syrian scholar, taught that any deviation or variation from the original teachings of Islam's Prophet and his earliest followers was apostasy and would alienate the hand of Allah in promoting the nation of Islam. These teachings and codes of conduct had been established by the "predecessors," or the Salaf. From there derives the doctrine of Salafism, that is, a return to the ways of the early founders of the caliphate. Mohammed Wahhab, a Salafist from the Arabian Peninsula resurrected Ibn Taymiya's strict fundamentalist teachings in the late eighteenth century, and his followers formed an alliance with the Saudi federation of tribes who established a state founded on Wahhabism, one of Salafism's major branches, that has been expanding ever since.

In the mid-twentieth century, when Egyptian intellectual and Muslim Brotherhood ideologue Sayyid Qutb studied for a time in the United States, he returned home fully convinced that Americans were entirely materialistic, morally debauched, and lacking any true belief in God. "I hate those Westerners and despise them!" he exclaimed. "All of them, without any exception." According to Qutb, secular Muslim leaders like Egypt's Gamal Abdel Nasser and Anwar Sadat were infidels and "near enemies," and they therefore had to be the first to be eliminated. Then the holy jihad would turn outward: "The white man in Europe or America is our number one enemy. . . . Let us teach these children from the time their nails are soft that the white man is the enemy of humanity, and that they should destroy him at the first opportunity." Osama bin Laden and Ayman al-Zawahiri were not breaking new ground; they have only espoused for modern listeners beliefs that are centuries old, and reminded them that it is holy to declare war on America and to ardently believe they will win.

This brief history of Islamist radicalism is widely accepted, but still it shocks many Americans who simply cannot conceive of such a religious ideology. Perhaps this explains in part why our national conversation about the threat from violent jihadists never seems to deal with the reality of their implacable hostility and enduring war against us.

Despite the weight and breadth of the jihadists' passion for destroying America, it's easy to dismiss them as a military threat; after all, they bring a slingshot to a battle we can wage with an Abrams tank and an F-16 fighter. But their strategy is asymmetric—they exploit our vulnerabilities and maximize their strengths. They can recruit and train from among the hundreds of millions of fundamentalist Muslims throughout the world. We don't need to know their exact numbers. We do need to understand the scale of the threat. And it is large indeed.

So, too, is the support that is expressed at times by segments of mainstream Muslims for jihadist warfare. This passive or latent encouragement of radicalism is almost as alarming as active violent jihadism. Following the 2005 subway bombings in Great Britain, *nearly a quarter* of all British Muslims polled said they supported the attacks. And a year later, a Pew Global Attitudes survey found that one in seven Muslims in Western Europe believed that suicide bombings against civilian targets are sometimes justified in the defense of Islam. Of course, jihadists do not need large numbers to wage their warfare—they need recruit only a tiny number from among pockets of these populations for their cells. By now, attacks have taken place in a shockingly large number of countries around the world, including Britain, France, Spain, Germany, Russia, the Netherlands, the Philippines, Lebanon, Pakistan, India, Indonesia, Malaysia, Saudi Arabia, Nigeria, Sudan, Somalia, Thailand, and, of course, the United States, Iraq, and Afghanistan. Jihadists may not have Abrams tanks, but that does not prevent them from executing fatal and devastating attacks.

The tactics of the various jihadist organizations take different shapes. Within Muslim countries, the priority is to gain adherents, particularly among those who can serve as fighters and suicide bombers. Sensational attacks in Western nations are designed in part to stir pride and passion, promoting recruitment at home. And the West's retaliatory, sometimes disproportionate strikes, which tragically but inescapably take innocent human lives, are extensively filmed and repeatedly broadcast by Al Jazeera and other militant television networks throughout the Muslim world, fanning flames of revenge. This cycle is part of the strategy of the jihadists.

Additionally, unstable Muslim nations such as Pakistan and Somalia, and part-Muslim countries like Nigeria and Lebanon, become targets for takeover by the jihadists because they can provide both territory and financing. Islamists today control both Iran and Sudan, and Afghanistan was firmly in their grasp until we invaded in 2001. (Again, there are crucial differences between the Shia Islamists of Iran and the Sunni Islamists of Sudan and al Qaeda, just as there were enormous differences between Nazi Germany and Imperial Japan. It is important to understand these differences, but the fact that jihadism has two ideological sources does not in any way diminish the overall threat.)

The value of controlling Iran, for example, is enormous for the Khomeinist jihadists. The oil-rich nation funds and directs Hezbollah's efforts to destabilize Lebanon, attack Israel, and plot terrorist acts across the globe. Iran funds Shia jihadists in Mesopotamia and Eastern Arabia but also Sunni jihadists such as Hamas in Gaza and Salafist jihadists in the Middle East and Africa. Iran funds and equips any Islamist radical willing to strike at the West. And Iran is a primary source of weapons and training for combatants that kill Americans and our allies in Iraq and Afghanistan.

The Iranian regime is not simply a *threat* to us. Any force that finances and orchestrates attacks and provides the bombs and bullets that actually kill American soldiers is our enemy. Much can be said about the diplomatic possibilities for convincing the Iranian regime to abandon this course, but we should not pretend for a moment that Iranian Khomeinists are not at war with the United States. The widespread public demonstrations following the 2009 Iranian elections made it clear that not all Iranians support the policies of the current regime. Given the ruthless suppression of these demonstrators and the show trials that followed, it is equally clear that the radical mullahs and their mouthpiece, Ahmadinejad, are not going to turn from violent jihadism.

Face-to-face military confrontations on fronts like Iraq and Afghanistan are also part of the plan, with jihadists convinced that despite our military superiority, they need only hang on and continue their insurgencies, and Americans and the West will eventually tire and retreat to go home defeated and demoralized, as did the Soviets. Wars like these boost recruitment of the young and adventurous, and when they are successful, they energize millions of the faithful. Even when they are defeated, they deftly transform their losses into at least a rhetorical form of victory. Following their defeats in Fallujah and elsewhere in Iraq, jihadist speeches boasted that "the infidels have been crushed and had to use greater technology, which signifies their weakness."

The jihadists' history with America justifies their confidence that we will abandon the fight. In 1983, jihadists attacked U.S. marines in Lebanon—and we withdrew. Then again in 1993, jihadists attacked U.S. marines in Somalia—and we withdrew. Next, jihadists placed bombs in the World Trade Center, but they were arrested and tried as if they were street criminals, not a real and present threat. Then the jihadists blew up an American facility in Saudi Arabia, without any reprisal. In 1998, al Qaeda blew up two U.S. embassies, killing hundreds of civilians, yet once again our response was temporary and pitifully ineffective—we launched missiles but failed to hit a single relevant target. In 2000, jihadists audaciously attacked the USS *Cole*, killing seventeen American sailors, but once more, we did nothing. Throughout these years, America also refused to carefully consider the dangerous implications of jihadist involvement in wars in Algeria, Bosnia, and Chechnya. With all this history as a backdrop for their lectures to the young, jihadists have become quite confident in the knowledge that, time and again, we have underestimated their threat, their capacity to kill, and their steadfast resolve. This is the lesson they pass on to young radicals in the making. Only in recent years has American resolve in Iraq and Afghanistan provided a counterexample of Western fortitude in the face of jihadist attacks.

Much has been written about the jihadists' use of asymmetrical warfare to offset our battlefield superiority. A former military officer related to me the result of an American war-games exercise in which a simulation of a U.S. navy task force in the Persian Gulf faced a "terrorist" team of small boats and planes. The enterprising team successfully defeated the navy group with a surprise attack. The lesson of this exercise applies in many theaters and across many different weapons platforms. Asymmetrical warfare does not aim for a single, decisive engagement of forces, the sort of central battle that has defined so much of Western military history. It aims to wound and enrage, then debilitate and demoralize.

Make no mistake: the jihadists have identified our vulnerabilities. They surely paid careful attention, in fact, when one heavily armed man and a boy, operating out of a single automobile, so terrified Washington, D.C., that the regional economy ground to a virtual standstill for days. (In that instance, in fact, convicted assassin John Allen Muhammad may well have been responding to a call to arms issued in an al Qaeda video.) Nor could the jihadists have overlooked the fact that most of the Eastern seaboard and Midwest went dark for an extended period following a single but catastrophic malfunction in our aging electrical grid. And what a lesson the subprime mortgage crisis has taught them: our economy is so fragile, interconnected, and opaque that a serious disruption in our nation's capital market can spawn a worldwide economic crisis.

Yet if that's the case, why haven't we suffered a major terrorist attack in the United States since September 11, 2001? In part, because we have prevented them: By the time of this writing, we had uncovered and averted plots involving local jihadists in Oregon, New York, Miami, Dallas, North Carolina, Georgia, and Virginia. British security prevented an effort to place bombs on multiple commercial aircraft on their way from London to the United States, and convicted the plotters in September 2009, though the occasion attracted little comment in the United States. Ironically, this series of counterterrorism successes has produced a prolonged period of uneasy calm at home which may well be responsible for our growing complacency.

Our increased security precautions and expanded intelligence networks may have delayed the decision to launch a major attack, or lengthened and complicated its planning. However, in the view of some people inside and outside our intelligence community, bin Laden will attempt to attack the United States again in a massive, potentially devastating way.

A future bin Laden attack on America could include the use of weapons of mass destruction. He has publicly claimed that "acquiring nuclear weapons for the defense of Muslims is a religious duty." Following the 2001 attacks, he boasted that he would soon have access to Pakistan's nuclear arsenal, and he promised that he wouldn't hesitate to use every weapon at his disposal—without exception—to defeat the infidels. The Iranian regime, the jihadists' prime sponsor, is on track to build nuclear weapons of its own, and—most chillingly—al Qaeda has proclaimed that it has been granted a *fatwa*, a legal sanction handed down by radical Muslim clerics, to kill four million Americans, half of whom may be children.

The American mind simply cannot conceive that bin Laden and his henchmen would carry out such butchery. Does he not understand the inevitable scale of our retaliation? Yet in a society that lauds martyrdom, that lives for rewards in the afterlife, and in which mothers celebrate the nobility of their suicide-bomber sons, there is little fear of retribution. If retribution were to occur, it would be Allah's will, and the glorious dead would watch the advance of jihad from their mansions in heaven. Dr. Phares predicts, "Should a cataclysmic weapon fall into the jihadists' hands, its use is more than just possible; it is almost a certainty." The Commission on Weapons of Mass Destruction, Proliferation, and Terrorism, established by Congress as a successor to the 9-11 Commission, unanimously concluded that it was probable that terrorists would succeed in attacking a Western city with a weapon of mass destruction within five years.

The pursuit of military power by China, Russia, and the jihadists is advancing, not retreating. Among the four contestants for world leadership, only the United States and the West are reducing their financial commitment to national defense. Given the consequences of falling behind, continued complacency could prove calamitous. We must strengthen the safeguards to our security, even as we face broad domestic challenges. And we must prioritize those sources of power that will be the most effective in providing an enduring defense.

4

Pathways of American Power

National power compels, convinces, or motivates other nations to act or to forbear from acting. While we generally associate national power with military strength, power can actually be derived from various sources.

China derives economic power from its large and rapidly growing market. The lure of access to their market as well as the growing global dependence on China for inexpensive manufactured goods has led nations like ours to effectively accede to China's demands that Taiwan be given something less than full diplomatic status.

Power can be diplomatic, as was the case when Senator John McCain led the U.S. threat to remove Russia from the G-8 as a way to stem its growing authoritarianism.

Persuasion, popularity, and personal affinity can similarly be forms of power. In the months prior to the beginning of the Iraq War, former president George W. Bush's cordial and influential relationships with a number of presidents and prime ministers surely helped expand the ranks of his coalition of the willing. Unlike so-called hard power, which flows from military might, these economic, diplomatic, and persuasive influences have traditionally been considered soft power.

Growing America's Soft Power

America consistently underperforms its soft-power potential. Our economy is twice the size of our nearest two competitors, Japan and China, and it is 80 percent as large as the combined economies of the twenty-seven nations of the European Union. Yet time and again, we have not been able to effectively exercise that power to our advantage. For example, while China's political stability in large measure depends on having free and unfettered access to our market, we have not been able to harness our soft power to deter China from its financial support of Sudan, nor to enlist its support in backing harsh sanctions against Iran.

Consider also our relationship with Colombia. It is a staunch ally, a democracy, a fellow combatant in the international war against drugs, and one of a shrinking number of Latin American nations that aggressively resist Venezuelan president Hugo Chávez and his totalitarian aims for his own country and hegemonic ambitions for the continent. We also sell more goods to Colombia than it sells to us. Colombia is a crucial economic and military ally. Yet the president and Congress have refused to date to enter into a free-trade relationship with Colombia, bowing instead to the political clout of American organized labor and its shortsighted suspicion of free trade agreements. This diplomacy by special interest is a blow to Colombia's pro-U.S. government and to our support among its people. So rather than employ our economic power to enhance our influence in the region, we have diminished it. In refusing to act, we actually strengthen Chávez, our announced enemy and a self-proclaimed partner of Russia and Iran.

(The day is coming when Chávez announces a "peaceful" nuclear program organized and supported by the mullahs in Iran. At that point, perhaps congressional Democrats will rethink their incredibly destructive treatment of our true friends in Colombia.)

This same pattern too often holds true in the use of our soft powers of persuasion and popular appeal—an arena in which America has substantial advantages. Our culture and brands are ubiquitous; our celebrities appear on billboards and magazine covers around the world. Students from nearly every foreign country are eager to attend our colleges and universities, which are ranked as the best in the world. Our technology in fields from software to health care is widely admired and sought. America's consumer market is the world's largest.

Our soft-power advantages should also be derived from our manifest generosity: Americans make up just 4.5 percent of the world's population, yet we donate 12 percent of global foreign aid, an amount almost twice as much as any other country. We provide the most funds for humanitarian relief and global charities, and former president George W. Bush's Emergency Plan for AIDS Relief is the largest international health initiative in history dedicated to fight a single disease. Pastors like Rick Warren lead churches like his to send thousands of Americans on mission trips around the world, bringing aid, comfort, and expertise to the most impoverished villages on the planet. American ships and soldiers are first to the scene of global disasters. In fact, whenever the world faces potentially insurmountable threats, military or otherwise, it turns to America.

Yet with all that we have done to help others, and with so much more that remains to be done, our popularity and persuasive sway are on the wane.

To some degree, of course, our flagging popular appeal is an inevitable result of our war on terror. And there is the predictable resentment engendered by our wealth and power, and even our generosity can arouse envy. But these do not excuse our ineffectiveness in promoting persuasive power. The appeal of liberty, the ability of free enterprise to lift people from poverty, and the demonstrated willingness of America to come to the aid of others could be far more compellingly employed in attracting other nations and peoples. The self-loathing of Western intellectuals should not hinder our sturdy defense of all that should make us the most admired and respected of nations. We must argue our case, leading others to eagerly join us in the cause of liberty and peace.

We often exercise diplomatic power well below its potential as well. As former UN ambassador John Bolton documents in persuasive detail in his book *Surrender Is Not an Option*, diplomats and State Department negotiators are often more motivated to secure an agreement—even those they know will become mere window dressing that will be ignored by the party across the table—than they are to push for actual, verifiable results favorable to America. When diplomatic success is measured by the agreements and documents we have produced rather than by behavior that has actually changed, we create a false sense of security that prevents us from recognizing and dealing with real threats. The multitude of North Korean agreements, celebrated by the scores of diplomats and politicians that secured them, harmed more than helped our national security. They had no appreciable impact on North Korea's pursuit of nuclear weapons and they prevented us from taking action that would have made a difference. Diplomatic power means successfully changing outcomes, not piling up meaningless agreements. Using this metric, American diplomatic power over the past two decades has been only partially successful.

One positive exception: the disarmament of Libya, which followed our invasion of Iraq. A suddenly chastened and fearful Qaddafi threw open his secret arsenal of chemical weapons and his nuclear program; American diplomats arranged for the transfer of it all out of the country. Here, military power opened the door to a diplomatic success and we took advantage of the opening to execute not a treaty promising disarmament of Libya's WMD, but actual disarmament.

We have been particularly ineffective in enhancing diplomatic power by exploiting the potential of our alliances and our associations with other nations. America is of course strongest when our friends are standing with us. We have a base of friends in NATO, yes, but to date we have found it difficult to bring together its member nations to jointly confront our most pressing threats. NATO does fully participate in the peacekeeping in the Balkans, but it was American resolve led by former president Bill Clinton that stopped the bloodletting there. And NATO has agreed to join the effort to stabilize Afghanistan, and that is no small accomplishment. But in the case of some nations, the commitment of fighting forces lags far behind where it ought to be. And the NATO countries have yet to adopt the kind of comprehensive, collaborative mission to defeat radical jihadism that has been proposed, for example, by Spain's former prime minister, José María Aznar. Even after repeated devastating blows from the jihadists across Europe, our alliance still balks at implementing the far-reaching strategy that is required.

It is not only in NATO and Europe where we have underperformed in constructing productive, results-oriented associations with our friends and allies. In Asia, our policies and initiatives often come off as ad hoc and uncoordinated. In Latin America, our friends are mystified by our inaction and inattention to the spread of Castro's and Chávez's radicalism and anti-Americanism. And in Africa, even as former president George W. Bush's humanitarian programs have won the admiration of tens of millions, we have seemed powerless in the face of genocide and perpetual civil wars.

There are some who look to the United Nations as a vehicle for us to exercise soft power. But looking at the appalling ineffectiveness of the United Nations and its inclinations toward authoritarian regimes, it may serve as a pulpit, but it is no actor in the cause of freedom and human rights. Its Security Council is hamstrung by China and Russia; even Syria, a state sponsor of terror, was only recently a member. The United Nations stood by as Hussein slaughtered Kurds and Shia, as nearly a million people were murdered in Sudan and Darfur, and as Syria flaunted the sovereignty of Lebanon and killed tens of thousands of Lebanese. Only when democratic Israel acts in Lebanon to defend itself from Hezbollah attacks does the United Nations snap into high dudgeon.

It is long past time for America to strengthen and effectively deploy our soft power. There should be no misunderstanding of the fact that soft power is *real* power; that it can and does affect world events. The Lebanon War in the summer of 2006 is only one example.

When conflict broke out between Hezbollah and Israel, many observers were surprised to see Hezbollah garner so much support among many of the Lebanese people. Hezbollah was launching rockets from Lebanese neighborhoods, making them the open targets of Israeli retaliation, but nonetheless, large segments of the Lebanese people, including a majority of Shia, cheered Hezbollah, even offering its soldiers refuge and logistical support. Many Americans were stunned by the deep well of support for the terrorists that began the war and that brought so much punishment down upon the Lebanese people.

A good deal of the support for Hezbollah stemmed, of course, from deep-seated anti-Israel sentiment and resentment. But it was also the result of Hezbollah's long effort to help the Shia community by building village schools, health clinics, and a wide array of other social services. Israeli officials with whom I spoke explained that Hezbollah contributed only a few million dollars a year to this effort, but it was money very effectively spent. In this instance, soft power meant real power for Hezbollah.

And where were we when Hezbollah were building their support? A few years before the war broke out, we had celebrated Lebanon's Cedar Revolution as a victory for democracy. But following the toasts and self-congratulations, we and our Western allies effectively declared victory over Syria and went home. When we did, the Iranian-backed Hezbollah and the Syrian secret police remained to go about the long-term work of changing hearts and minds, and in some cases, to wield the intimidation of assassination. Why didn't we or other nations like France, which has long and still-important ties to the country, invest in the villages and families of Lebanon? Why didn't we aggressively promote soft power, particularly when democracy was so fragile and just gaining root? And why didn't we push Syria out, firmly and finally, when we had the chance to do so?

Perhaps the simple and unacceptable answer is that no one of substantial stature and clout was paying attention. Beyond assistant secretaries and State Department bureaucrats, who in the United States is charged with thinking about Lebanon every day? Who will be held personally accountable if Lebanon retreats back into its status as Syria's puppet? Who has the resources—including money—to implement a soft-power strategy? Who can direct experts at the U.S. Agency for International Development to partner with the Department of Health and Human Services to help design a medical clinic? Who can direct the Department of Education to help design a school for a Lebanese village? Who can hire local contractors to build a clinic, a school, or a water project? No one.

If an official in this country wanted to secure funds for medical clinics and schools in Lebanon, he or she would have to go before committees and subcommittees of Congress, before agencies and departments of the executive branch, and then—if by some miracle money was authorized and appropriated—they would have to follow federal-contracting rules to get them built. By that point, Hezbollah would be firmly ensconced. Given the encouraging Lebanese elections of 2009, we have an opportunity to learn from and rectify our mistakes of the past.

Global strategist Thomas P. M. Barnett has written important books on the past and future uses of American soft power. In *The Pentagon's New Map* and subsequent volumes, Barnett argues that "connecting the gap" to the developed world is the most effective and important of all American initiatives. Barnett is an apostle of soft power, and while his message cannot replace the necessity of a robust military establishment and the willingness to use it when required, the soft-power doctrines he extols should become routine components of the projection of American power abroad.

Our government is not presently configured to allow for such deployments of soft power. Beyond State Department bureaucracy, who in the United States with authority and power is focused every day on Latin America, for instance, and is responsible for moving its nations toward freedom and free enterprise? Who can draw on already appropriated funds to support charities, initiatives, and projects throughout Latin America in order to encourage people and politicians to adopt and abide by the principles of liberal democracy? No one.

You can be sure that opposition forces are not so inattentive or powerless in the deployment of soft-power initiatives. Go anywhere in Latin America and ask people if they have heard of Operation Miracle, for example. "Of course," they will tell you, "that's the surgery Fidel Castro provides to cure cataracts." America spends far more on humanitarian aid in Latin America than does Castro, but his aid is known, branded, promoted—and is therefore more *effective*. Our relative ineffectiveness in the battle for the hearts and minds of South America's emerging powers is startling.

Our nation's military once faced a similar problem of "accountability gaps" when it came to performance. No one person was responsible for pursuing our military objectives in a given region. Each branch of service had its own command structure, and the regions of the several service commands often had different boundaries. Plans, priorities, and budgets regularly ran up against the barriers erected between the services. In other words, the situation was similar to our soft-power failures today.

After World War II, President Truman moved to impose accountability on the military, and approved a plan that divided the world into military regions and selected a single commander to be responsible for each region— for establishing military priorities, programs, objectives, and foreign-military relationships—across every branch of the service. And it has worked. Astonishingly well. Military success and failure are never orphans in the world of the American military. Every breakthrough or setback is owned by a very specific chain of command that ends in a very specific commander.

The same thing should be done to advance our soft-power effectiveness. The world should be divided into regions, preferably the same regions as those of the military. One individual—only one—would have responsibility to lead the promotion of democracy, freedom, stability, and free enterprise in that region. We might call this person a regional presidential envoy or the ambassador from CENTCOM or any of the other regional military commands. The title doesn't matter. The authority and the accountability do.

Every year, an independent agency would gauge progress in that region using defined metrics and then report to the nation whether and to what extent the envoy was succeeding. The envoy would be given a budget, and he or she could call on the resources of federal agencies and departments to support this effort, using previously authorized budget dollars to compensate that department. The envoy could act innovatively, implementing plans and programs that were uniquely positioned to succeed in that region. The envoy's sole mission would be to exercise soft power throughout their region, building more effective alliances, strengthening friendships, coordinating with NGOs, and working collaboratively against common adversaries. President Obama appears to have addressed this opportunity with the appointment of special envoys like former senator George Mitchell, Richard Holbrooke, and Dennis Ross. But these ad hoc arrangements lack the enduring commitment that will enhance credibility and success. The long-standing State Department bureaucracy, often staffed with wonderfully intentioned but hamstrung career diplomats, have seen special envoys come and go on a regular basis. We need to overhaul the country-by-county ambassador/career/CIA divisions within our embassies—a nineteenth-century system that was outmoded even before twenty-first-century communications systems revolutionized soft power.

It would be ideal if other allied nations created similar regional positions, and if we coordinated our efforts with theirs. France, for example, might play a leading role in Lebanon and among a number of nations in Africa; Spain could exercise its soft power with Cuba; and Britain could sustain important relationships with former colonies in Africa and Asia. NATO and new alliances could move beyond military missions to the promotion of stability, modernity, and democracy—alliances that would collaborate in addressing regional and global concerns.

There is growing urgency for the United States and the West to strengthen our soft-power effectiveness. Radical forces are competing with us to indoctrinate and mobilize large impoverished communities such as those in Somalia, Gaza, Bangladesh, and the Sahel region of Africa. These are areas, among others, where jihadists are being recruited in large numbers and where anti-Americanism is on the rise. The intelligent application of our soft power is critical if we are to counter the campaigns that have been unleashed by the radicals.

In the Islamist world, soft power is real power. The Muslim Brotherhood invests heavily in soft-power initiatives, as do Hamas and Hezbollah. Radical Saudi interests have long directed large appropriations of petro dollars into the penetration of Muslim communities in both Muslim and non-Muslim nations. Our soft-power responses to these initiatives, on the other hand, have either been nonexistent or applied ineffectively. Indeed, in many instances where U.S. funds were sent to help local communities, they were directed to the very people and organizations that had been indoctrinated by the radicals. In the war of ideas, our enemies have used our own soft power against us.

In a world in which we encounter both regional and global challenges, America must act decisively to build and exercise greater soft power. It is relatively inexpensive, it can help us promote freedom, and it may spare us from the tragedy and cost of armed conflict.

The Weight of Hard Power

"Depend upon it, sir," the great Samuel Johnson remarked, "when a man knows he is to be hanged in a fortnight, it concentrates his mind wonderfully."

It is, of course, hard power—military might—that concentrates the minds of our adversaries. Nations with substantial hard power are generally the most able to influence the actions of others.

It is American military might that dictated the outcome of World War I and World War II, and which steadily but surely wore down the Soviet Union until the cost of the attempt to keep up with us exhausted their energy and brought about the Evil Empire's collapse. Military might has always counted most when nations compete. Military power influences events even when it is not actually used.

This fact has not been lost on nations like North Korea and Iran. They have pursued nuclear weapons at great expense and some risk in part to satisfy their military aims, but also because of the influence that hard power can give them. It is Russia's hard-power prowess, particularly its nuclear arsenal, which accounts for a measure of its disproportionate sway in global affairs, along with its energy stranglehold on Europe

If military might is the core of hard power, America is in a league of its own. Even so, there are those who like to overstate the extent of our military advantage, believing as they do that our military investment is excessive and disproportionate with our needs. One of the most frequent sights along the 2008 national campaign trail was a billboard trailer pulled behind an activist's car that claimed that the defense budget is a shocking 50 percent of the national budget. But the chart is the product of accounting hocus-pocus. Their figures include only the budget's discretionary spending. When all federal spending is included, defense is 20 percent of the total.

Reports of America's share of worldwide defense spending can also be misleading. According to official budgets, we are responsible for about 48 percent of the entire world's defense spending—approximately ten times the amount spent by China or by Russia. But again, reported numbers do not tell the real story. First, some countries simply do not report all their military expenditures. China, for example, does not include expenses for strategic forces, military purchases from foreign countries, or the cost of military-related research and development. So while its reported military budget in 2007 was $46 billion, its actual annual spending is estimated to be in the range of $100 billion to $140 billion.

Some analysts make an additional currency adjustment when comparing spending and resources in China with our own: rather than converting the Chinese yuan into U.S. dollars at the official exchange rate, they use the Purchase Power Parity (PPP) exchange rate, which compares the cost of a basket of goods in the United States with the same goods in China and then adjusts the currency accordingly. Because things generally cost less in China than they do here, applying the PPP exchange rate to Chinese military spending produces a Chinese defense budget range of approximately $240 billion to $340 billion—quite a different figure than the $46 billion that is reported.

But even the PPP adjustment is misleading when comparing the relative cost of specific resources like soldiers and ships and airplanes. For example, it costs the United States $129 billion a year to field 1.5 million troops. China, by contrast, can raise an army of 2 million troops—33 percent more men and women than in our combined services—for only about $25 billion annually. If their cost per soldier were the same as ours, instead of spending $25 billion for their troops, they would have to spend $172 billion. China's lower troop cost is largely the result of conscription and the nation's low wage rates.

For all these reasons, if you were to accept the argument of the activists opposed to the defense budget's size and you were to look at reported defense spending figures as a measure of the military strength of the two countries, you would get a very inaccurate impression. If China's cost to employ a soldier and to purchase an item of military hardware were identical to those that are paid in the United States, *its budget would be closer to half the size of ours, not the one-tenth that is reported.*

China and other nations also enjoy other cost-saving advantages. The United States invests heavily to ensure that we continue to lead in defense technology—which we must—but our invention and research is regularly incorporated by foes and friends alike, at no cost to them. Sometimes it's stolen through espionage, and sometimes it simply becomes widely available in the marketplace. In 1967, I attended the Paris World Air Show at Le Bourget Airport. America's Grumman F-11 fighter was proudly displayed on the tarmac, cordoned off by velvet ropes and closely guarded by a number of U.S. military personnel. And oddly, it seemed to me, its landing gear was partially retracted, so it sat quite low to the ground. I asked a friendly soldier why, and he explained that the landing gear's design was innovative and his superiors didn't want people with cameras to get too close a look.

America's military innovations go far beyond landing gear, of course, and foreign nations employ decidedly more sophisticated techniques for stealing them than simply snapping photos at air shows. The FBI identifies China, in fact, as having an "aggressive and wide-ranging effort aimed at acquiring advanced technologies from the United States." So aggressive has the People's Republic of China's quest for our technology been that the U.S. Immigration and Customs Enforcement agency lists China as our leading espionage threat. The weapons we spend billions of dollars to develop for our defense are often simply appropriated at a fraction of the cost by our competitors.

One of the greatest disparities between our military cost and that of other nations results from the scope and breadth of our respective military missions. The U.S. military provides global humanitarian relief, for example—and we are often the only nation with resources that can be deployed worldwide at a moment's notice. Our military is also charged with deterring nuclear attack whether from rogue nations or a future would-be superpower; preventing space attack and cyber-attack; protecting world shipping routes; supporting nations in their defense against insurgencies and helping failed states avoid becoming bases for terror; stopping ethnic cleansing and genocide; and maintaining the capabilities to respond to conventional wars wherever they might occur on the globe. No other nation's military takes on so many diverse missions in so many parts of the world. Our total defense outlays reflect our total responsibilities.

Defending all fronts from attack is far more expensive than mounting a single offensive against a point of attack. Consider the relative costs of protecting the whole nation against a biological attack versus the cost of obtaining and dispersing a toxin or virus. At the Salt Lake City Olympics in 2002, for example, we spent $320 million defending against possible terrorist attacks that could have cost our enemies a small fraction of that amount to deploy. And this cost was for a single event in a single city staged over less than three weeks.

America spends more on our military than other nations simply because we have so much more to protect and defend—not only for ourselves, but also for our allies. We cannot let "official" military-spending figures make us overconfident or complacent. Nor should they be considered credible evidence that we spend too much on defense. We should always determine the proper levels of U.S. defense spending only after carefully examining our actual and projected military capabilities relative to others, our present conflicts and future risks, and the specific requirements of our many missions at home and around the world.

A Strong and Dynamic American Defense

Americans have paid more for freedom than for anything else. The price for Alaska was $7.2 million and the Louisiana Purchase cost only $15 million. In national treasure alone, however, the cost of liberty has been in the trillions. In the cost of American lives, our greatest treasure, the sacrifice has been far greater. Almost 50,000 lives were lost in the War of Independence and the War of 1812 with Great Britain. More than 600,000 people gave their lives in the Civil War, which brought freedom to the slaves and preserved the Union. And since the close of the Civil War, our costliest conflict, more than 600,000 more lives have been lost in the many battles in distant places to ensure liberty for America and other freedom-loving peoples.

There has never been a time when our liberty was "free." From the founding of the Republic forward, wars have followed wars. It is foolish and dangerous to assume that human history has changed for the better when it comes to its unbroken record of strife and war. For a time after the collapse of the Soviet Union, the dream of freedom in a world at peace seemed to be on the brink of unfolding. Instead, new tyrants emerged, new wars and threats broke out, and our men and women in uniform once again were forced to enter harm's way. They expelled Saddam Hussein's army from Kuwait, fought extremists in Somalia, secured peace in Bosnia, then in Kosovo, and cleared the skies over Iraq. Then came September 11, 2001, and we were in Afghanistan and, soon thereafter, in Iraq once more.

It has always been the case that we have been unable to predict with anything approaching certainty when or from which corner of the earth would come the next threats to freedom.

We thought that we could avoid being drawn into the first great war of the twentieth century, but we were wrong. Confident that the ghastly toll would never be forgotten and that World War I would be "the war to end all wars," we turned our attention to our domestic travails and dramatically reduced our army and limited our navy. Japan's 1941 attack and Hitler's worldwide aggression proved these to have been very unwise indeed.

When the peace was won in 1945, we failed once again to learn from experience and we disarmed once more, only to be called on to defend South Korea from invasion. More recently, our dismissive attitude toward the threats posed by the jihadists throughout the 1990s left us unprepared for the horrific assault that followed. The 9/11 Commission declared that our lack of preparation was a "failure of imagination." In fact, ours has been a long history of failing to imagine the very real threats to freedom and peace. Perhaps what was most unusual about the failures that led up to September 11 is that we remained complacent even though the jihadists had declared open war against us, had killed marines in Beirut, had bombed our embassies in Africa, had nearly sunk a destroyer, and had previously bombed the World Trade Center.

As President Obama proposes to once again reduce our investment in national defense, I acknowledge the public fervor and widespread wish that world peace will prevail nonetheless. But history, the growing threats around us, and the reality that even now the jihadists are killing Americans, all demand that the truth of our peril must trump hope.

The truth is that we are at war with a formidable enemy and that nations like Russia and China are intent on neutralizing our military lead. The truth is that hatred and tyranny are pervasive; that we will be attacked again and that we cannot confidently predict the nature of the attack, or when or from where it will come. And so the truth is that for our freedoms to endure, we must pay a large price to maintain our freedom, and if we do not pay enough in dollars, we may be forced to pay the price in blood.

When former secretary of defense Donald Rumsfeld said that "you go to war with the army you have," he was roundly criticized because it had been the administration's decision whether and when to go to war with Iraq. But the statement itself was correct, of course. You may do your best to rapidly power up once you know the enemy and the nature of the conflict, but in the interim, you can fight only with the soldiers and equipment that have previously been readied. Years ago, the training of soldiers and the production of armaments of warfare were rudimentary. Washington's minutemen had muskets at home and they already knew how to shoot. Munitions and cannons could quickly be cast in crude foundries. Even decades later at the commencement of World War II, the production of aircraft, tanks, and small arms was relatively straightforward—auto plants were transformed into tank and aircraft plants in just one year. Even so, because we significantly dismantled our military prior to World War II, the investment required for us to catch up and confront our enemies was massive. The defense budget reached 34.5 percent of the GDP in 1945, about nine times today's 3.8 percent, and the delay prolonged suffering and loss of life.

Given the lead times necessary to produce the advanced technology of modern warfare and the extensive training required by today's fighting forces preparing to wield those technologies, wars of the future will necessarily be fought with the soldiers and armaments at hand and long delays will accompany even the most pressing mobilization. An F-22 can't be built anywhere but in a specialized and dedicated facility by highly skilled engineers and workers; substantially ramping up production could take years. Our F-22 program began in 1986, but the first fighter wasn't battle-ready until 2006. The Joint Strike Fighter, commissioned in the mid-1990s, is not expected to join our fleet until 2013. Similarly, the training, equipping, protecting, supporting, and even feeding of our personnel are highly sophisticated and time-consuming endeavors. An officer corps and noncommissioned officer corps take years to put in place. To protect America against the many threats we may face in the future, we cannot wait until they are upon us. We must build a military today that is capable of defending against the threats of tomorrow.

Some people argue that we should sharply narrow the scope of our military and defend against only our current menaces—terrorist insurgences and asymmetric warfare. Their motivation is unquestionably budgetary. If we spend less on the military, they reason, more money will be available for entitlements and social programs. But because we have never been able to accurately predict the nature and timing of the next war, and because it takes years of research, procurement, and training to build military capacity, following such a course is certain to be dangerous and quite possibly disastrous. Optimism as to the prospects of peace could cost tens of thousands of lives, and maybe even more. I can think of no social program that is more valuable than the lives and freedom of our sons and daughters. Rather than scale our military according to our hope for peace or out of a desire to shift funds to domestic priorities, we should build it to be capable of fulfilling each of the missions necessary for our sure defense. Only then can we be confident that we will secure America's place in the world and preserve life, liberty, and prosperity. Those missions should include the following:

1. Strategic Defense

America's strategic defense relies on credible nuclear deterrence. Accordingly, our nuclear arsenal must be updated—comprehensively and soon. While other nations from France to Pakistan have been testing and updating their nuclear capacity, we have done little to maintain our deterrent power. The bipartisan Perry-Schlesinger Commission concluded in 2009 that our nuclear facilities are in urgent need of repair and transformation.

Russia is insistent that nuclear reduction talks encompass only strategic nuclear weapons, not theater nuclear weapons, which are currently config-ured for short-range deployment. Their position is understandable, as they have many times the number of theater nuclear weapons as does the United States; they'd like to cement that superiority into place. You can always count on the Russians to bargain in their own interest. We must bargain in our interest, however, never permitting Russia or anyone else to secure nu-clear superiority.

Just as important, we must develop and install a robust missile defense system. Progress achieved in the Bush years in building a shield to protect the United States from the missiles of rogue states and in preparing for a missile shield in Europe was a good start. The Obama administration's de-cision to reduce missile defense funding and to abandon our defense sites in Poland and the Czech Republic is inexplicable—especially as Iran and North Korea are working overtime to deploy nuclear-tipped missiles that could threaten the world.

The Cold War doctrine of mutually assured destruction was an effective deterrent against the Soviet Union, a nation intent on its long-term sur-vival. But when unstable nations like Pakistan and North Korea are armed with nuclear weapons, when North Korea attempts to sell nuclear technol-ogy to other rogue nations like Syria, and when the Islamic fundamentalist leadership of Iran pushes hard for nuclear capability, we face a risk of nu-clear blackmail or worse.

As important as our missile shield, however, is our pressure on would-be nuclear powers. Iran must be prevented from obtaining nuclear weapons. Unfortunately, it is unlikely that the Obama administration will exert the necessary force to avert this catastrophe for the world. Not only will Israel's very existence be threatened, but the entire region and world will be destabi-lized. A nuclear Iran will precipitate a nuclear race throughout the Middle East. Iran's Supreme Leader Ayatollah Ali Khamenei has boasted that his nation is ready to provide nuclear technology to others, suggesting that Su-dan's Omar al-Bashir may be one of them. In a world in which its signatories have abandoned the Nuclear Non-Proliferation Treaty and rogue nations and terrorist organizations will eventually have nuclear weapons, a missile defense capability is a clear and urgent priority for the United States.

Ideally, we would rid the planet of nuclear weapons. But we are unlikely to be successful in doing so, at least within the coming decades. To begin with, because Russia's conventional capabilities have badly deteriorated, it derives its power from its nuclear stockpile and strategic weaponry and it has no interest in losing its place in the world by eliminating its nuclear weapons. It does, however, have a great interest in paring down the U.S. arsenal. Iran is committed to becoming a nuclear nation because it believes that achievement will vault it to superpower status among Middle Eastern nations, perhaps securing its candidacy as the twenty-first-century caliphate. And with nuclear power in hand, Iran is virtually guaranteed that no foreign power will invade, as the United States did in Iraq. Iran learned its lesson from North Korea: No matter its size, a malevolent country can thumb its nose at the world with impunity—if it has the bomb.

Global nuclear disarmament also has the problem of verification. Deceptions are routine. Both India and Pakistan developed their programs in secret, and there are believed to be many other nations that could "go nuclear" in a relatively short period of time. Nuclear technology is so widespread that it could be harnessed by any number of foes. Could America, or even Russia for that matter, ever realistically rely on signed treaties and agreements to guarantee that no group, no terrorist, and no nation would secretly develop nuclear weapons? It is inconceivable that jihadists would ever abandon their pursuit of nuclear weapons, regardless of agreements. As long as even one country or one group of fanatics pursues nuclear weapons, the United States must maintain robust nuclear capability.

We must not allow wishful thinking to obscure the truth. We are not on the verge of nuclear disarmament; we are on the cusp of greater and extraordinarily dangerous nuclear proliferation. North Korea and Iran's nuclear arms will compel others to follow suit. While America and the world still have a chance to stop Iran, neither the current administration nor the global powers have yet shown the stomach for deploying and enforcing the truly withering sanctions that goal would require. As a result, the American nuclear deterrent—updated, tested, and ample—and a highly effective missile defense system are essential not just to our security but to the security of the world.

We must convincingly make clear to friends and foes alike what our response will be if any nation or group chooses to use a nuclear device or other weapon of mass destruction. During the Cold War, each side understood the stakes: A nuclear attack by one superpower would result in massive retaliation by the other. Nations like Iran that may be inclined to provide fissile material to others must be entirely certain that we will hold any nation that supplies nuclear material just as responsible for its use as a country or group that deploys it. Iran's rulers and its people must be made to understand that developing nuclear technology carries with it a very real risk: If its fissile material gets into the hands of a group that uses it, Iran itself will suffer devastating retaliation. Now is the time to state this plainly, as a deterrent and as a warning—not following an attack when voices are crying for restraint and a "proportionate" response.

2. Counterinsurgency and Land War Capacity

America must be prepared to fight and win land wars and counterinsurgencies, including the ones we are now fighting, and these conflicts rely on ground troops, tanks, field artillery, helicopters, and close air support. The logistical support requirements are complex, numerous, and expensive. In the future, land forces may be required to stabilize a collapsed state—and Pakistan is certainly a possibility in this regard given its nuclear arsenal. Land forces may also be required to again remove a government that is enabling attacks on America, such as was done with the Taliban in Afghanistan and in Saddam's Iraq. Of course, the existence of a readily deployable military also helps deter attacks on our allies.

Iran's direction and support of Hezbollah's rocket attack against Israel, as well as Russia's invasion of Georgia, illustrate just how quickly aggressions around the globe can escalate into wars that demand American responses, though in these two instances, American troops were not involved. But scenarios triggering the need for "boots on the ground" are far less inconceivable than they once were. A military capable of successful ground fighting is *not* a thing of the past. Even those who insist that we never repeat a mission like that in Iraq should not forget that ground forces remain vitally important in Afghanistan, and in 1990, they were needed to thwart Saddam Hussein's invasion of Kuwait. The Desert Storm conflict employed over 500,000 U.S. troops and over 2,000 tanks and other combat vehicles. It would be foolhardy to rule out the need for ground forces capable of winning a decisive victory.

Former secretary of defense Donald Rumsfeld held to the view that conflicts like those in Iraq and Afghanistan can be successfully waged with a relatively small number of ground troops. That course has failed in both places. As noted by conservative *New York Times* columnist David Brooks, this path is an "illusion" with "simply no historical record to support" it. He continues: "The historical evidence suggests that these middling strategies just create a situation in which you have enough forces to assume responsibility for a conflict, but not enough to prevail."

To fulfill missions of this nature, a good deal of work and investment lie ahead of us. Our ground forces have been stretched, their equipment worn down, and their stockpiles of crucial materials depleted. The demands of the two-front war in Afghanistan and Iraq came after an era of deep cuts in our military preparedness. After the end of the Cold War, the army was cut from eighteen divisions to twelve and consequently, our army and marines were stretched to the breaking point in Iraq and Afghanistan. Most army brigades have been deployed to Iraq or Afghanistan more than once, and fully a quarter of them have been deployed three or more times. Soldiers' rotations have been extended, critical training shortened, and recovery and recuperation times have been sharply reduced. Early in 2008, General Richard Cody testified to Congress that the demand for our forces "exceeds the sustainable supply."

The result has been that our Reservists and National Guard have had to fill the gap, and they've borne a heavy and unanticipated burden. Designed to be held back in the event of a sudden threat or dire emergency, our Reserves and Guard instead have been repeatedly called upon for regular operations. These are not just young single men and women; they are more often middle-aged fathers and mothers. Their service represents a particularly heavy sacrifice, for them and for their families and employers. As governor, I attended a number of National Guard troop send-off ceremonies. The audience was typically overflowing with spouses and children; along with their tears, I almost always saw pride in their eyes. And the soldiers were proud of their skills: one A-10 Warthog Air National Guard pilot boasted that their wing's kill rate would be better than that of active-duty fliers; when they got home, they confirmed it. But long rotations took a heavy toll on the families, including reduced earnings for already strapped budgets, missed birthdays and anniversaries, and an absent parent or spouse.

When our armed forces are short-staffed, the inevitable results are higher casualties, more long-term health impacts, greater risk to our security, and more adventurism by tyrants. These human and national costs are simply too high to bear. We must add at least 100,000 soldiers to the army and the marines, and given the growing need for counterinsurgency capabilities, we must significantly expand soldier training.

Gordon Adams, a former fellow at the Woodrow Wilson International Center for Scholars, argues that we won't need a larger army if we simply avoid getting into conflicts like Iraq. But entering wars will not always be our choice. And if foes perceive a weakness, they will exploit it. The stronger our army, the less likely it is that it will have to fight.

We also need to increase our investment in the weapons of ground warfare. The conflicts in Kuwait, Iraq, and Afghanistan have destroyed, damaged, and worn out a large share of our armament. The army needs to upgrade all of its tracked vehicles and many of its tanks. And the Army National Guard reports that it currently has at its disposal only 40 percent of its needed equipment stock. The air force reports that it has lost 40 percent of its Predator unmanned aircraft, and that it cannot "meet the demands for battlefield surveillance." In rearming our military, Secretary of Defense Gates is right: we must focus first on what we need to win the wars we are currently fighting. It is inexplicable and inexcusable that the 2009 Stimulus Act, with $767 billion in spending, devoted almost no funding toward this effort. In the defense of liberty, there is no substitute for the brave men and women of the U.S. military—and we should start taking better care of them.

3. Control of the Commons

"Control of the commons" means that our military is able to move freely on the seas, in the air, and in space—allowing us to protect trade, respond to humanitarian crises, provide essential support to our ground forces, enhance our credibility as an ally, and project the power necessary to restrain the ambitions of tyrants. This freedom of movement is the direct result of the superiority of our navy and air force, and of our alliances around the world. While our lead remains great, we should not forget that China and Russia are investing heavily to close the gap that exists when it comes to international mobility, not necessarily by matching our strength head-on, but by creating asymmetries.

Following the Cold War, we reduced our navy by over half, from 570 ships in 1990 to the current 283-ship fleet. The size of our navy has been permitted to shrink dangerously. The navy's stated minimum requirement is 313 ships. Unless the shipbuilding budget is substantially increased, we will see a navy with 210 to 240 vessels, numbers that no one believes are consistent with America's security and global responsibilities.

America is a sea power. The seas have not grown smaller nor have our responsibilities shrunk. We are inviting the challenges on the oceans that a dominant navy deters. We must rebuild our fleet.

Our air force flight squadrons were cut from 76 to 50. The average age of our military aircraft is now twenty-nine years, and the average age of our long-range bombers is thirty-three years—the same vintage as an AMC Pacer or Chevrolet Vega. The air force's main bomber, the B-52, is now fifty years old. The Clinton administration boasted that they would change "government as we know it" by reducing the federal payroll. What it did not advertise nearly so loudly was the fact that 90 percent of the cuts were in military employment. Nor did they trumpet that our human intelligence resources were cut by one quarter—including those in complex and dangerous places such as Pakistan, Egypt, and Syria.

Despite the cuts to our land, sea, air, and intelligence capabilities, and the growing ambition of China, Russia, and others, our lead in military power remains substantial. But according to Secretary of Defense Gates, other nations "are developing the disruptive means to blunt the impact of U.S. power . . . and deny the U.S. military freedom of movement and action." In particular, he continued, China's investments in space-warfare, cyber-warfare, missiles, and submarines "could threaten the United States's primary means to project its power and help its allies in the Pacific." America's lead will endure only if we remain committed to the research and procurement of our sea, air, and space defenses. This is not the time for another procurement holiday.

4. Defending Against Discontinuities

Other nations are actively pursuing new technologies that hold the promise of leapfrogging them into superiority and making our military capabilities ineffective and obsolescent. China's investments in cyber-warfare, antisatel-

lite warfare, and antiship weaponry, for example, are calculated to neutralize our military's many strategic advantages. The devastating implications
if such hostile strategies succeed can't be overstated. A successful Electro-
magnetic Pulse (EMP) attack, for example, effectuated by a single ballistic
nuclear missile exploded above the United States "could result in airplanes
literally falling from the sky; vehicles could stop functioning, and water,
sewer, and electrical networks could all fail—all at once," according to the
Heritage Foundation's Jena McNeill and the Hudson Institute's Richard
Weitz. The area affected might be a single region or virtually the entire
nation, leaving our military utterly unable to respond because all electronic
and communications systems would be inoperable.

   A cyberspace attack could similarly cripple our defenses. The Department of Defense manages a hundred thousand networks on five million
computers in sixty-five countries around the world—a system that could be
attacked at any point by hackers, hostile governments, or terrorists. As with
all advances, our dependence on information technology is both a strength
and a vulnerability that potentially can be exploited in a new kind of warfare. It is essential that we invest the considerable resources in developing
technologies to defend against these threats. The fact that America's government and commercial computer systems have repeatedly been hacked
by foreign entities does not instill confidence that this investment has yet
been made a priority. In 2009, it was reported that foreign hackers had
gained access, *over a period of two years,* to computer files containing design, performance, and electronic data for the F-35 Joint Force Fighter.
Depending upon which data was obtained, such information could potentially enable an enemy to determine how to compete with, defeat or disable
the aircraft. The F-35 is no ordinary fighter. At a price tag of $300 billion,
the program represents the most expensive weapons system that has ever
been undertaken by the U.S. military. The Department of Defense claimed
that the most critical aspects of its design were not compromised, but the
credibility of the military's optimism is surely suspect given its failure to
prevent the cyber-attacks in the first place or to detect them over such a
long period of time. *The Wall Street Journal* reported that former military
officials indicated that the incursions "appear to have come from China."

   If we choose to minimize the effort to defend against cyber-threats,
everything we have invested in our army, navy, and air force could be

rendered useless in an attack in which not a single shot is fired. Space and cyberspace are the twenty-first century's new battlefields.

5. Counterinsurgency Forces

The jihadist strategy of insurgency and destabilization of nations throughout Asia, Africa, and the Middle East means that counterinsurgency support from the U.S. military will be in great demand in the coming years. In situations like our current effort to stabilize Afghanistan, we must draw upon the resources of our entire military. But in other cases, such as the terrorist threat in the Philippines, a smaller footprint can be more effective.

In 1991, the terrorist organization known as Abu Sayyaf was formed by Philippine members of the Islamic International Brigade, the predecessor of al Qaeda. Osama bin Laden charged it with waging jihad and establishing sharia in the southern region of the Philippines. By some estimates, Abu Sayyaf amassed more than three thousand terrorists and enjoyed widespread public support, resulting in years of brutal strikes and kidnappings. In 2002, the Philippine government asked the U.S. military to join its counterinsurgency and we responded. But instead of assuming command and deploying numerous combat forces, our military assembled a small team of special operations forces and intelligence personnel who worked in partnership with the Philippine military. And rather than immediately engaging Abu Sayyaf combatants, these forces first extensively evaluated geographic, economic, and political conditions in each of the affected communities and trained Philippine troops in counterinsurgency warfare. As regions were systematically cleared of hostile forces, our troops initiated public works projects and built schools, water systems, and bridges. As a result, the local population became increasingly supportive of the Philippine government and individuals increasingly began to offer intelligence. Little more than a year later, Abu Sayyaf had shrunk to a band of only about three hundred fighters and had moved entirely out of the region.

These small military teams composed of special operations forces and intelligence personnel—working in collaboration with a foreign nation's military—may be a model for supporting countries under threat from jihadists. In an address in 2007, I called such teams Special Partnership Forces, a term that highlights not only their distinctive capabilities but also their relationship with the host nation's military. We and other NATO nations should act quickly to raise such forces and place them on call to help needy governments repel insurgent jihadists before they become entrenched. Supplying them with the specific tools and armaments they will require for successful counterinsurgency must be a very high priority. Any reader of Robert Kaplan's chronicles of the post 9/11 modern American military will know the incredible effectiveness of our special forces deployed in partnership in nations as diverse as Mongolia, Algeria, and Colombia. This "small footprint-huge impact" approach may well be necessary in Pakistan, Malaysia, Nigeria, Somalia, and throughout the Horn of Africa. When a nation that is threatened by violent jihadists calls for such assistance, we must have the capability of sending it.

Alliances Capacity

America alone is strong. America standing with its allies is a good deal stronger. But as Thomas Donnelly and Frederick Kagan observe in *Ground Truth*, our allies are disarming at the same time that our potential foes are rearming. China and Russia are spending more than 4 percent of their GDP on their military, but France and the United Kingdom spend less than 2.5 percent, Italy 1.8 percent; Germany allocates only 1.3 percent, and consistent with its postwar commitments, Japan spends less than 1.0 percent on defense. Raising the United States defense budget from 3.8 to 4 percent of our GDP would add about $30 billion to defense. Raising defense spending by these five allies to 4 percent of their GDP would add *ten times* that amount to our combined defense. It is time for our allies to increase their investment in national and global security in order to assume their fair share of the load and to strengthen our combined capabilities.

When added together, the troop-strength and armament figures of our allies appear quite competitive, but the numbers may be deceiving to the public. They do not fool our potential adversaries. Low levels of modernization, disparate command structures, and divergent rules of engagement prevent the various forces of our allies from becoming a coherent collective military power. When NATO joined the effort to stabilize Afghanistan, for example, many European armies lacked the airlift capacity to actually get their troops there. Instead, they had to charter flights *from Russia*. In theory, the European

Union could become a credible military superpower. That would be as welcome as it is improbable. The countries of the EU spend far too little on defense, face demographic and budget crises, and experience little public sentiment that favors more significant military investment. A region that has witnessed war close at hand throughout its history is nevertheless more inclined to favor hope and wishful thinking than to vigorously support adequate defense. And the expenses of a vast welfare state are simply easier to carry when, by default, America is picking up a large share of the cost of Europe's national defense. We recognize and appreciate the extraordinary sacrifices made by some of our allies in the war against violent jihadists, especially Great Britain, which lost scores of brave soldiers and Royal Marines in both Iraq and Afghanistan, but the fact is that Great Britain and, to a greater degree, our other NATO allies simply have not budgeted for a military establishment equal to the challenges that face our alliance.

Despite the disparity in the conventional and strategic capabilities of our allies in comparison with the world's potentially hostile major powers, their capabilities are in fact critical to the defense of freedom. Allies provide bases that are essential to moving military resources to hot spots around the world, and they impede the movements of potential foes. Those countries like Britain, France, and Canada that have invested in substantial numbers of trained ground forces can significantly augment our troops, particularly in peacekeeping and stabilization missions. In some cases, our allies have particular skills—such as naval minesweeping—that we have in only short supply. Some have intelligence, communications, and political resources that may exceed our own. America is strong alone, but not strong enough to overcome alone all the challenges that are likely to confront freedom and security in the next half century. "America has no leadership role in the twenty-first century without a basic partnership with other democracies in Europe and Asia," writes Dr. Henry Nau, a professor at George Washington University. We need strong allies.

NATO's initial decision to engage in Afghanistan was a major accomplishment. Again, we cannot ignore or diminish the losses of life that our allies have suffered there to protect freedom. But the lack of decisiveness and the disunity among NATO members, coupled with its exclusive focus on the security of Europe, have led some observers to suggest that we bypass NATO and create a new global consortium of democracies. This is not the right course. Instead, the history, achievements, and current commit-ments of NATO make it the preferred foundation for such a body. Includ-ing other democracies like Japan, Australia, and South Korea could be accomplished by forming regional security councils and establishing a worldwide charter, but the NATO alliance should remain its foundation.

A great deal of political hay has been made of our diplomatic failures with NATO nations in the lead-up to the Iraq war. President Obama has an oppor-tunity to strengthen our NATO ties and leadership. The right way to do so, however, is not by apologizing for every one of America's mistakes or by simply acquiescing to the opinions of others. America has earned its leadership of the world's free nations, and we have nothing to apologize for when the balance sheet of our contributions is weighed against whatever mistakes we have made. Our job remains the unapologetic leadership of the globe's most decent, most free states. It is, in the words of Dr. Nau, to "pay more attention to the interests of others, but then, after hearing those interests, to clearly assert our own." The objective of the United States of America is strength, not popularity.

Effective application of our soft power and the modernization and reinforce-ment of our military power will be neither easy nor inexpensive. President Obama, however, drops the defense budget to 3.7 percent of the GDP in 2010, and sets it on a course to approach 3 percent of the GDP in ten years. During the fifty years of the Cold War, defense budgets averaged 6 percent of the GDP. The budget comparison itself is not enough to make the case for higher spending, but the gaps in our current military capabilities and the threats we face certainly do. It is time to commit to an annual defense budget of at least 4 percent of the GDP. The troop reductions of the 1990s, the de-pleted state of our military equipment, the threats posed by new technol-ogies, and the growing list of potential military missions mean that if we continue to underfund our military, we cannot sustain the level of American leadership that peace requires and that our national security demands.

In some respects, the long and very expensive Cold War simplified the selection of military priorities. The arms race was a two-party contest; we could assess where we stood by counting the Soviet Union's comparable weapons. The end of the Cold War and the resulting eruption of conflicts around the world, however, have expanded the number and the nature of threats. Today, even at a moment when we remain the world's only true superpower, our military has more missions, not fewer.

At the same time, we face enormous challenges at home, and I anticipate a growing outcry to reduce or cap our security spending. Some will support their argument by comparing defense budgets with those of other nations, but when they are properly calculated, the figures simply do not support cutting back. Others will insist that dialogue and diplomacy can free the world of grave threats, but history proves otherwise, and an honest threat assessment augurs for the opposite outcome: Iran and its jihadist colleagues present a real and serious danger; Russia is retooling and rearming its military and paying the bill with its massive energy resources; China's military expansion is the largest peacetime ramp-up since prewar Germany's; and the proliferation of nuclear weapons and disruptive technologies is expanding, not shrinking.

While our diplomacy and leadership can influence the world, we cannot control the world. What we can control is the size and sophistication of our military power and its deterrent effect, which in turn determines whether we remain free, safe, and prosperous.

One of President Reagan's first and most important actions was to secure two double-digit increases in the defense budget. For this, he was widely criticized by those who thought his actions were provocative. But history proved Reagan right and his critics wrong. The funds were used to recapitalize America's military, using the information-age technology that American ingenuity had brought to the marketplace. It was that modern military that pressured the Soviets into a corner and paved the way for unprecedented years of global peace, prosperity, and progress for democracy.

The same opportunity is available to us today. America has the capability to protect against the full spectrum of threats that confront us. The question is whether America's leaders have the clarity of vision to stand for a renewal of the defensive power necessary to protect the cause of freedom in the twenty-first century.

5

A Free and Productive Economy

Americans can only be as secure over the long term as our economy is strong. An inferior economy cannot indefinitely support a superior defense. Mathematically, the scale of our military can be no larger than the product of our total economy—the GDP—and the percentage of that economy that is spent on defense. And the size of our economy is a function of the number of people in the workforce and the *productivity* of that workforce.

As virtually every American discovered beginning in fall of 2008, a strong economy is also the foundation of our citizens' prosperity: Americans have experienced the impact of a weakened economy. But beyond the lows of recession and the highs of expansion, the sustained wealth of our families and communities is also driven by workforce *productivity*.

Productivity is so central a concept, so crucial an ingredient to national well-being, that a focus on productivity should be a constant in the media and in the minds of citizens. And the importance of productivity transcends ideology. Whether you are interested in spending more on benefits or you want to add to defense, achieving your objective depends on the nation's productivity.

Given its significance, productivity doesn't get much attention. In fact, many people with whom I speak aren't quite sure what it means. I once asked a class of college students to define "workforce productivity," and their best guess was that it was a measure of how hard and fast people work. Americans are in fact hard and skilled workers, but the work ethic in some other countries is also quite impressive.

Several years ago, I toured a factory in southeast China that manufactures small appliances like hand mixers, bread makers, and toasters. The plant employed about 20,000 people—mostly young women between the ages of eighteen and twenty-four. A tall barbed-wire fence surrounded the facility and guard towers anchored each corner; factory officials claimed that the security was needed to keep people from coming in—large numbers wanted very badly to work there. The women worked ten-hour shifts, six days a week, and they lived in dormitories on the company "campus."

Never before had I seen people working with such concentration, speed, and efficiency. As we toured the assembly lines, not one person glanced up at us as we passed. No radios offered potential distractions, and not once did I see a pair of workers sharing even a few quick words—everyone was intently focused on their work. When I asked the plant manager what was the reject rate for finished products, he didn't immediately understand what I was asking—because there are *no* rejects at his factory: Every single appliance is in working order when its assembly is complete. The manager explained that every bread maker, for example, is individually tested and actually bakes a loaf of bread before it leaves the factory—there are 0 percent defects.

When my American colleagues toured a competitor's small-appliance plant in the United States, they described it as operating at a much less frenetic pace. If productivity were solely a measure of how fast and hard people work, and if these plant tours were at all representative, you'd have to conclude that Chinese workers are highly productive, perhaps even more productive than our own. But, in fact, the American workforce is more productive—much more productive.

The reason is because workforce productivity is a measure of the *value* of the goods and services produced by a worker, not just how fast or intently someone works. For facilities like these small-appliance plants, workforce productivity is the total value of the appliances produced divided by the number of workforce hours. And despite the fact that the Chinese workers were dedicated and hardworking, the Americans were more productive. Why? One reason may have been because the American workers were more skilled or experienced. Another was that the American plant was more automated. In China, I observed women actually hand-winding copper wire to make small electric motors—something that's done by machine in America.

On a national scale, workforce productivity is the value of all the goods and services produced in the nation, divided by the number of people in the national workforce. The average income or wealth of our workers is the same figure. If this seems confusing, perhaps it's best to think of it this way: If American workers produce twice as much "stuff" every year as workers in another country, on average our workers will *earn* about twice as much as well. There is only one way to raise the income of the average person, and that is to increase national productivity—the value of the goods or services we collectively produce.

We devote a great deal of thought and emotional energy to the question of how best to divide the income pie at both a company and a national level—how much to pay and tax the CEO, the stockholders, and the factory workers—but we should also be very interested in how these decisions have an impact on our national productivity. Over the long term, national productivity will determine how much money the average citizen can make and whether the nation is able adequately to provide for the national defense. Again, the *only* way that America's wealth will grow and our personal incomes and standards of living can be raised is by increasing national productivity.

While almost everyone agrees that growing *overall* productivity is a good thing, some don't like to see productivity rise when the changes required affect them personally. To illustrate, imagine a tiny imaginary nation where a hundred workers raise the food and a hundred others build the houses. One day someone discovers how to make a plow and harness it to a draft animal. From then on, only fifty workers are required to produce the same amount of food. Is this a good development or a bad one? Fifty people are suddenly out of work—and they certainly aren't enthusiastic about the improved productivity. If there's a meeting of all the workers, you can count on fifty votes against the plow.

But what's certain is that someone will discover new things for those fifty unemployed workers to produce: tools, clothing, entertainment, or perhaps a chair in which individuals can rest comfortably at the end of a hard day's work. Some of those new jobs will pay less than the old job of farming. Some will pay more. Some of the displaced workers will thus be better off and some worse off. On average, the people in the society will become better off; in fact, much better off. The nation's overall productivity rises a great deal because more is being produced per person; per capita GDP increases, as does average personal wealth, all because someone invented the plow and because someone else created new goods or services that employed the displaced workers. This is the principle upon which individual and national wealth are built.

The Innovation That Propels Productivity

Raising the productivity of a nation and the prosperity of its citizens depends on two types of innovation—one that improves existing goods and services and another that invents new ones. The former may result in reduced employment; the latter generally adds employment. It's a two-part system: improve the old, invent the new.

In the effort to make existing products better and to make them more efficiently, innovation in the use of capital has long been a major source of productivity growth. When I was a boy, I remember touring a Rambler auto factory with my father and watching as components were lowered by hand-operated cranes, fit into place, then fastened, or welded. The assembly plant looked like a human beehive—skilled men and women worked shoulder to shoulder to build every car. But when I visited a modern automotive plant a number of years later, I found that a great deal of what had previously done by hand was now performed by robots. Capital innovation had led to fewer workers, better product quality, and greater productivity.

The steel industry has seen just as dramatic a transformation. In the 1980s, it took ten man-hours to produce a ton of steel; today it takes about an hour. The president of the United Steelworkers of America says that "when you go into a modern mill, it's as high tech as NASA . . . our members are able to bring their brains to work."

A similar kind of change has taken place in hospitals. Nursing stations today resemble a NASA control center: Computers monitor dozens of patients at a time, and signal when, where, and why a nurse's attention is needed. The initial investment in capital to upgrade a hospital is large, but the result is that fewer nurses are needed to simply look in on patients. And because patients are constantly monitored, they receive better care. In hospitals, auto plants, steel factories, and hundreds of other settings, innovation through technology, purchased with capital, has increased productivity.

Innovation can also enhance the *value* of the product itself. Alfred Sloan introduced automobiles with annual style changes and in a greater array of colors than Henry Ford's "he can have it in any color he wants, so long as it's black." Sloan thereby made cars more valuable to the consumer. When Intel discovered how to put more computing power on smaller and smaller chips, it made them more valuable and raised the company's productivity. Flat-screen TVs invented by the Japanese in the 1980s were perceived as having greater value and commanded higher prices; the TV manufacturers consequently enjoyed a boost in productivity. (A huge surge in productivity awaits the manufacturer who simplifies television remotes!)

Innovation may also improve the way in which labor is organized and utilized. When I was a teenager, we cruised Ted's Drive-In on Woodward Avenue near Pontiac, Michigan. Particularly on weekends, the cars circled, waiting for a slot to open where you could pull in and place your order. Ted's hamburgers were hand-shaped, cooked on a griddle, and delivered by carhops. But then McDonald's arrived with machine-made hamburgers and French fries that were frozen and trucked in from out-of-state factories. Fewer workers were required to prepare the food, and no one was needed to serve it to us. Ted's is gone. The Golden Arches are recognized around the world.

In the auto world, Toyota innovated what we now call "quality manufacturing"—placing such consistent attention to each detail at every step of the manufacturing process that flaws and rejects virtually disappeared. In doing so, they not only improved the value of their products, they also reduced the number of workers needed to rework defective cars. Productivity soared.

Many people find it hard to imagine how labor organization and management can have such an enormous impact on the cost of making or doing something. When I was serving as the governor of Massachusetts, for example, I suggested that we look into the possible benefits of hiring a private company to manage our state prisons. But almost uniformly, I was met with a very negative reaction. People invariably presumed that if we did, the state's costs would rise because a private company "would have to make a profit." It was hard to convince people that the private companies that manage prisons have learned how to safely do so with fewer workers than state-operated prisons—and that the money they save through productivity innovations more than makes up for what they earn in profit. In fact, it's the profit motive that led them to find ways to improve their productivity. The tax dollars we would save could either be returned to the people who paid them or be spent on additional government priorities. Either way, productivity would increase.

Organized labor made sure that private sector productivity would never disrupt government jobs in Massachusetts prisons, or anywhere else in our state government for that matter. In response to former governor Bill Weld's initiatives to open up state functions to competition from private enterprise, the legislature passed an act that effectively ended the practice.

It has been my experience that almost always government is far less productive than enterprises in the private sector. That's why private companies build roads for governments and make equipment for the military. It's also part of the reason why FedEx and UPS can make a profit shipping and delivering packages while the U.S. Postal Service loses money, even with its inherent competitive advantages. Local, state, and federal governments could save a great deal by hiring private contractors to provide a wide range of goods and services in which better organization and management of the workforce is a major source of productivity improvement.

In addition to innovating by creatively applying capital and by organizing workers effectively, productivity enhancements also come from new designs, new materials, new technologies, new sources of capital, streamlined process flow, better worker training, improved supply chains, and many other sources. There is simply no end to the ways in which innovators have improved products and services, thereby growing productivity and improving our standard of living. It is the inevitable, inexorable course of a consumer-driven, free-market economy.

For innovation to make a difference, it takes more than a good idea. It takes a good idea that is actually adopted and implemented. For years, IBM dominated the computer industry. Their strategy was based in part on building the fastest and most powerful computers—that way, they could best meet the large and growing processing needs of America's biggest companies. But then companies like Digital Equipment Company (DEC) had the idea that for many companies and in numerous applications, a fast but smaller minicomputer was a better match, a better idea. For whatever reason, IBM just couldn't adopt that way of thinking, so it began to lose its grip on the market. Then Wang came along, with its idea to create even smaller computers that met only the needs of an individual workstation. But neither IBM nor DEC embraced Wang's innovation. Dell and Apple soon pioneered microcomputers and laptops, but like IBM and DEC before it, Wang didn't jump on the new idea. Wang and DEC went out of business. IBM staged a comeback, reinventing itself by embracing the kinds of new ideas and technologies it had eschewed during its decline.

Again, good ideas alone don't automatically lead to innovation. First, there's the idea, but there must also be the conditions that lead it to be adopted and exploited. As Clayton Christensen, a Harvard Business School professor and one of the nation's leading scholars on innovation, has shown in his book, *The Innovator's Dilemma*, those conditions didn't exist at IBM, DEC, and Wang.

The same principle holds true when it comes to inventing an entirely new enterprise—an entrepreneur must have a good idea, but the conditions that will allow him or her to use that idea to build that new business must also be present. One of the most influential entrepreneurs of all time was Christopher Columbus. His good idea was to sail west to reach the Orient, but the conditions for implementation of his idea in Italy, his home country, weren't favorable, so he had to get financing from Spain instead. Similarly, although the Chinese developed the printing press, political conditions in China prevented their innovation from becoming truly revolutionary; it

fell to the Europeans to rediscover and popularize the printing press several
centuries later. Hero developed a steam engine in Rome in the year AD 50,
but the technology would not power machines until the Industrial Revolution more than one and a half millennia later. It is certain that valuable ideas
arise in the minds of people all over the world, but that many of them simply
lie fallow because conditions for their implementation aren't favorable.

Innovation and Creative Destruction

The key to increasing national prosperity is to promote good ideas and create the conditions that can lead them to be fully exploited—in existing
businesses as well as new ones. Government is generally not the source of
new ideas, although innovations from NASA and the military have provided frequent exceptions. Nor is government where innovation is commer-
cially developed. But government policies do, in fact, have a major impact
on the implementation of innovative ideas. The degree to which a nation
makes itself productive, and thus how prosperous its citizens become, is
determined in large measure by whether government adopts policies that
stimulate innovation or that stifle it.

The government policy that has the greatest effect on innovation is
simply whether or not the government will allow it. It's sad but true: Government can and often does purposefully prevent innovation and the resulting improvement in productivity. Recall my hypothetical example of a
society in which half the farming jobs were lost due to innovation in the use
of a plow? Some nations accept and encourage such "creative destruction,"
recognizing that in the long run it leads to greater productivity and wealth
for its citizens. But other nations succumb to the objections of those in danger of becoming unemployed and prevent innovation that may reduce short-
term employment.

Two centuries ago, more than three-quarters of our workforce actually
did labor on farms. Over the succeeding decades, innovations like irriga-
tion, fertilizer, and tractors were welcomed, and eventually large farming
corporations were allowed to prosper, despite protests from family farmers
and the often heart-wrenching dislocations that accompanied consolidation
of farmlands. The result was the disappearance of millions of agricultural

jobs and the large-scale migration of Americans from rural regions to our cities. Once there, they provided the labor that powered America's new industrial age. And at the same time, because farming innovation and productivity were allowed to flourish, America became the leader in agriculture education, research, and industry. Innovations from these sources have enabled us to produce sufficient food to feed not only our growing population but other parts of the world as well.

In contrast, Japan resisted many of the same innovations we embraced. In that country, small farmers held such political power that Japanese leaders enacted laws and regulations that stymied agricultural productivity. Japan similarly prevented the adoption of higher productivity innovations like supermarkets, not to mention big-box stores and hyper-markets. Retailers were historically governed by the so-called large-scale store law, which restricted store size to one thousand square meters or less. Today, strict environmental regulations on new retailers achieve the same objective, and a skilled bureaucrat can keep a supermarket out of virtually any Japanese town. According to a comprehensive study by former McKinsey & Company partner William Lewis, the result is that productivity in retailing is about half of what it is in the United States.

Yet Lewis also found that in heavy industry and manufacturing, Japan's productivity is well above our own. In that sector of the Japanese economy, a total of only about 1.5 million workers manufacture steel, cars, consumer electronics, auto parts and computers, compared with over 8 million workers in the country's retailing and food processing sectors. The net result is that Japan's innovation and productivity disadvantages in those two sectors—as well as in agriculture—swamp its achievements in industry, depressing Japan's overall economy and the wealth of its people. Japanese governmental policy that is purposefully designed to prevent creative destruction also inevitably blocks innovation, lowers productivity, and depresses the income and wealth of its citizens. Japan's leaders surely understand the consequences of their job protection policies, but the politics are simply too compelling for them to resist.

In post–Soviet Union Russia, it appears that the nation's leaders failed to fully appreciate the beneficial implications of creative destruction. Lewis's productivity analysis of that country found that in 1990, it produced virtually as much steel as the United States. Three large-scale plants had adopted world-class technology that enabled them to achieve productivity equal to 95 percent of that of the U.S. steel industry. But across Russia, thirty-three small, highly unproductive steel mills operated with antiquated open-hearth technology and subscale production. The Russian government attempted to protect them with subsidies, massive tax and energy-cost breaks, and by allowing them to reduce worker wages. The result was that in 1997—just seven years later—Russian steel productivity had fallen from near parity with that of the United States to 28 percent of our level.

Had the Russians followed one of the two better alternatives—either by investing in new facilities and technologies to make the small mills competitive or by allowing them to fail and devoting financial resources and available labor to new and more productive enterprises—the outcome would have been far different for the Russian economy and people. It takes a leap of faith for governments to stand aside and allow the creative destruction inherent in a free economy, but it's a leap that has been successfully made by every advanced economy in the world. As Alan Greenspan has observed, "Deep down that is probably the message of capitalism: 'Creative destruction'—the scrapping of old technologies and old ways of doing things for the new—is the only way to increase productivity and therefore the only way to raise average living standards on a sustained basis."

Creative destruction is unquestionably stressful—on workers, managers, owners, bankers, suppliers, customers, and the communities that surround the affected businesses. The pressures these groups put on political leaders to block game-changing innovations can be intense. Back when I worked as a venture capitalist, I was approached by an entrepreneur whose new company had developed software and an integrated system that could complete the legal work required by banks to close a mortgage—and the company could do it for a fraction of the cost being charged by lawyers for the same service. My partners and I invested in the company, convinced that the huge cost advantage it could offer would quickly build business, and we were right. Banks soon signed up for the service, and it looked like we were on our way to taking over the lion's share of the industry. Borrowers saw much lower closing costs, and the costs for banks came down as well.

But the company's growth was *not* good for real-estate lawyers. And because we were not yet fully appreciative of the realities of state government, we were surprised when legislators—many of them were part-time real estate lawyers themselves and many others had friends and contributors who were real-estate lawyers—enacted legislation that put us out of business.

Despite the benefits to the country, the consumer, and the overall workforce from productivity-enhancing innovations, they often face considerable opposition. Managers of corporations that are disadvantaged by a competitor's productivity-enhancing innovation may lobby to prohibit the innovation or the competition. Walmart, for example, pioneered a retailing concept that has propelled it to national leadership, but mom-and-pop and Main Street retailers often do their best to get local governments to prohibit or forestall Walmart's stores from being located in their vicinity. Unions as well often oppose productivity innovations that will lead to reduced employment; understandably, they aren't persuaded by arguments that workers will eventually find employment in new enterprises. And they may worry that even if new jobs are created, these jobs will not be in their union. Typically, they work to block such innovations in two ways. First, they threaten to strike the company that wants to adopt a productivity-enhancing new technology. Second, they exert their considerable political clout to convince government to impede the innovation.

In the hotel industry, for example, hospitality managers have learned that productivity is improved if they cross-train and cross-assign—doormen, bellmen, and the check-in staff are trained to do one another's jobs. If there's a backup at check-in, the person at the bell desk can cross over to help, and if the bellmen are busy, the doormen can take luggage to a guest's room or even fill in at the check-in desk. Because of this ability to move workers to different posts as needed, the overall staffing level needed by the hotel is lower, creating higher productivity.

But hotel unions routinely oppose cross-training and cross-assignment, even though such training increases the skill sets of the employees. At union hotels, the result may be that larger staffs are needed, productivity is lower, and hotel guests are more likely to be irritated while they stand in long lines and observe hotel employees who aren't busy. These kinds of work rules pervade many companies and most managers say such artificial barriers to productivity exact higher cost penalties on their business than do the typically higher wages won by the union. In fact, nonunion hotel companies typically go to great lengths to make sure their nonunion workers receive the same or higher wages than their competitors' union counterparts.

Government often supports union efforts that block productivity gains by prohibiting government contracts from being performed by nonunion companies. And it can bolster them, too, by requiring a certain staffing ratio by law, as is the case with proposed legislation that is being aggressively promoted at both the state and national levels to establish minimum levels of nurse staffing at hospitals. As hospitals have begun to adopt telemetry and monitoring technology that reduce the number of nurses needed in wards and other hospital settings, nursing unions have lobbied hard to see legislation enacted that fixes the ratio of the number of patients per nurse throughout the hospital. Under these rules, a hospital would be obliged to staff to the mandated level whether or not that number of nurses was necessary for the care of patients and the effective operation of the hospital, thus adding to the cost of health care for everyone.

Sometimes the government's complicity is even more direct. The most naked pro-union power play in decades is the AFL-CIO demand for Congress to change the process by which a union enters a company's workplace as the designated bargaining unit. The proposed statute, known as "card check" legislation, would represent a massive imposition on the freedom of workers to choose whether or not to become part of a union. Currently, the decision about unionization is made by a secret-ballot vote by the company's employees, but because unions haven't been winning a lot of elections lately, they want to change the rules. Under the AFL-CIO plan, there would no longer be any secret-ballot elections where employees can vote without the union knowing how they voted. Instead, the union would collect pro-unionization signature cards from a majority of employees, cards that could be collected over an extended period of time and without the knowledge of the employer that an organizing effort is under way; thus, employees could be targeted and pressured, one by one. This is a remarkable departure from one of the prerequisites of any democracy—that of a secret ballot.

It's easy to imagine how this system could lead to employee harassment and coercion. Ironically, the proponent's name for this proposed "card check" legislation is the Employee Free Choice Act. But what are the chances that it would promote free choice rather than stifle it? I'm convinced that in some cases it would effectively impose unionization on reluctant workers, as well as on small and big businesses across the country. It would also slam the door on countless innovations routinely opposed by unions, driving down or stalling completely productivity growth, and virtually ensuring that, over the long term, America's economy and household incomes would suffer.

There is no intrinsic reason why unionization must reduce productivity, of course. Some unions go to great lengths, in fact, to provide their members with training and skills that make them more efficient and productive. Forward-thinking unions look for ways to help their employer become more competitive.

Unfortunately, some union CEOs are less concerned about an industry's competitiveness than they are with how many of their union's jobs they can protect, how much they can increase wages, and how they can impose even more favorable work rules. In some cases, this mind-set has contributed to companies or to entire industries falling so badly behind their competition that they lose market share or fail altogether, resulting in even greater job losses. Airlines, textiles, tires, steel, aluminum, consumer electronics, and autos include cases in point. The decline in unionized workplaces in the private sector reflects a recognition by working people across America that continual improvement and innovation are required in order for an employer to survive in the global marketplace. Unionization continues to grow in the public sector, however, because there is no competition to drive out a government entity that is inefficient, unproductive, or high cost—government is a protected monopoly.

How Government Can Help

Again, the most important thing government can do to promote innovation and productivity is not to block it, as by preventing creative destruction. Likewise, if government prevents or impedes foreign competition it depresses productivity. Trade improves a nation's productivity and raises its citizens' incomes. But as with creative destruction, embracing the often disruptive and painful effects of foreign competition can be more than a bit counterintuitive.

Imagine that a foreign television maker develops a manufacturing process that improves the quality of televisions and makes them less expensive as well. You can bet that the U.S. government would immediately hear from our own television manufacturers. In the 1950s, America was the home to ninety different television companies, including RCA, Magnavox, Zenith, General Electric, and Motorola. They would argue that they would be driven out of business if the foreign TVs were allowed into the U.S. market without the imposition of a hefty tariff. The electronics-workers union would join the outcry, as would parts suppliers and the mayors of communities where American television plants are located. From their perspective, if the government didn't "protect" the U.S. industry, jobs would be lost. The collective outcry would be loud and sustained.

What is less clear to many is what the government should do: What is best for the American economy and for our people? Obviously, lower-priced and better-quality televisions would be good for American consumers. And if the U.S. companies were unable to match the foreign competition, jobs lost by U.S. television manufacturers would be replaced by jobs in industries making goods in new or growing businesses in which American companies were more productive and more successful than their foreign counterparts, leading to growth here and abroad. The inefficient manufacturers would inevitably disappear, but new ones would grow and thrive.

The math here is quite straightforward: replacing jobs in low-productivity industries with jobs in high-productivity businesses raises the nation's average productivity and per capita wealth. "The process of expanding exports from more productive industries," Harvard Business School professor and author Michael Porter concludes in his cross-nation study, "shifting less productive activities abroad through foreign investment, and importing goods and services in those industries where the nation is less productive, is a healthy one for national economic prosperity.

"Employing subsidies, protection, or other forms of intervention to maintain such industries," Porter continues, "only slows down the upgrading of the economy and limits the nation's long-term standard of living." The best course for the nation—and for our citizens collectively—is not to obstruct foreign competition.

U.S. companies faced with innovative and less costly products from overseas have to make one of two choices. They can invest in new technologies, innovations, and productivity improvements themselves and beat the foreign competition at its own game—a process that usually necessitates convincing investors to back them with new capital. It also often requires unions and suppliers to make adjustments. When Finnish manufacturer Nokia entered the American market with its high-quality and inexpensive mobile phones, for example, U.S. manufacturer Motorola didn't panic or cave in; it fought back with new investment and the cooperation and dedication of its workers and suppliers. Motorola continued to thrive.

Alternatively, U.S. companies can argue for protection, hold on as long as possible, and slowly watch their market share wane—aware all the while that sometime down the road they will be forced to liquidate, at the expense of their workers' jobs and the investment of their shareholders. Sadly, the foreign-television scenario wasn't hypothetical. In the nation that patented the first electronic television, very few if any TVs continue to be manufactured.

The case for trade, like that for creative destruction, makes good economic sense—trade improves the wages and standard of living for the average citizen. Trade also strengthens the overall economy. But trade can disrupt and devastate those individuals directly affected. Owners and shareholders may lose money, of course, but that is not an unexpected or unfair aspect of investing—they have encountered the unfortunate half of the "no risk, no reward" maxim. But it is the employees and managers, from the shop floor to the drafting tables to the delivery trucks, who take the brunt of the pain. Trade is good for the nation and for the average citizen, but it is decidedly not good for everybody.

Some years ago, I served as a lay pastor. In the Mormon Church, we don't have full-time or paid pastors, so individual members like me are asked to assume that responsibility. I served a congregation or a group of congregations in the Boston area for about fourteen years. Among these were inner-city and Spanish-, Chinese-, and Portuguese-speaking congregations. I cannot count the number of times I consoled or counseled a person who had lost a job. Not one of them, of course, saw their unemployment as "a good thing for the national economy." It was instead a deeply traumatic personal experience. The resultant stress caused a few people to gain weight, but most lost quite a lot. When the unemployment lingered, people often aged. Sometimes problems in the marriage or at home developed.

And these things occurred even though these people were not destitute; when needed, they received help from the church and from family as well as unemployment benefits they may have earned.

For some, when they found new jobs, they received better or at least equal opportunity and pay. For many, that was not the case. When the new position was an upgrade, people tended to overcome the unemployment experience. But when people could not find at least equal opportunity in a new position, and do so relatively rapidly, there often were sustained and meaningful personal costs. Marriages faltered, faith dwindled, illnesses appeared, countenances changed. Ever since these experiences, unemployment is not merely a statistic to me.

Given the beneficial effects for the economy, for the nation and for the average citizen, we should not restrict trade or burden productivity. But as a nation we must do everything we can imagine to help the affected people transition to new and more productive employment. Effective employment centers can help. For those who lack English proficiency, language programs at community colleges or similar institutions are essential. Other adult education programs can, of course, be extremely helpful. In my own experience, I have seen that the best training often occurs in the workplace where it is targeted to a job that is actually needed. That is one reason why I favor programs that incentivize employers to hire and train people who have been out of work for an extended period of time, who have disabilities, or who have been affected by the failure of a company or industry. As governor, I was able to establish a program that paid employers $2,000 toward the cost of training anyone they hired who had been out of work for more than a year. For all the benefits that productivity improvements bestow on the many, we need to make sure that the cost is not borne by the few.

Personally, I don't like to see America lose *any* good jobs. But when I see an American company challenged by a foreign competitor, I don't look for protectionist policies as an answer to the company's problems. Instead, I look to see how that company can become competitive once more, drive off its foreign foe, and propel its own products into foreign markets.

The first serious blow to the U.S. car industry that I remember—back in the days when my father and his team at American Motors made Nashes and

Hudsons—was landed by the German automaker Volkswagen. Its innovative, low-priced, and high-quality "Beetle" was first imported in 1949. But by the early 1960s, it had captured public attention as well as market share. American Motors responded by promoting its own compact car, the Rambler, but the Big Three took their time, continuing to bank on "gas-guzzling dinosaurs," as my dad and later millions of Americans called them.

Then in the 1970s, the Japanese invaded the American auto market, offering better-quality cars at lower cost than their American competitors. The domestics eventually adopted labor-organization and inventory practices that had been pioneered by companies like Toyota, and that helped. Nevertheless, the Japanese—and later the Korean—automakers enjoyed a substantial cost advantage over their U.S. competitors. Discussions I have had over the years with consultants and executives who have worked for the automakers estimated that disadvantage to be about $2,000 per vehicle, despite the cost of shipping cars from foreign locations to ports in California. Japanese, Korean, and German carmakers then took advantage of the market gains they had achieved to build assembly factories in the United States—bringing attractive jobs to thousands of U.S. workers and partially blunting the anti-foreign-car backlash. Even then, these "transplant" vehicles continued to enjoy a sizable cost advantage.

Foreign automakers don't generally pass their cost advantage on to their customers in the form of lower prices. Instead, they use it to add better features and put higher quality into their vehicles, keeping their prices competitive with domestic vehicles. The result is a perception that Detroit just can't make cars that Americans want to buy. Yet imagine the challenge the Big Three face in attempting to build a car as good as their competitors' when those foreign makers get to spend an extra $2,000 on their models. I believe U.S. engineers and designers have done a heroic job trying to compensate for the cost penalty. The Ford Mustang and Fusion and the Chevrolet Malibu and Silverado are examples of their ingenuity. And in my mind, there is nothing that has come out of Japan that can compare with the look and throaty growl of my 2005 red Mustang convertible.

What are the sources of the cost disadvantage? Among the many, the foremost is that the United Auto Workers has negotiated, and management has agreed to accept, very expensive pension and health benefits for its retirees. Next, UAW wage rates and work rules result in significantly higher costs per vehicle in a UAW plant. And third, the federal government's failure to adopt a predictable energy policy and its ad hoc imposition of fuel economy standards made it more difficult for domestic automakers to plan for market needs and legal standards. Simultaneously, it gave a distinct advantage to foreign companies that had engineered and developed fuel-efficient automobiles for their home markets, which had never embraced America's love for big cars and the open road.

As long as the American manufacturers suffer a severe productivity disadvantage, they will continue to lose market share. If the cost disadvantage were allowed to persist, Detroit would eventually go out of business—and that would be a terrible shame, a human tragedy, and an avoidable outcome. There is no inherent reason why America can't build competitive automobiles. There is every reason why we ought to be able to reclaim our leadership in the national and international automotive market. If we were to remove excessive retiree burdens, eliminate costly work rules and wage penalties, allow investment in new productive technologies, and adopt at last a *predictable* energy policy, the American automobile industry would vigorously rebound and many of thousands of jobs would be preserved and, over time, more thousands would be added.

I opposed Washington's bailout for the industry in 2008 because it enabled GM and Chrysler to avoid the restructuring and productivity improvements essential for their success. The managed bankruptcy that I proposed ultimately occurred, but only after tens of billions of taxpayer money had been wasted, and only after sweetheart deals and paybacks for favored interest groups had been engineered with the public's money. The question now is whether or not the administration's heavy hand has protected political and UAW interests in such a way that the industry's burdens persist. There are encouraging reports that General Motors's average hourly labor rate was reduced by 30 percent and that retiree burdens have been shed. If so, the company will have a "second chance," according to the *Wall Street Journal*'s former Detroit bureau chief, Paul Ingrassia. If, on the other hand, burdens have been permitted to remain, we will watch further loss of market share, further layoffs, and further subsidies. A CEO of an automotive industry corporation told me that in spite of what is said in public, the government is calling the shots on every major decision at GM, including which plants to expand and which to close. Management by politicians is a losing proposition. As a son of Detroit, I find the decline of the industry and of the great state of Michigan painful to watch. If the bitter but necessary medicine of restructuring has been taken, and if Washington politicians are removed from the management of the companies, there will be a turnaround. If not, we will watch the final chapter of the American automotive industry unfold.

There may be extremely rare occasions when government properly should protect a domestic industry from foreign competition. These would be in only very selective circumstances and then only temporarily. If foreign firms are engaged in predatory or monopolistic practices, our antitrust provisions should penalize them. When a country has artificially held down the value of its currency so that its products have a sizable cost advantage when they enter the American market, we must act to persuade that nation to allow its currency to adjust to market rates. Government should also act to stem dangerous foreign environmental policies and to block products produced by child labor or in inhumane conditions. In some cases, an industry may request short-term—*very* short-term—breathing room so that it can adjust to a new competitive threat. Such requests should be granted only when it's clear that the affected American industry can and will act decisively to regain a truly competitive position. But for every request for protection or subsidy that is warranted, a hundred or more others are not. The Bush administration's decision to protect the U.S. steel industry is a case in point—I agree with those who have concluded that it did more harm than good. President Obama's action to defend American tire companies from foreign competition may make good politics by repaying unions for their support of his campaign, but it is decidedly bad for the nation and our workers. Protectionism stifles productivity.

Encouraging trade does not mean entering into agreements that disadvantage the United States or being soft with trading partners who ignore our agreements. For years, Japan effectively prevented American products from entering their market despite our trade agreements. Others like South Korea keep out our agricultural products under the pretext of health concerns. And the World Trade Organization litigation process has been singularly unreceptive to American interests. None of this is reason to embrace protectionism, but it is reason for tough bargaining and strict implementation.

There is nothing so sought after by companies and unions as protection from competition, and yet there are few things so beneficial for an economy and its citizens as competition. It is rational for special interests to seek special treatment—and they do. The largest companies inevitably want antitrust laws relaxed so they can breathe easier and grow their market share even further. Companies facing tough competition from abroad crave tariffs, quotas, or restrictive product requirements so they can lessen their risks and avoid the cost and pain of restructuring and innovation. Companies that see their competitors invent productivity improvements want those innovations blocked by legislation.

Innovation means *change*. Change that makes a genuine difference means greater productivity. Improving productivity often results in the loss of jobs en route to the creation of new, better, and more sustainable jobs—a difficult process nationally and an often devastating one for individuals. Political, business, and union leaders who deny or minimize this fact of economic life do the country and its businesses and employees no favors.

Where Innovation Comes From

Increasing productivity begins with innovation and innovation begins with good ideas. More often than not, good ideas come from educated minds. America's post–World War II commitment to public higher education directly contributed to the burst of productivity that rocketed our economy beyond every other. But in important respects, other nations have made as great or greater a commitment to higher education than we have, particularly in engineering, computer science, and information. Fifteen years ago, China and India awarded about half as many master's degrees in these fields as did the United States. Today, they graduate more than *two times* the number of students in these fields as we do. The Chinese accomplishment in Ph.D.s during this time period is even more impressive. While our annual number of degrees has hovered around 7,000 to 8,000, theirs has risen from 1,784 to 12,130—50 percent greater than ours.

This is a stunning reversal of global preeminence in the priority attached to the highest level of educational attainment. Not surprisingly, China, Japan, and Taiwan claim a growing share of the world's patents.

Beyond the long-term consequences of this quickening eclipse, the short-term implications are devastating. Microsoft's founder Bill Gates, for example, told author Thomas Friedman that within a few years of its opening in 1998, the company's research facility in Beijing was already more productive than any of its other three research centers in India, England, and the United States.

A nation's collective priority for higher learning also impacts the type of innovation a country pursues. Germany's education prowess in engineering translates into innovative product engineering. England's success in chemical industry innovation is likely the product of its distinctive excellence in chemical-related advanced education. America's most advanced learners, by contrast, increasingly choose to specialize in the liberal arts. If the trend continues, we may produce innovations in writing, entertainment, and finance but be less likely to generate the newest innovation in such fields as chemical engineering and computer science. Not surprisingly, those who study something in depth are the most likely to make discoveries about it.

Education is more than a factor in generating productivity-enhancing ideas. It also figures into our ability to successfully implement those ideas in the marketplace. The use of computers, electronics, and statistical analysis have become commonplace for workers across the globe, even in blue-collar occupations. But America's decline in elementary and secondary education—where we now rank well below other developed nations—puts our workers and our businesses at a distinct disadvantage when it comes to the skill sets our youngest blue- or gray-collar workers possess. Michael Porter reports that Japanese managers at U.S. manufacturing plants complain that American college graduates are often confounded by techniques that Japanese *high-school graduates* readily comprehend. American companies increasingly have to devote substantial resources to the most basic kinds of training, often simply to bring their American workers up to global standards.

The lead America enjoyed in all levels of education fifty years ago, and which powered our industries to world leadership, has vanished. If we do not make dramatic improvements in our educational system, it will be almost impossible for our lead in innovation and productivity to be sustained. We owe every American child a chance at a great education, and not just because of the inherent, God-given value of that child, but also because our entire society depends upon the collective output of our citizenry. The world's developing nations long ago recognized the necessity of broad-based educational excellence. They learned it from us. Tragically, we have allowed politics to weaken the schools that powered our generation's economic success.

As important as education is to innovation, we are fortunate that other factors, such as culture, also play a vital role. These are factors less susceptible to the ill-effects of special interest politics, and thus our advantages in these areas are more resilient. One example: Americans aren't afraid to fail. There's no loss of face if it occurs, as there is in Japan and Germany. The innovative and entrepreneurial spirit in America compensates, at least to some degree, for the present failures of our public educational system.

It seems as if virtually everyone in America dreams of starting a business. More Americans are engaged in entrepreneurialism per capita than in any other country—it's an advantage we must strive to preserve. Over 12 percent of us are entrepreneurs of some sort; the British come in second, but only at about half that rate. When I asked the dean of the Harvard Business School whether the majority of his recent graduates sought banking, consulting, or industry as their field of choice, he replied, "None of the above. It seems that about 90 percent of our students want to start their own company!"

Most entrepreneurs I've met didn't find their niches straight out of college or business school. The majority of them came from jobs from which they saw a need and had a bright idea about how to meet it. America's industries and domestic markets are, in fact, breeding grounds for innovation. A young Eldon Roth held a blue-collar job in a cold-storage plant where beef was frozen soon after it was butchered. His idea: Instead of slowly freezing the meat in walk-in freezers, why not place the beef on conveyors and pass it between two supercold drums, instantly freezing it to lock in flavor? Eldon now owns a very large jet. Far more important than that, he has created hundreds of jobs.

No one likes to lose a job; no one likes having their back to the wall. But if "necessity is the mother of invention," it may be that there are occasions when the risk inherent in our free enterprise system leads to innovation. When Todd Pederson injured his shoulder, he couldn't continue drywalling to pay for college, so he started doing door-to-door selling of security systems.

High-school graduate Jimmy John borrowed $25,000 from his father, promising to pay it back with interest after a year. If he could not, he agreed to enlist in the army. Both men are now extraordinary success stories, Todd as the founder of APX, a 9,000-employee security company, and Jimmy with his nationwide chain of Jimmy John's Gourmet Sandwiches. America has tens of thousands of others like Todd and Jimmy.

Since American innovation comes from people who are educated, experienced, and motivated, we should eagerly welcome individuals from other countries who possess those qualities. But our current immigration policies do not. In order for some foreign students to come to America to earn a degree in physics, for example, they will not only have to endure necessary—but unnecessarily long—Homeland Security screenings. They may also have to agree to *leave* the United States when their degree has been awarded. That just doesn't make sense. If a young woman from India or Sri Lanka or Argentina earns a degree from an institution like MIT, Cal Tech, or dozens of other fine American universities, we should staple a green card to her diploma and encourage her to stay. We want her to use her talents to innovate and create new technologies and new jobs here in America, not to take her skills elsewhere. Duke University reported in *USA Today* that there is a new reality in *reverse* immigration among highly educated and skilled individuals: "What was a trickle has become a flood."

We follow the same deeply counterproductive course when we strictly limit the number of visas we award to scientists, technicians, and other foreigners with advanced degrees and valuable skills. If we want to continue to lead the world in innovation, we need the most intelligent, educated, and accomplished individuals we can find or develop. What we now do instead is strictly limit how long and how many highly skilled foreign applicants can be admitted and how long they can stay, even those that have specifically been requested by an American employer. At the same time, millions of people without these skills enter the country illegally. Our immigration practices are literally upside down. The best and the brightest wait in line to come here, then are forced to return home after we educate them with the very skills we desperately need, but those with only little education and skill enter by the hundreds of thousands and are permitted to stay. No wonder the immigration system is a source of such controversy and frustration. Our borders are effectively unguarded, a failure that has not only economic but national security implications as well. At the same time, legal immigrants who want to live within the rules, and who have the most to contribute to the economy, are forced to deal with a system that is difficult if not impossible to navigate. *The Economist* magazine calls ours "a policy of national self-sabotage." Immigration is an important source of innovation and productivity; in addition to the focus on illegal immigration, we should also concentrate on expanding legal immigration for students and individuals with advanced education and critically important skills.

Funding Research and Innovation

Education, culture, and motivation play key roles in spurring innovation, but spending on innovation also makes a difference. Federal investment in science and basic research, typically carried out in universities and research institutions, has led to numerous innovations and commercial successes— from lasers to MP3 players, and from the Internet to MRI scanners. Most national research spending is concentrated in health, defense, and space technologies, and, not surprisingly, the United States leads the world in all three sectors. Numerous by-products from work in these fields have made it into the commercial economy.

Government funding for basic science and research in universities and research laboratories has been declining for years. It needs to grow instead, particularly in engineering and the physical sciences. Research in energy, materials science, nanotechnology, and transportation are vital to the economy and to our nation's competitiveness. Government should not, however, attempt to pick winning ideas or technologies in which it would invest funds for development and commercialization. Ted Williams famously said that the hardest thing to do in sport is to hit a baseball, and in my experience, the hardest thing to do in business is to hit a home run with a new business. Some of our best and brightest people start up new businesses, finance them, and bring them into the marketplace. Then the realities of that marketplace sort out those that have potential for growth and sustainability and those that do not. Attempting to substitute government for the roles carried out by entrepreneurs, angel investors, and venture capitalists while also bypassing the unforgiving test of the free market is a very bad idea indeed. It would inevitably lead to investments that had no real potential in the market. Then, as their commercial failure became apparent, politicians would subsidize their mistakes with even more investment, hoping to hide their errors. Ultimately, we would be devoting huge resources to ideas that don't improve productivity, wages, or national economic vitality.

We are used to thinking of research and development (R&D) as one activity. In fact, it refers to two categories of activity. Research seeks new understanding and ideas. Development takes these ideas and transforms them into products or services that can be sold in the marketplace. Research itself covers a broad range of activities. At one end of the spectrum is basic research or science. This is work that is devoted to fundamental learning about science that may or may not be pursued with any commercial application in mind. Examples are the space program's Hubble telescope or missions to Mars. Some research, on the other hand, is highly focused on potential commercial application, as with that carried out by pharmaceutical companies. During the period of my career in business, I have seen a reduction by many enterprises in the amount of resources they devote to research of either type. I'm convinced that the short-term personal financial incentives of executives are a fundamental part of the problem. Because research takes years to pay out, managers are often inclined to trade their company's future prospects in exchange for near-term but shortsighted profits.

When management and owner incentives are aligned with the long-term value of a business, R&D becomes a much higher priority. Back when I worked as a private equity investor, my partners and I acquired a very unprofitable business from a publicly traded company—it had lost over $70 million during the prior year, and its public parent had slashed costs across the board to reduce the losses. The company, which made equipment for oil production, was losing market share at an alarming rate to a competitor that produced superior products. Because we had taken the company private, we didn't have to worry about short-term stock price. We hired a new CEO who, like us, would primarily be compensated based upon the long-term value of the business, not its short-term annual earnings. He opted to invest heavily in R&D, which predictably depressed short-term earnings, but he was banking on the opportunity to leapfrog our competitor with better-quality products. His plan worked—the company began to regain market share, stopped shrinking, and became a thriving and profitable business once more.

As with government funding, if corporate funding of research does not accelerate, we will lose a good portion of our lead in technology and innovation. For us to see rising private investment in research, shareholders and boards need to reorient executive compensation toward the long-term value of the enterprise. It's in their interest, and it's in the nation's interest.

Government's Impact on the Capital That Fuels Productivity

Fortunately for all of us, innovation and entrepreneurism are deeply embedded in the American DNA. But more often than not, it also takes capital for an idea to be implemented. Where capital is scarce, hard to find, or not available to entrepreneurs and innovators, good ideas simply die in the mind.

Having grown up in Detroit, I tend to think in automotive terms. If we imagine that the economy is an engine, then capital is its fuel. If the fuel is too expensive, if shortages occur because it is being diverted to less-productive purposes, or if it's simply being drained away and wasted, the engine may be unable to get enough fuel to operate. In that case, it will sputter and stall, with no capital, no fuel to grow productivity. Productivity, in fact, is a measurement not only of the performance of the workforce, but of capital as well. And government plays an awfully big role when it comes to the availability of capital.

Most fundamental, government manages the currency and the financial system. If people don't have confidence in the future value of the currency, they may not be inclined to invest because they can't be sure what value their money will have when they get it back—their return from their investment. No one would deposit money in a bank if the only guarantee it made was that you'd get back 90 percent of what you deposited. But that's the effect of inflation. That's why the Federal Reserve must be committed to a monetary policy that promotes stability and seeks to prevent inflation from rising above approximately 2 percent. When inflation is high and volatile, people worry about making investments that take time to mature and to return their capital. Given this worry, they may ask for a return on their capital that is very high—so high that the entrepreneur or business can't afford it. When this happens, capital isn't available to start new businesses or to expand and innovate in existing ones; productivity and the economy grind to a halt.

The same unfortunate outcomes occur if the financial system through which capital flows is lethargic, unreliable, or unpredictable. One of the reasons why America has so many entrepreneurs, start-ups, and small businesses is because we enjoy by far the largest and most responsive venture-funding market in the world. Our largest corporations also have an investment advantage relative to those in many other countries thanks to our substantial equity markets, commercial paper market, and the extensive number of commercial lending institutions.

Clearly, if the financial system were to shut down entirely, the free market couldn't operate, and the entire economy would collapse. This is what we were facing at the end of former president George W. Bush's term in late 2008. When Lehman Brothers went bankrupt, it was not only shareholders, debt-holders, and employees who lost out. Billions of dollars in commercial paper lost its value. Unlike equity and long-term debt, commercial paper—unsecured bank promissory notes—from an institution like Lehman Brothers was considered to be virtually risk free, "as safe as cash." When that long-standing assumption turned out to be false, the entire commercial-paper market dried up, making it extremely difficult for some companies to pay their employees or to secure vital financing. It also precipitated a run on other financial institutions. Commercial paper is one of the instruments in which many money market funds had invested. The millions of Americans who owned money market funds had every confidence that their money was entirely safe. When the Lehman bankruptcy put that into question, people and businesses began pulling their money out of money market funds—and banks. The shock of the collapse had ricocheted around the nation and the globe. Wachovia and other banks began to fail. Former treasury secretary Henry Paulson was getting phone calls from banks all over the country warning of imminent peril. A cascade of bank collapses was on its way. That's why President Bush and Secretary Paulson rushed to Congress just before they left office to ask for billions of dollars. It wasn't to bail out Wall Street, but rather to attempt to keep the entire financial system from failing.

I understand why so many people were and remain outraged at the emergency measures. They are offended by the idea of a bailout, and they don't much like Wall Street, either. The suspicion of bailouts is entirely sound. It doesn't make sense to bail out individual companies or banks or financial institutions that get in trouble. As we've seen, creative destruction is part of a growing, productive economy. Bailing out sick enterprises is a lot like what Great Britain did in the first few decades after the war—by using precious resources to prop up unproductive businesses, it was unable to invest sufficiently in emerging ones and therefore failed to keep up in the global marketplace. Subsidizing failure doesn't stop the failure—it merely prolongs the final act.

But Secretary Paulson's proposal was not aimed at saving sick Wall Street banks or even at preserving jobs on Wall Street. It was intended to prevent a run on virtually every bank and financial institution in the country. It did in fact keep our economy from total meltdown.

A majority of senators and congressmen understood the gravity of the situation, and the reality that what was at stake ultimately was every home, every dollar of savings and every job in America. It was in the middle of John McCain's campaign for president. He knew that the measure was not good politics. He voted "yes" because it was right for the country.

But TARP as administered by Secretary Timothy Geithner was as poorly explained, poorly understood, poorly structured, and poorly implemented as any legislation in recent memory. Even to this day, the American people have not been given a clear explanation of how the funds were used. It was originally sold as a program to acquire financial institution assets that were temporarily depressed in value—assets that could later be sold, potentially at higher values. But now we are given to understand that direct balance sheet investments were made, sometimes in equity. Institutions were informed after the fact that TARP funds brought government "big brother" into management decisions, even when banks hadn't requested TARP funds in the first place.

Secretary Paulson's TARP prevented a systemic collapse of the national financial system; Secretary Geithner's TARP became an opaque, heavy-handed, expensive slush fund. It should be shut down.

In addition to government's role in managing the currency and keeping the financial system intact, its policy directly influences our four major sources of capital: individual savings, corporate savings, savings from abroad, and government surpluses

The government affects how much money we save, and savings are a key source of capital for loans and equity investments. By definition, when you *tax* something, you get less of it—tax savings and people will save less. In the United States, we tax savings and investment twice. Imagine that your uncle starts a software company with an investment of $1 million he raises from family, friends, and an angel investor. Let's say that each year, the business earns $100,000. Combined, the federal and state governments charge the company an income tax of about 40 percent, leaving the investors with an annual dividend of $60,000 to take home. But then, each investor is also taxed personally as well—say, another 40 percent, leaving them with just $36,000 in net earnings. Considering the total of both taxes, your uncle and his investors have paid nearly two-thirds of what was earned from their software investment to the government. If they had opted to forgo their dividend and reinvest it in the company, they could have eventually taken their profit as a capital gain, taxed at 20 percent, and in that case the government share would *only* have been about half. Either way, your uncle and his investors would likely find themselves thinking long and hard about their decision to invest in a new business to begin with: the government would get half to two-thirds of the profit even if the business was good enough to be successful in the first place. When government heavily taxes investment, innovation, and entrepreneurship, we get less of those things—and fewer new high-paying jobs.

If we want to make more capital available for investment, we will have to lower taxes on saving and investing, either at the corporate or the individual level, or preferably both. Our current corporate tax rate is tied with Japan's as the highest in the developed world, but lobbyists and a willing Congress have seen to it that myriad tax breaks are available, which can lower the rates some companies pay. They hire teams of lawyers and accountants to take advantage of every legal means to lower their tax bill. This is rational behavior, but the process is an enormous waste of time and money—a lower rate would accomplish all that the special breaks do, and improve the incentives for investment and entrepreneurship as well, creating growth and jobs.

As noted, the obvious solution is to simplify the code and reduce the rate across the board. Personal taxes on dividends, interest, and capital gains for all middle-income families should be completely eliminated—something that wouldn't cost the government a great deal because most of this tax today is paid by high-income individuals. What this change *would* do is increase the size of our national capital pool and foster a mutuality of interests between our employers and our citizens.

Some people advocate the "fair tax" as a means of boosting savings, a system that would entirely replace federal and state income and payroll taxes with a consumption tax—a kind of sales tax. If we funded the government with the fair tax, your uncle and his investors in the software company wouldn't pay any tax on its $100,000 in earnings—until they spent some of it. That's a big incentive to save. They would instead be taxed on all their purchases of goods and services, such as food, cars, housing, movies, landscaping, and haircuts—everything.

Fair tax proponents estimate that a tax rate of 23 percent would be sufficient, but detractors claim that it would be closer to 40 percent. With the federal government consuming 22 percent of the GDP and with exemptions for lower levels of income, it's logical that the rate would be between 25 and 30 percent. If a consumption tax were to replace taxation at the federal, state, and local levels of government, the rate would probably be near 35 percent.

Under the fair tax, the Internal Revenue Service would be eliminated—to the objection of very few people, of course—but a government agency of some kind would have to ensure that people weren't bartering or finding other means to avoid paying such a substantial tax on the goods and services they purchased. And just as happens with our current system, tax cheaters would suffer rather severe penalties. One challenge with the fair tax is that the very rich would see their taxes go down—a lot. If Bill Gates makes about a billion dollars a year on his investments, for example, his current taxes would be at least $200 million. Let's say he spends $50 million on himself and his family every year—which is a huge sum and I doubt he spends that much, but let's use it for illustration: Under the fair tax, Bill Gates would pay "only" about $17 million in taxes—his tax bill would thus drop from $200 million to $17 million. *The Wall Street Journal* found that the enormous amount saved by the wealthiest under the fair tax would be made up by a higher tax burden on the middle class. This is not an outcome that will or should gain traction with the American public.

The fair tax would boost savings. The effect on consumption is less certain. Some people would work hard not to buy anything because products would look much more expensive with the tax added to them. They'd be cutting hair at home, eating at home, painting their own houses, and passing things along to family members rather than buying new. That doesn't sound so bad—in the abstract. But the effect on the economy and jobs of such a dramatic change in consumption patterns is hard to predict. What if the new system didn't work as well as promised? What if it produced massive cheating and the sales tax rates had to jump, spurring even more cheating? And if national consumption dropped precipitously, we could be thrown into a recession deeper than the one we've recently experienced.

It would be instructive if we could give the fair tax a fair test, but that would be difficult. In concept, the idea of a consumption tax is very appealing because of its potential to propel economic growth, but there are a number of potential drawbacks that will have to be worked out. At a minimum, the fair tax would have to be structured to avoid a windfall for the very rich and the extra burden which would fall on the middle class.

A Value Added Tax (VAT) is a flat tax on consumption, like the Fair Tax, but it can be implemented in a way to reduce the compliance problems. Because it is collected in stages along the production process, tax evasion is much more difficult. And because it would not entirely replace the current tax system, it would not mean a windfall for the wealthy. As attractive economically as is the VAT, its drawback is that big government spenders could simply add it to the current tax burden. That is why we should not open the VAT door.

The best course in the near term is to overhaul and to dramatically simplify the current tax code, eliminate taxes on savings for the middle class, and recognize that because we tax investment at both the corporate and individual level, we should align our combined rates with those of competing nations. Lower taxes and a simpler tax code will help families and create jobs.

Government policies also directly affect our second major source of capital—corporate profits reinvested by the business that earns them. Technically, these are personal savings—shareholders could theoretically demand that a company they collectively own pay them all its earnings as dividends. But practically, if a company has good investment opportunities and the management is persuasive, it will invest its profits back into the company. Corporate profits—retained earnings—are a source of our national savings.

If you're a Republican running for office—and particularly if you've made a living in the private sector—one of the lines your opponent is certain to throw at you is that "you put profits ahead of people." But I think recent economic events have led voters to understand a more fundamental truth. They've seen all too clearly what happens when our nation's employers don't make profits—they lay off *people*, shrink, fail, and go out of business. Even though this hard truth is much more widely appreciated in 2010 than it was in 2008, many people still don't know where a company's profits actually go. In the first six months of 2009, for example, Comcast reported a profit of $1.7 billion. How much of that goes to pay bonuses for the company's executives? None. Profit is what's left after compensation of every kind has been paid to management and employees. How much did stockholders receive? About 22 percent was returned to them as dividends. The remaining 78 percent of Comcast's profit was reinvested in the business, financing the accounts of new customers, expanding the network and equipment, purchasing capital products from others—in other words, doing things that mean more jobs for *people*. Profits ahead of people? No, profits *for* people.

High corporate tax rates reduce the amount of a company's profit that can be devoted to new investments, new hiring, and greater productivity. And high corporate taxes also encourage companies to move elsewhere. There's a misconception both in Washington and around the country that if business taxes are raised, companies will simply knuckle under and pay. That may have been true at a time when businesses required large physical assets—blast furnaces, machining equipment, transfer lines, and the like. But manufacturing makes up only 11 percent of our employment today, and much of that 11 percent is light manufacturing and assembly that is not very difficult to move. Businesses today look carefully at comparable tax rates when they decide where to locate new plants or facilities. Daniel Vasella, CEO of Novartis, the multibillion-dollar pharmaceutical company, has explained that his company doesn't have a headquarters. Instead, Novartis's upper-level executives work from offices all over the world. Increasingly, companies choose where to incorporate—and where to pay their taxes—based on state and national tax rates.

Interestingly, I think that governors understand this quite well. States actively compete with one another for businesses, and we have learned that the taxes we charge can be a major factor in company's decision about where to locate. Soon after my friend Governor Arnold Schwarzenegger took office in California, he came to Massachusetts to see if he couldn't poach some of our employers. He even put up a billboard of himself, inviting our companies to move to his state. So I had billboards of my own placed near California's airports, where I knew his businesspeople would see them. The signs had me saying, "Smaller muscles, but lower taxes."

Businesses often do very thorough calculations to compare the cost of doing business in one state as compared with another. While I was serving as governor, we went to work to convince Bristol Myers Squibb to locate its new biotech manufacturing facility in Massachusetts. We wanted the one billion dollars that were reportedly going to be spent to build the facility to go to our construction trades, and we wanted the permanent jobs that the facility would create. Just as important, we were anxious to make Massachusetts not just a leader in biotech research, where we were second only to California, but in biotech manufacturing as well. We figured that if we won, it could mean that other biotech manufacturers would follow suit. It could make a big difference to us in the long term.

Our team went to work to find a good building site, to accelerate the construction-permitting processes, and to demonstrate the depth of our pool of skilled labor. Those things mattered, but in my calls and meetings with their CEO, it was clear that this would come down to dollars and cents—cost of construction, property taxes, corporate taxes, and incentives. His team had built a model that boiled it all down to one number, and he told me that we were still high compared to one other state. The legislature and I went to work to put together the best tax and incentive number we could, and having done so, we won. Now several years later, the plant is about ready to open.

Now and then, companies make location decisions on a less quantitative basis—where the CEO wants to live, who knows who, or where some key skills or suppliers are located. But most of the time, I have found, it comes down to the numbers.

There's a good deal of rhetoric today from liberal politicians who say that we need to heavily tax those corporations that "send jobs overseas." I'm afraid they don't understand that companies with subsidiaries in other countries are doing business in those countries and that they pay taxes there. Requiring them to pay still-higher U.S. taxes would make them less competitive in those markets, making it bad for their business overseas, and also for jobs here. Sales made by subsidiaries of U.S. companies are often supported by high-paying jobs in finance, accounting, research, and management here at home. And if a company's tax burden under such legislation grew too high, it could simply move overseas to avoid it—resulting in a loss of tax revenue for the United States, not a net gain. Those of us who want to see corporate tax rates lowered to the levels of other developed countries aren't trying to fill the pockets of executives. We're trying to keep businesses—and jobs—here in the United States, and to expand savings and investment, personal incomes, and our entire national economy—all of which are very good things for everyone.

Savings and investment that come from abroad are a third source of national capital. In his book, *The World Is Curved*, economist David Smick demonstrates that Japanese families have been a major source of America's capital. Up until 2008, interest rates had been so low in their country that Japanese households bought American treasuries to get a better return. Japan's national savings rate was twice our own; China's was almost four times greater. Without foreign savings and investment in America, our economy could not have continued to grow, given our own low rate of personal savings. Initiating a trade war with the rest of the world or erecting barriers to foreign investment would almost certainly result in reduced flows of foreign capital into the U.S. and would have serious unintended consequences for our pool of capital and for our economy as a whole.

The fourth source of capital is surplus government funds. Our government deficits, on the other hand, drain away capital. Michael Porter argues that "controlling government deficits that are not being used to finance productivity-enhancing investments in the economy is perhaps the most direct way in which government can influence the pool of investable capital." The huge and ever-growing federal deficits shrink the amount of capital that could otherwise start and grow businesses, and when the government is forced to borrow heavily, it inexorably drives up the interest rates that individual and corporate American borrowers pay, which slows the economy at every level.

Deficits aren't an imaginary problem that affects only imaginary dollars. They act to drain the lifeblood of the American economy. The bigger the deficit, the greater the loss of economic vitality in the private sector.

Some analysts believe that given the global flow of capital that exists today, our economy is less dependent on our own national pool of capital than it otherwise would be, and that's undoubtedly true to some extent. But foreign investors tend to focus their investments on U.S. government debt and other securities that are rated very safe, because it's difficult for foreign investors to know American markets, consumers, competitors, and regulations in great detail. They are thus far less likely to take risks and play a major role in financing productivity improvements in existing businesses or in providing capital for new enterprises.

In fact, risk capital tends to be invested quite locally. California's venture capital firms invest almost 60 percent of their funds in California businesses, for example. Firms in Massachusetts, the number-two venture state after California, invest nearly 40 percent of their capital in Massachusetts; they spend more than six times as much at home as in New York, a nearby state with a much larger economy.

America's relatively plentiful venture capital resources are one reason we have become such a successful entrepreneurial nation. For the last ten years, America's share of worldwide venture capital spending has exceeded all other nations combined. Capital does flow around the world—absolutely—but local and national boundaries still matter a great deal when it comes to the availability of the risk capital needed to launch new businesses and to increase productivity.

The tendency of foreign risk capital to stay at home may ultimately be heightened by the recent financial crisis. Of course, as long as fear of a severe disruption exists, capital will flow to the dollar as a "safe haven." But as that fear continues to subside, foreign investors will reassess their willingness to invest in securities and markets that were so incorrectly rated by our agencies and poorly overseen by our regulators—and where they lost money. For us to confidently grow our economy, we must grow our own pool of capital and make it available at a reasonable cost. To do that, we must preserve the value of the dollar by defending against inflation, rein in government's excessive deficits, simplify taxation, and reduce taxes on enterprise and investment.

Dynamic Regulation

The Republican Party has long been an opponent of overregulation, and rightly so. But I believe some people in my party are overly fond of bashing regulation as the constant enemy of growth and competition. They are certainly right about some regulations, but they are wrong when it comes to others. The rule of law and the establishment of regulations that are clear, fair, and relevant to contemporary circumstances provide the predictability and stability that is needed for investment and risk-taking.

Back when I was at Bain Capital, one of our first venture capital investments was in a technology that allowed machining companies to reuse their cutting oil—the cooling lubricants that are used in drilling, routing, and cutting metals. New government regulations had just been established to prevent companies from simply throwing used oils down the drain. The regulations ultimately led to better machining industry practices, but because they weren't *enforced* for almost a decade, we lost our investment. Michael Porter is convinced that, far from being a drag on the economy, "National advantage is enhanced by stringent standards that are rapidly, efficiently, and consistently applied." I wish more Republicans and Democrats alike understood that important truth.

Labor regulations can also help the economy or hurt it. Equal opportunity regulations increase the inclusiveness of our economy, drawing people into the workforce who might otherwise have stayed on the sidelines. Occupational safety regulations, for example, protect the individual from accidents and disability, preserving the economic benefit from workers with skill and experience. The requirement for unemployment insurance provides a benefit not only to the worker but also to the economy. This insurance helps workers who have been laid off, perhaps due to an improvement in productivity, while they find new employment that will benefit from their skills and experience. The overall impact of unemployment insurance thus can smooth the individual and national transitions that are an inevitable part of the changing global marketplace.

But much labor regulation—both in the United States and among our Western allies—actually works against workers' best interest. In France, for example, government regulations prevent an employer from terminating an

employee "at will"—the employer must have one of specific, legally established reasons for doing so. On its face, the measure appears to be laudable
and of much benefit to workers, but what it means in practice is that French
employers have an enormous incentive to delay hiring new employees as
long as possible. The result has been relatively high unemployment, which
is the exact opposite of what the regulation intended. The regulation also
makes it far more expensive for French companies to implement productivity measures. In his best seller *The World Is Flat*, Thomas Friedman observes that "the easier it is to fire someone in a dying industry, the easier it
is to hire someone in a rising industry.

"This is a great asset," Tom notes in a burst of candor that not many
politicians would ever indulge; they would fear a YouTube snippet that would
make them appear indifferent to the pain of unemployment. Friedman also
reports that the United States has some of the most flexible labor regulations in the world. I agree with him that it's in our best interest to keep
them that way.

Regulation can have a particularly pernicious effect on the formation of
new businesses, particularly in the developing world. A World Bank study
found, for example, that it takes just two days to start a business in Australia, but it takes 195 days in Haiti and 149 days in the Democratic Republic
of Congo. Consider what this means to new business formation in these nations. Americans have a significant advantage over many developed countries in this regard when it comes to starting a new business—it takes only
six days to complete the federal paperwork required to start a company in
the United States, compared with eighteen days in Germany and twenty-
three in Japan. And we do a good job of keeping the federal cost down as
well. Less than 1 percent of income per capita is required for new business
fees and filings here, while the costs in Germany and Japan are over 5 percent and 7 percent respectively.

States and municipalities, on the other hand, can have their own damp-
ening effect on business creation and expansion, something I personally
discovered when I was governor of Massachusetts.

I had been invited to sit down with a CEO who had just opened a new
facility in our state. I expected him to offer me his thanks for the role that
the state and the city had played in the process. But instead, he bluntly
informed me that if he had it to do over again, he wouldn't locate in

Massachusetts. "It took almost ten years to get the permits and approvals from the state and the city and then finally to build," he told me. And then he rehearsed some the burdens and delays our state and city regulatory bureaucracies had placed on him, even as he was bringing us good jobs. His revelation led me to inaugurate a guaranteed 180-day approval process for any employer planning to expand or build in the state. I wanted it even faster and I wanted more of our cities to follow suit, but any step in the direction of getting businesses open in a safe, efficient fashion is a step in the right direction.

What was an irritant to big business is often an insurmountable obstacle for small business. Labor regulations, tax filings, permits, approvals, and delays can be financed and navigated by a major corporation. But to the people who just want to open a store or a garage or a restaurant, that kind of hassle and time costs money they may not have. Taking a weed-wacker to small-business regulation should be a regular agenda item for every growth-oriented state, city, or nation.

Excessive regulation that slows the creation of new businesses and the expansion of existing businesses, as Friedman notes, "tends to hurt most the very people it is supposed to protect." At the same time, in order to provide the structure and predictability that business needs and to protect against abuses, we need *dynamic regulations*, which are up-to-date, forward-looking, consistently applied, and free of unnecessary burden.

We certainly suffered from the absence of dynamic regulation in the 2008 economic collapse, particularly in the area of housing finance. While some outdated regulations had been eliminated, modern replacements had not been put in place. Mortgage banks had become loan-origination offices rather than true banks and were allowed to churn out mortgages without any meaningful regulatory oversight. Commercial banks bought new asset classes—derivatives and mortgage-backed securities—that likewise were not regulated to reflect either their risk or their lack of transparency. The wholesale failure at the federal level to revise and refine outmoded regulatory structures even as the ever-aggressive private sector sought out new profit centers allowed the risks in the system to overwhelm the collective good. We know the bill we have all paid as a result. What is odd is that some are looking to the same people in Congress as a source of wisdom on how to avoid a repeat of the fiasco—one about which they had received many warnings, failed to act, and actually abetted with the worst sort of populist

boosterism that facilitated adding even more risk into an already overleveraged sector. We have to fully understand what happened in order to protect
against its recurrence, and we need a sober and balanced assessment, not
political rhetoric and posturing.

What Went Wrong and What to Do Now

For the fifty years from 1950 to 2000, average U.S. housing prices, after
inflation is removed, rose by less than one half percent a year (*see* graph on
following page). The growth was remarkably steady over five decades. If the
index for a home price in 1950 was 105, it had risen to about 120 by
2000—again, taking out inflation. So, 15 points of growth in fifty years.
Then suddenly, beginning near the year 2000, real home prices took off like
a rocket. By 2006, the home price index was almost 200! That means about
80 points in six years—five times more price growth in six years than had
occurred in the previous fifty years. No bubble like that has ever endured; it
simply had to pop.

What created a bubble like this in the first place? The true answer is "a
lot of things." Politicians wanted low-income families to be able to buy
homes, so they pushed the federal government's mortgage guarantors, Freddie Mac and Fannie Mae, to ease up on their loan requirements. As far back
as 1999, *The New York Times* reported that Fannie Mae "has been under
increasing pressure from the Clinton administration to expand mortgage
loans among low and moderate income people." The *Times* went on to accurately predict the peril: "Fannie Mae is taking on significantly more risk,
which may not pose any difficulties during flush times. But the government-
subsidized corporation may run into trouble in an economic downturn."

Mortgage banks and other originators generally didn't care whether the
loan could be repaid or not because once a loan was closed, the originator
sent it off to Wall Street, which sliced it into parts to resell to investors. At
most stops along the way, commissions were paid. To help home buyers get
a mortgage, originators made loans with no or very low down payments—
the average down payment on a home in 2007 was 2 percent! (By contrast,
in 1971, the bank in my town required that I put 20 percent down on my
house.) Some buyers were not asked about their earnings or their ability to

U.S. Housing Average Price 1950–2000
(Excluding Inflation)

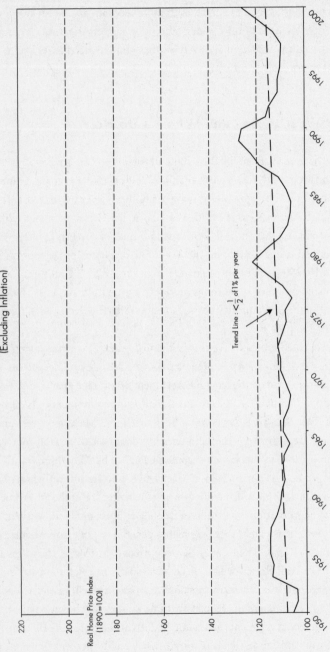

Real Home Price Index
(1890=100)

Trend line : $<\frac{1}{2}$ of 1% per year

Source: Robert J. Shiller, *Irrational Exuberance*, Princeton University Press 2000, Broadway Books 2001, 2nd edition,
2005, also *Subprime Solution*, 2008, as updated at http://www.econ.yale.edu/~shiller/data.htm

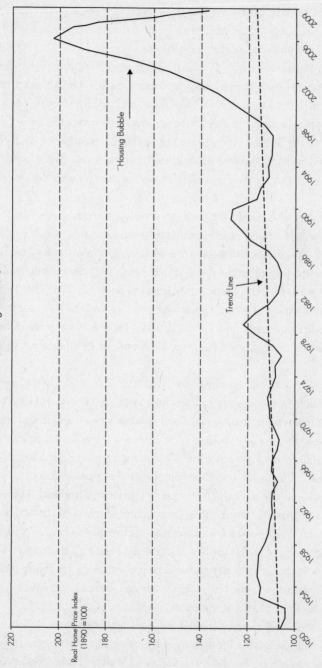

U.S. Housing Average Price 1950–2009
(Excluding Inflation)

Real Home Price Index
(1890 = 100)

"Housing Bubble

Trend Line

Source: Robert J. Shiller, *Irrational Exuberance*, Princeton University Press 2000, Broadway Books 2001, 2nd edition,
2005, also *Subprime Solution*, 2008, as updated at http://www.econ.yale.edu/~shiller/data.htm

repay the loan. By 2006, over half of all mortgages originated in the United States were subprime, jumbo, seconds, or other nonconforming loans—in other words, more risky than normal loans.

Wall Street was happy to take the mortgages from the originators because they made enormous amounts of money by bundling them up, reslicing them in new and complicated ways, and selling those slices off to others—a technique that most believed spread the risk while in fact it was spreading the disease. And to boost their returns even higher, Wall Street leveraged itself far beyond historic and prudent levels. When mortgages turned sour, this leverage meant there was virtually no ability to absorb the losses.

Investors who bought the packages from Wall Street were so anxious to get the higher interest rates provided by these securities that they failed to look into the creditworthiness of the borrowers. And investors were blindsided by the private rating agencies that inexcusably never understood the risks or at least never went out of their way to publicize them. One Harvard economist told me that in a discussion he had with one of these agencies, he asked what their risk model showed would happen if the price of houses went down. Their answer: "Our model doesn't let us input negative numbers."

In his capacity as chairman of the Federal Reserve, Alan Greenspan made a decision to hold down interest rates for an extended period that didn't help, either. He was motivated by a desire to avoid deflation—and in that respect, it worked. But the low interest rates also meant low mortgage payments, which allowed borrowers to afford a bigger mortgage and pay a higher price for a home. Those who sold their homes were very pleased, indeed.

And all of this was helped along by a big dose of irrational exuberance, which accompanies the growth of every bubble. Average Americans became speculators. Debt looked cheap and easy to refinance as long as prices kept going up. A lot of people made a lot of money, creating a contagious craving to get in on the game: mortgage bankers, real-estate agents, rating agencies, Wall Street firms, home sellers, home builders—even the politicians benefited from fuller campaign chests.

Then in 2008, interest rates ticked up, housing values stalled or declined, and hundreds of thousands of high-risk borrowers began to default on their mortgages. Suddenly the securities Wall Street had sold here and around the world plummeted in value. Investors dumped the securities at huge losses. Others tried to catch the last train leaving the station and flung their securities into a market that was rapidly retreating. Panic replaced exuberance, one of the most dangerous of all macroeconomic forces. Many of the banks and Wall Street firms that still held some of the securities were pushed toward insolvency.

Who's to blame? Well, just about everybody. The Federal Reserve should have seen the problem when it realized how many of the mortgages issued in 2006, for example, were substandard. Bank regulators should have recognized that these mortgage-backed securities were very high risk and should not have been allowed to constitute a large percentage of an institution's reserves. The ratings agencies should have done their jobs and busted the pretenders. The politicians should have realized that when you interfere with the market—as they did with Fannie Mae, Freddie Mac, and with their home-ownership initiatives—*bad* things can happen. Wall Street should have done enough due diligence on the enormous pool of high-risk mortgages to appreciate the risk they involved, and the buyers of the securities should have done some due diligence as well. The Treasury secretary and congressional oversight committees should have been on the watch for this kind of game-changing discontinuity, and yes, because the buck stops at the top, former president George W. Bush can't escape some of the blame, either. Nor to his credit has he tried to. It would be a wonderful thing if Senator Chris Dodd, Congressman Barney Frank, and the others who had actually pushed for the destructive government policies would own up to their share of the responsibility for the fiasco that so deeply wounded millions of Americans.

Some argue that blame rightfully ought to be assigned more narrowly—usually as part of their effort to deflect blame for their own failures. Wall Street greed is a common and easy target. That greed is surely part of the story. So are massive Wall Street miscalculations. Investment banks were overleveraged. Some of them had sought to identify and evaluate the risk that they had on their balance sheets, but their risk models famously were based on the 99 percent range of possibilities. But as Nassim Taleb, author of *The Black Swan*, has explained, the bankers didn't adequately consider the *1 percent* probability that national housing prices would collapse. There were voices of warning, but for the most part, they went unheeded. That's why so many firms—and tens of thousands of investment bankers—have disappeared.

The human cost of all these errors is staggering. Millions of men and women have lost their jobs. Millions have lost their health insurance. Millions have seen lifelong savings and investments drop precipitously or even vanish. As homes have plummeted in value, millions of Americans owe more on their mortgage than their home is currently worth. The trillions of dollars in wealth that have been lost is only a partial measure of the hardship. Seniors worry that insufficient retirement funds could mean they may be forced to enter a nursing home, where Medicaid will pay the bills. Parents worry that they will be unable to afford to send their child to college. Without health insurance, families fear that a sickness or disease could impair not only finances, but also health and life. Parents who had sacrificed and invested themselves in new homes, new neighborhoods, and new schools for the sake of their children have followed the sheriff out their front door.

The issue now is how to end the hardships, how to help the economy recover. First off, it is necessary to say again that the economy will in fact recover. Downturns are *always* followed by recoveries and there is nothing so uniquely terrible or discontinuous in this recession as to suggest that there will never be a rebound. As I write this, encouraging signs have begun to appear. But the depth and length of the downturn, the rate of the recovery, and the long-term effects of both will be very much influenced by the actions which government takes and has taken.

President Bush signed a $152 billion stimulus bill early in 2008, but as the magnitude of the economic slide became more pronounced, a second stimulus was called for. The $12 trillion reduction in individual net worth meant that annual consumption would fall by over $500 billion. This would not be made up by rising exports because the dollar had strengthened, due to the flight to safety. Nor would investment fill the gap; lenders with capital and equity investors had become scarce. The second stimulus could have been passed in 2008. Then, too, President Bush would have had a hand in shaping it. But congressional Democrats were too wary of allowing Bush to participate in fashioning such a package, because he certainly understood much more than they the crucial role played by tax cuts in reversing the post 9/11 recession.

The "all-Democrat" stimulus passed in early 2009 has been a failure. The administration takes great pains to argue that the stimulus helped grow the economy. The relevant question is whether it performed according to the Obama administration's own standards—and that answer is "no." President Obama and his economic team said that it would hold unemployment below 8 percent. But unemployment soared to 10 percent and has remained over 9.5 percent for more than a year. Rather than focusing on incentives to create private sector employment, the stimulus funded federal programs and bailed out state governments. Washington, D.C., became a boom town as the government added 127 thousand new jobs. People throughout the rest of the country suffered, however, as private sector employment plunged by 2.4 million jobs. The 15 million Americans out of work as of August 2010 would constitute an unemployment line reaching from Washington, D.C., to California and back again. The Obama stimulus, funded with a mountain of debt, was a bust.

Borrowing money to stimulate the economy is quite clearly a two-edged sword. The money you borrow can get things going again, but the borrowing will eventually drive up interest rates and divert future resources to service the debt and repay the principal. That's why every stimulus should be crafted with care and exactitude; every dollar should immediately create jobs, encourage business expansion, or provide for essential needs such as equipment for our troops at war. Instead, Congress crafted and the president acceded to a stimulus that funded unnecessary pet projects, long-term programs, and delayed employment initiatives.

In 2009, I spoke with the director of stimulus funds for a mid-Atlantic state. He candidly acknowledged to me that less than 10 percent of the federal funds his state received would actually create jobs. This has been true across the country. What a disheartening diversion of resources that could have instead powered a meaningful set of investments, protected our troops in combat, and created new jobs.

Given the shortcoming of the current stimulus, voices may emerge to craft another one. That would be the wrong course. The right course would be to fix the current stimulus by removing programs and by substituting tax incentives that create employment, such as a robust investment tax credit, a one-year write-off for 2010 capital expenditures, and a lower payroll tax. The answer is not to repeat the stimulus but to repair the stimulus. We need to stimulate the economy, not the government.

The administration's economic missteps went well beyond its poorly designed stimulus. Rather than focus on the economy, the president embarked on a dizzying array of initiatives intended to "change" America and install his liberal agenda. The economic crisis was to be exploited, not solved. Unfortunately, the initiatives were decidedly anti-investment, anti-growth, and anti-jobs. Obamacare was slated to raise taxes by one-half a trillion dollars, to place heavy administrative burdens on small business, and to radically change health insurance and healthcare. Cap-and-trade would rocket energy prices by an indeterminable amount. Financial reform legislation would fundamentally change the rules for financial services companies—sometime in the future. Individual and small business taxes were set to sharply rise: The tax on dividends, for example, would jump from 15 percent to 39 percent. The administration would slant the employment field toward labor unions by installing a labor stooge at the NLRB and by promoting "card check" and mandatory arbitration.

This legislative assault introduced new layers of uncertainty into the private sector. Most businesses can handle bad news, but they can't handle lack of predictability. All the while, the president toured the nation to scapegoat and demonize the private sector—everyone from insurance managers, auto managers, health-care managers, financial managers, bankers, bond holders, and doctors felt his wrath. With the economy in the doldrums and with the president piling on, small business in particular retreated. Even large companies held back new investments and hiring: A record amount of capital has been frozen on corporate balance sheets. In the past, we have had government declare war on poverty and war on drugs, but this is the first time government had declared war on free enterprise.

Of course the financial system itself must not be allowed to collapse, but individual institutions that do not show the capacity to right themselves should be allowed to fail. Nonfinancial businesses should also be allowed to fail; if they have future prospects, bankruptcy will allow them to reemerge as stronger, viable employers. General Motors shares should have been immediately distributed to the public rather than being held by the federal government. Meddling politicians and bureaucrats aren't the answer to Detroit's woes. The sooner the IPO, the better for GM.

To speed a sustainable recovery, we must also demonstrate to the world that we have become financially responsible. The president has done just the opposite with plans that would double the national debt in five years. Massive trillion-dollar deficits could take us beyond the tipping point and lead to a worldwide crisis of confidence in America. Accordingly, our currency could experience very high rates of inflation, wiping out savings, further devastating the pool of capital needed to grow jobs, and threatening our economic vitality. We must rein in our trillion-dollar deficits, solve our looming entitlement liability problem, and show an unwavering commitment to stop spending what we do not have. New expensive programs and entitlements must be off the table. If we do not bring government finances under control, our recovery will be long and slow, and we will risk another downturn precipitated by a severely weakened dollar.

Ultimately, the recovery depends on the very same things that strengthen our long-term economy: investing in productivity, stimulating investment and innovation, exercising fiscal discipline, and securing our energy needs. There are no quick fixes, only enduring values.

Despite the huge role our nation played in the financial crisis and the resulting global recession, America's economy remains the most powerful and productive in the world. Our GDP, GDP per capita, productivity, and standard of living are the highest of any other major economy. We have generated more patents than the rest of the world combined. Over the last two decades, our economy has grown faster than that of any other developed nation, accounting for almost one third of the entire world's economic growth. U.S. per capita disposable income, adjusted for inflation, rose 37 percent between 1986 and 2005. The poverty rate fell from 22 percent in 1959 to 13 percent in 2005.

Despite our accomplishments, our record is not perfect. Our poverty rate, before counting welfare, health, and transfer payments, is high for a developed nation. Far too many American families live below the poverty line, and many more live with worry and insecurity. Racial minorities especially have not shared equally in the nation's economic success, and there is a growing gap between the highest-earning households and the lowest. In his book *Income and Wealth*, Alan Reynolds points that the gap is even greater between those who have college degrees and those who do not. In the fifteen years between 1989 and 2004, individuals with college degrees saw their real earnings rise by 61 percent, compared with only 12 percent by those who had a high-school diploma or less. Education pays—particularly in a world where two billion uneducated, unskilled workers have joined the workplace.

We must also be concerned about our continuing loss of manufacturing jobs and the impact this has had on many middle-class families. Today, manufacturing employs only 11 percent of our workforce, but manufacturing output continues to grow because of productivity improvements. National output per employee more than doubled from 1987 to 2005, propelling America's manufacturing output to grow by 77 percent, excluding inflation. But despite that growth, some major manufacturing sectors have declined sharply, and others have disappeared altogether.

Some people contend that it's acceptable to lose manufacturing jobs to offshore sites as long as American firms keep their high-paying research, engineering, and development staffs here at home, but I don't agree. My experience is that ultimately, development and manufacturing will take place in the same locale—there's simply too much need for collaboration between the engineer and the manufacturer to make any other arrangement viable. This has ominous implications for America. In a recent survey, most CEOs said they would prefer to carry out their R&D in China, rather than in the United States. As I have discussed above, the best way forward is not to erect trade barriers but instead to facilitate innovation and productivity that will sustain our global manufacturing competitiveness.

For the past three decades, we have imported far more goods than we have exported. Prior to that time, the United States was the world's largest exporter; today China is. Much of what America produces is intellectual property, and a good deal of it is simply stolen by companies in other nations. In a service and technology driven economy like ours, we must ensure that ideas, discoveries, inventions, patents, designs, and trade secrets are protected, and that their use is properly compensated when they are incorporated by others; so far, this is something we have failed to do.

The most pointed criticism of our economic achievements is directed at the financial crisis that began in 2008. In fact, our economy has endured a number of recessions in its history, though this one has been the most painful since the Great Depression. No other developed nation or economic system of which I am aware has escaped downturns and contractions, except those few countries that base their economies on the sale of natural resources. This is the nature of the economic cycle, which we have not yet determined how to overcome. But the cycle can be managed much more adroitly than our government did in the years leading up to 2008. The key is that we learn from the painful years behind us. We also have to remain confident that, even recognizing the imperfections, it is undeniable that America's economic success is an unparalleled accomplishment.

The issue is not where we have come, but where we are going. If I may return to my engine analogy from earlier in this chapter: Our economy is powered by two pistons—the first is productivity improvement in existing businesses and the second is the creation of new businesses. To operate efficiently, the engine requires the rule of law, dynamic regulation, a stable currency and financial system, skilled labor, and adequate low-cost capital. It's an engine that is driven by innovation, which in turn is the product of creative, educated, and highly motivated people.

As with all engines, there are things that make it run faster and things that slow it down. On the acceleration side, there is education, especially in disciplines that generate productivity-enhancing innovations. There is research, development, competition, trade, thoughtful immigration policies, and a culture that promotes entrepreneurship.

Thankfully, we don't have to deal with economic decelerators like rampant corruption, risk of nationalization, or the civil wars that stall many developing nations. But there are a number of things that slow our economy down. Wasteful spending by government drains capital that could otherwise fuel growth. Excessive taxation and outmoded regulation are economic brakes. Efforts to impose unions, restrict competition, and limit trade retard innovation and productivity. Frivolous and excessive litigation burdens businesses and discourages invention. And annually draining hundreds of billions of dollars from our economy to buy foreign oil slows our economic growth. Unfortunately, a number of these are components of the economic agenda that prevails today in Washington.

To strengthen America's economy, we must minimize those things that retard economic growth and promote those things that accelerate it. A growth agenda favors low taxes, dynamic regulation, educational achievement, investment in research, robust competition, free trade, energy security, and purposeful immigration. And it seeks to eliminate government waste, excessive litigation, unsustainable entitlement liabilities, runaway health-care costs, and dependence on foreign oil. This, in a nutshell, ought to be the economic agenda for America.

A productivity and growth strategy has immediate and very personal benefits: economic vitality, innovation, and productivity are inexorably linked with the happiness and well-being of our citizens. While it is undoubtedly true that "innovativeness raises uncertainties," Nobel laureate Edmund Phelps observes that an innovative, capitalistic economy like ours also "promotes 'vitalist' lives. It produces the stimulation, challenge, engagement, mastery, discovery, and development that constitute the good life." His research bears out his conclusion: Compared with workers in European countries, those in America have greater opportunities at work for taking initiative, take greater pride in their jobs, and have higher levels of satisfaction not only with their jobs but also with their lives. So promoting innovation and productivity undergirds a good share of our happiness. It permits us to enjoy a high and rising standard of living, and it makes possible our dream that our children will enjoy lives even more rewarding than our own.

But there is much more that compels us to pursue a productivity and growth agenda—it is essential to preserve the America we know. For if Washington were to continue to depart from this strategy, acting in ways that depress productivity and growth, America would decline. We would be surpassed as the world's leader, and lament as freedom is stealthily stripped from our descendants and from our friends around the world. It was not for this that the Founding Fathers established the nation, nor for this that hundreds of thousands of our brave men and women shed their blood.

America is freedom, and freedom must be strong.

6

The Worst Generation?

In his 1998 book, journalist Tom Brokaw coined a term for those Americans who survived the Great Depression, defeated the Axis powers in World War II, and created the most prosperous society in history: "the Greatest Generation." These men and women—our parents and grandparents among them—succeeded in these epic tasks, not out of a desire for personal glory or a comfortable lifestyle, but because they simply believed that vision, sacrifice, and success were vital for their children and to the generations that would follow them.

Today we find ourselves at a very different moment in history, and I fear that if we remain on our current track, history will come to know us as this nation's *worst* generation—because we will force our children and their children to bear the brunt of our recklessness and the willful neglect of the problems we created. The problem is so deep-seated that relatively few of us in the postwar "boomer" generation even understand at a basic level how we are compromising future generations. If we did, I'm convinced that we would do whatever it takes to set things right.

Gail Sheehy observed in her book *Passages* that as people age, the issue of what they will leave behind as a personal legacy becomes vitally important.

Right now that legacy is looking grim indeed, in large part because politicians and the leaders of special-interest groups have purposefully and consistently over many years hidden the truth from us.

Avoiding the fate of becoming "the worst generation" won't be easy, particularly given how long we've been on a collision course with debt and decline. But I'm convinced it will be worth it if we face this stark truth: The debts and financial obligations we are on track to leave the next generations will be so huge that they will preclude our children from achieving the American dream. Never before has there been a generation of Americans that has imperiled the following generations' opportunity for achievement and advance as we have done. And America's ability to preserve individual freedom and the nation's security is also in jeopardy, because unless things dramatically change, our debts and obligations will imperil our economy and our military—not because of fierce foreign competitors or the need to engage enemies militarily, but simply because of our own woeful negligence.

The Entitlement Nightmare

The term "entitlement" is one of those bits of government jargon that everyone has heard, but only some people understand. In simplest terms, an entitlement is considered to be a guarantee of access to government benefits by right or by agreement through law. Almost everyone is familiar with Social Security; the other two of the so-called Big Three entitlements are Medicare and Medicaid. Medicare is a health-insurance program for seniors and certain disabled people provided by the federal government and partially funded by payroll taxes and shared premiums. Medicaid is a health-insurance program for the poor and disabled. While we think of Medicare as the health program for seniors, Medicaid is actually the program that covers the elderly poor when they need the long-term care of a nursing home. On average, and in normal economic times, Medicaid is funded about 57 percent by the federal government and the remainder by the individual states. But the ratio between federal and state Medicaid spending isn't the same for all states; some, like Massachusetts, pay 50 percent of total Medicaid costs, while others, like Tennessee, pay 40 percent.

These three entitlement programs create a safety net for seniors and citizens who are poor or have special needs. But they have become immensely expensive. President Franklin D. Roosevelt signed Social Security into law in 1935 as part of his New Deal, but even he would be surprised to see how much it has grown. In his book *Running on Empty,* former commerce secretary Peter G. Peterson explains that Roosevelt's original Social Security program "has spawned a gigantic federal benefit system that is 50 percent larger, as a share of today's (vastly larger) GDP, than the entire federal government was at the height of the New Deal." Social Security grew exponentially as Congress in the 1950s and 1960s added more and more benefits to the original program.

But when it comes to benefit expansion and out-of-control growth, Social Security doesn't hold a candle to Medicare. When Medicare became law in 1965, President Lyndon Johnson estimated that it would cost American taxpayers only about $500 million dollars annually. But in 2010, total Medicare costs are projected to approach $500 *billion*—almost a thousand times larger than what it looked like to President Johnson.

Medicaid became law during the final weeks of the Medicare legislative process. Projections were that it would cost less than $250 million by the time all fifty states had implemented the program. That figure was exceeded when only six states had done so. Since then, Medicaid growth has far outpaced the expansion of our overall economy because of dozens of congressional expansions and additions to the original program.

At present, the total cost of U.S. entitlement programs accounts for more than *half* of all federal spending. Combined with the interest payments on the national debt, so-called mandatory spending is over 60 percent of all federal spending. Entitlements consume more than 11 percent of our entire economic output, while the defense budget, by way of comparison, is less than 4 percent of our GDP.

Because entitlement spending grows so quickly—much faster than either the GDP or total federal tax revenues—it effectively crowds out spending on other priorities. State governors have to deal with only one of the entitlements, Medicaid, but I can report that one is more than enough. When I became governor of Massachusetts, the first time I met with my cabinet members to begin drafting a budget, my secretary of health and human services brought charts that outlined massive projected growth in our Medicaid spending. He noted that when it came to Medicaid, we had no choice in the matter: It was federally mandated. One of the other cabinet secretaries quipped, "So I guess all the rest of us will simply preside over permanently shrinking agencies."

He was right. We began to refer to Medicaid as "Pac-Man," because it grew more than twice as fast as our state tax revenues, eating its way through everything else in the budget.

Because of the disproportionate growth of the big-three national entitlements, this "Pac-Man effect" is even more pronounced at the federal level. The General Accounting Office calculates, in fact, that entitlement spending and interest will constitute more than *three-quarters* of all federal spending within a single decade. By mid-century—if tax rates remain unchanged—entitlements alone would consume all other government spending. Nothing would be left for national defense, infrastructure, medical research, education, science, or anything else. Nothing.

But that won't happen, of course. Instead, there will be a campaign to raise taxes by a massive amount. Today payroll taxes totaling 15.3 percent cover the cost of entitlements. To keep pace with the projected growth in entitlement spending, the tax would have to more than double by mid-century, then rise to 44 percent after that. That would make the federal tax rate for entitlements alone greater than the combined rate of all federal taxes we pay today!

Our grandchildren would watch helplessly as 44 percent of their total earnings were taken simply to maintain mandated Social Security, Medicare, and Medicaid payments to their grandparents and parents. Given the scale of this tax burden, only a very few of them could expect to earn enough to buy a home or to build a business. Their total federal tax burden would far exceed half of what they earn. In practical terms, America would cease to be the land of opportunity. The American dream would be over.

The Political Shell Game

This untenable outcome is the simple result of promising ourselves the moon—not directly, but through commitments imposed on future generations that were made in our behalf by the men and women we have elected to office. I can't imagine that we would have done this intentionally. How is it that we didn't know? Most Americans are aware of the budget deficits, the national debt, and our trade deficit, but this entitlement nightmare has been virtually unnoticed by our generation, or by the ones who will be stuck with it.

Part of the problem is that the federal government has a habit of hiding its long-term liabilities. It publishes the equivalent of an annual budget, but it doesn't publish a balance sheet. In the private sector, anyone who wants to understand how healthy a company is begins by looking at two reports. The income statement shows the company's annual profit or loss, but that doesn't tell the whole story. If a hypothetical business made a $10 million profit last year, is it healthy? Perhaps, but you'd want to learn more. If its balance sheet shows oversized debt and undersized equity, it may not be so healthy. Enron was very profitable until it collapsed. So were Lehman and AIG. So have been a great number of now-bankrupt companies. The balance sheet tells a good deal about "the rest of the story."

If the federal government published a balance sheet—just as it requires public companies to do—it would be forced to show its entitlement liability. And if it amortized that liability, it would also appear in the annual budget. We would see it, we would talk about it, and we would be more likely to do something about it. But the politicians keep it well hidden instead.

Washington politicians have also perfected the use of another budget trick to hide their excesses. All new bills are "scored"—which means evaluated for their impact on the budget—based upon their cost to the federal budget over only the next ten years. So when proponents of a big entitlement expansion of some kind draft their legislation, they are careful to make sure that the major financial impact doesn't hit until eleven years out. That way, the cost won't even be considered.

A case in point is the CLASS Act, designed to provide long-term care insurance for seniors. Individuals must pay premiums for five years to qualify for the program, so benefits don't start until at least five years out, and even then, they will initially be paid to only a small portion of the people who are in the program. Thus, when the bill was scored over ten years by the Congressional Budget Office, it looked like it would make money. Of course everyone knows it will cost an enormous amount over the long term. Ironically, and outrageously, CLASS was included in Obamacare legislation as a source of funding.

Hiding long-term liabilities makes sense for politicians with short-term goals, like reelection. It allows them to give big gifts to their friends, donors, or special-interest groups without the public at large becoming aware of them. When I ran for governor, for example, I paid a visit to the firefighters' union to pitch for its support. Union leaders had endorsed Massachusetts's two prior Republican governors, so I imagined I could count on them as well. During the meeting, I discussed at length my commitment to fire safety, low taxes, interoperable communication systems, and a range of issues that I supported and knew the union supported as well, but the union representatives in attendance appeared entirely unmoved.

Finally, I got the big question from the union leadership: Would I support "25-75"? Someone had to explain that it was shorthand for a proposed state law mandating that after twenty-five years of service, firefighters could retire and receive annual pensions that would equal 75 percent of the average of their highest three years of compensation, plus inflation—a pension that would be paid regardless of whether the retired firefighter got another job, even another job in state government.

I did a quick calculation. A firefighter who was hired at twenty years of age would retire at forty-five, then be paid for the remaining thirty years of his or her life expectancy, plus receive health-care insurance. The state would actually pay this person more during retirement than he or she had earned during their years of employment. It made no sense—not just the money, but also the notion that a public employee could retire at forty-five with a full pension. I declined to offer my support for "25-75." It would have been very easy to say yes and win the union's support because the cost to the state wouldn't have become significant until many years after I'd left office. It wouldn't show up on my budget, and because we don't publish a balance sheet, it may have hardly been noticed.

Something similar has gone on for decades in other political campaigns, in statehouses, and in Washington. Lobbyists for seniors, for example, justify their own large salaries based on what they "get" from government, and they explicitly or implicitly offer their considerable support to those politicians who agree to pile on obligations that bring benefits to older Americans. Today that same highly sought-after support goes to those office-seekers who agree not to disturb the mound of entitlement obligations already in place. And because those obligations are well hidden, it's easy for politicians to comply.

Some politicians are able to convince themselves that they are doing the right thing when they ignore looming problems like entitlement finance. In public, they mount elaborate and specious arguments meant to discount the extent of the problem, but in private, among friends, most will admit the truth. The combination of compelling short-term political self-interest and a veiled means of delivering a favor to key special interests in order to get a favor down the road are irresistibly potent for many in public life. These are not criminal transactions. They are not the sort of bribes we see hit the front pages. But they are insidious incentives to act contrary to the interests of future generations of Americans, and their enticing power goes a long way toward explaining how we have reached this point. The public generally has no idea that politicians acquiesce to such things as excessive public-union pensions and runaway entitlement growth, leaving the coming unsuspecting generations to suffer the consequences of this political hide-and-seek.

The entitlement liability can be rectified, and the first step is to create public awareness that pushes the issue to the front burner. That will require political leaders who believe that their next election is less important than their children's future to speak out. It will also require able and relentless investigative voices in the media to refuse to let candidates off the hook who do not confront this issue. Prior to the 2008 economic collapse, there was reason to be hopeful that these voices would emerge. But the turbulence and uncertainty surrounding the financial crisis may keep the entitlement emergency in the shadows, allowing politicians to continue to ignore it for a while longer. Unfortunately, President Obama has done nothing to call attention to this looming crisis or to advance any solutions.

As noted above, public awareness would certainly grow if we required the federal government to publish a national balance sheet and to annually amortize its long-term liabilities. It would help make the voting public—and particularly those young Americans just entering the workforce—aware of what awaits them if we don't take a different course. And it would mean that new programs and entitlements would be evaluated not just on their effect over the next few years, but over their lives. I suspect, for example, that if former president George W. Bush would have had to declare the actual balance-sheet impact of his Medicare Part D prescription-drug program—now estimated to be approximately $8 trillion—it would not have passed. Politicians love to talk about transparency and accountability, but when they do, they are rarely referring to themselves. The time has come for that to change.

In 2008, the liberal Brookings Institution and the conservative Heritage Foundation joined forces to recommend that our elected officials stop considering all entitlement spending as "mandatory and automatic," because it is not, after all. Congress and the president have the power to appropriate spending as they see fit, even for so-called mandatory programs like entitlements. The two cooperating think tanks called for the creation of an annual budget for these programs, a performance review of each to determine whether it was effective and on budget, and extensive analysis and debate before it is funded. They concluded that "automatic spending in these programs is preempting the policy discussion we should be having about our national priorities and how they should be funded. . . . From diverse points on the political spectrum, [we] sound an alarm: if America is to remain strong, such evasions must end."

Another fiction that's often used to obscure the extent of the crisis is the so-called Social Security Trust Fund, which the American public is assured has a large positive balance composed of U.S. treasuries. Yet it is not a fund in the conventional sense of the word. From the fund's inception, money collected from payroll taxes hasn't been "locked away," but rather has been used to pay the benefits of current beneficiaries. When payroll taxes for a given year have exceeded that year's Social Security payout, those excess funds have been immediately made available for the rest of the government's spending. There simply is no "fund" safely invested somewhere that will reduce the specter of our children facing ever higher taxes, and therefore entitlement programs will consume an ever larger share of our economic output. There is no fund, and there is no silver bullet.

To put it in a nutshell, the American people have been effectively defrauded out of their Social Security. In 1982, the government raised Social Security taxes with the intention of creating a surplus that could be set aside in some fashion for the baby boomers when they retired. But for the last thirty years, the surplus has been spent, not on retirement security, but on regular budget items.

Let's look at what would happen if someone in the private sector did a similar thing. Suppose two grandparents created a trust fund, appointed a bank as trustee, and instructed the bank to invest the proceeds of the trust fund so as to provide for their grandchildren's education. Suppose further that the bank used the proceeds for its own purposes, so that when the grandchildren turned eighteen, there was no money for them to go to college. What would happen to the bankers responsible for misusing the money? They would go to jail. But what has happened to the people responsible for the looming bankruptcy of Social Security? They keep returning to Congress every two years.

It is important to conduct the entitlement discussion without scaring our senior citizens, which is why the reforms that are necessary must be made concurrent with guarantees to our elderly that their benefits will not be slashed and the promises they relied upon will not be broken. They are worried already because they are more aware of the enormity of the entitlement problem than the rest of us—candor will be the best assurance we can give them that the solutions will not be crafted with them as targets.

Sustainable Entitlements

From a mathematical perspective, there are at least four ways one could repair Social Security. First, Congress and the president could raise the Social Security tax rate or apply it to a greater share of an individual's earnings, or some combination of both. But as Social Security benefits are proportional to what an individual has paid into the system, raising taxes would also raise benefits and compound rather than solve the existing problem. Even if we were to decouple an individual's Social Security benefits from their contributions—raising taxes to solve our entitlement crisis—we would be saddling the next generation with the very tax burden we are seeking to avoid.

Alternatively, we could gradually increase the retirement age. This does have a certain logic to it: The average American's life expectancy has risen by more than ten years since Social Security was created. Increasing the retirement age by even one or two years would help get the system closer to sustainability. Because some people would be physically unable to work beyond today's retirement age, the system would have to allow for exceptions, but most people I know in their sixties want to keep working; they're simply happier when they do. I keep hearing that "sixty is the new fifty"—at least that's what I've been telling myself for the last few years. Many older Americans are healthy, vital, and want to stay engaged in meaningful work. If we increased the retirement age, we would encourage seniors to stay healthier longer, keep their minds active and alert, and at the same time, we would relieve the terrible Social Security burden our children and grandchildren face.

I've also been intrigued by an option proposed by Bob Pozen, who served in my state cabinet in Massachusetts and is the former vice chairman of Fidelity Investments. He currently heads MFS, a Boston-based financial services company. His idea is to simply change the way high-income individuals' initial Social Security benefit is calculated. At present, the initial benefit for all recipients is keyed to the total amount of their lifetime employment income and the Social Security taxes paid on it, adjusted to reflect the inflation that occurred up to the date of retirement. But the inflator that is used in the calculation isn't the consumer price index (the CPI), as you might suspect, but rather the wage index. Because wages have gone up a good deal faster than consumer prices, the wage index raises the starting point for Social Security benefits faster than would have been the case had the CPI been used. The rationale for using the wage index was that people who rely on Social Security for most or all of their retirement need it to keep up with their current wages, not a lower figure based on the change in the cost of goods. The Pozen Plan proposes to continue to use the wage index as the inflator for low and middle-income citizens, but he now applies the CPI index to compute the initial benefits for higher-income individuals who are not living predominantly on Social Security benefits.

The Pozen Plan tends to sit better with conservatives than it does with liberals because, while the former don't like anything that looks like a tax increase, the latter aren't fond of anything that looks like a benefit reduction. To make the plan as palatable as possible to everyone, one could let high-income individuals make the choice themselves. If they wanted the higher wage index to be used to determine their initial benefit, then they would be charged a higher Social Security tax. If they preferred the CPI method, their tax would remain the same. Few would object to being offered a personal choice, and the active involvement of citizens in the calculation of their benefits would greatly enhance the understanding of the system as well as the trade-offs on which it is built.

When the United Kingdom faced a retirement-system crisis similar to our own, the British Parliament opted to switch to the CPI index inflator for all beneficiaries, not just those with higher incomes, and the country effectively solved its problem. Pozen's graduated inflator plan wouldn't solve our entire Social Security shortfall, but he calculates that it would remedy most of it. Together with a gradual increase in the retirement age, it would preserve the government's ability to meet Social Security obligations without taking a rising share of wages, and it would be phased in over time so current and near retirees would not be affected in any way.

Individual retirement accounts offer a fourth option, one that would allow today's wage earners to direct a portion of their Social Security tax to a private account rather than go entirely to pay the benefits of current retirees, as is the case today. The federal government would make up for its lost Social Security revenue by borrowing that amount through the sale of treasuries, just as it currently does for the rest of its deficits. Owners of these individual accounts would invest in a combination of stocks and bonds and—presuming these investments paid a higher rate of return than the new treasuries—the return on these investments would boost the payments to seniors. I also like the fact the individual retirement accounts would encourage more Americans to invest in the private sector that powers our economy.

The 2008 stock market collapse is proof, however, that we can't always count on positive returns from these investments. But it is not, as some critics claim, proof of the folly and danger of individual accounts. It is evidence that such a system would have to be phased in over time so that the market's inevitable ups and downs—by far more ups than downs over a lifetime—do not endanger a secure retirement. But given the volatility of investment values that we have just experienced, I would prefer that individual accounts were added to Social Security, not diverted from it, and that they were voluntary. Former commerce secretary Pete Peterson has proposed that such individual accounts be mandatory, pointing out that voluntary savings programs like 401(k)s and IRAs tend to be underutilized. But if the accounts were linked with Social Security, set at

1 percent of wages as the annual contribution, and required an annual "opt-out" by both the individual and his or her spouse to be inoperative, I believe they could be effective, while at the same time giving taxpayers personal choice.

One or a combination of these last three options will put Social Security on track to sustainably meet its obligations to current and future retirees, and they will keep us from raising taxes that would stifle our economy and encumber future generations.

On to Medicaid. When I was governor of Massachusetts, the Bush administration's then secretary of health and human services Tommy Thompson proposed a straightforward and uncomplicated plan to fix the Medicaid program. Appearing at the annual governors' conference, he proposed that each state annually be given the Medicaid dollars it had received during the prior year, adjusted for inflation and changes in the state's population of the poor. The state would be allowed to fashion its health-care program for the poor as the state chose.

You might imagine that the fifty Republican and Democratic governors would have recoiled at the idea; after all, overall inflation rises far more slowly than does health-care inflation. In fact, however, the proposal was welcomed by many in both parties. A number of us had already filed requests at the Department of Health and Human Services for waivers that would allow us to adjust our states' Medicaid program because, over the years, we had watched as its intent to care for the poor had been distorted by some very creative people.

Have you seen advertisements by lawyers claiming that with their help, the government will pay for nursing-home costs regardless of one's assets? They have found ways to turn wealthy retirees into poor people—at least for the purposes of qualifying for Medicaid nursing-home care. Now millionaires can give their fortunes to their children, become "poor," and qualify for Medicaid. And as a result, middle-income retirees see no need to purchase long-term care insurance. An operator of a chain of nursing homes said that twenty-five years ago, Medicaid paid the bills for about 20 percent of the people in their nursing homes, while 80 percent were covered by their own private insurance. Today those numbers have been reversed. If the government is willing to give away money, there will always be a long line to get it.

These distortions and inequities in Medicaid have become so severe that governors like me were willing to trade the federal government's open check-book for the ability to control our own state's program. We were convinced that we could save money and provide better care for more people who really needed it. Yet Congress rejected Thompson's plan. Since then, I haven't seen a better idea for fixing Medicaid come so close to becoming law.

There are other cost-saving options for Medicaid as well. Recipients could be moved to managed care plans. A 2004 report from the Lewin Group found savings in the range of 6 to 12 percent could be achieved via this route. Or states could pay a standard fee for each covered individual to a primary care practice or community health center. This would provide cost certainty and better care for the poor.

Rather than allowing Medicaid members to go to any hospital, states could negotiate with fewer providers to obtain better rates. Or we might let Medicaid recipients opt out of the Medicaid program, give them an equivalent voucher, and allow them to purchase private insurance instead. The best way to see which of these or other ideas is most beneficial is to allow states to experiment, evaluate the results, and share them with the other states. Using the states as the laboratories the Constitution intended under our federal system is exactly what led us to meaningful and effective welfare reform in the 1990s. Such experimentation can lead us to the right result again. But Congress and the president must advocate for such a move and pass and implement it before such reforms can begin.

Returning Medicare to solid footing represents our greatest entitlement challenge. If we make no changes to the current system, payroll taxes would have to increase by 40 percent to meet our Social Security bill in 2040, but the increase to meet *Medicare* costs in two decades would be a staggering *250 percent*.

Like Social Security, Medicare is currently being rocked by the swelling numbers of baby-boomer retirees. By the middle of this century, the number of people age sixty-five or older will more than double—to nearly 80 million people. That means that one of every four Americans will be over 65. Have you noticed how many seniors live in Florida? In 2050, the senior share of the *entire* U.S. population will be the same as it is for Florida today. Simple demographic math will drive up the Medicare load borne by every individual still in the workforce, just as it does for Social Security and Medicaid. There are now 3.3 workers for every retiree, but in forty years that ratio will drop to 2 workers for every retiree.

The rising cost of health care adds just as much to the weight to the Medicare burden as does the age wave. When I was a young consultant to a health-care company in the late 1970s, I predicted that health care would reach 20 percent of the GDP by 2050. At the time, health care made up 11 percent of the nation's GDP, and my client scoffed at me, insisting that the economy couldn't possibly accommodate that much spending on health. "Something will have to give before that happens," he assured me. But, as it's turned out, health care *already* accounts for nearly 18 percent of the economy. It won't reach 20 percent in forty years, as I had projected, but in only eight. As health care costs outstrip the growth of the rest of the economy, it gobbles up a larger and larger share of the GDP. So it is health care itself that has to be brought under control if we are to keep our Medicare bills from overwhelming the next generation.

The debate over health care raged in Washington during most of 2009. Sadly, that consensus as to the problem did not result in a consensus as to the solution. The real tragedy was that it wasn't the sort of bipartisan and genuine search for solutions that I experienced in Massachusetts in 2006 and 2007. Our reforms in Massachusetts didn't produce a perfect system, just one that was much better than what had been there before, and it taught us all valuable lessons on how to work collaboratively to reform health care. But the most important lessons—involve everyone, demonize no one, and be transparent—were never adopted by President Obama, Speaker Nancy Pelosi, Senator Harry Reid, and their surrogates. As a result, we have not achieved the kind of reforms that will tame health-care cost inflation.

In addition to top-to-bottom health-care reform—which is the subject of the next chapter—there's also a great deal that we must do to repair Medicare itself.

As noted above, Congress must set an explicit budget every year for Medicare; the mandatory-spending mind-set simply isn't conducive to the kind of productivity improvement and cost reduction that we so critically need.

Second, we must begin to move Medicare away from the current fee-for-service reimbursement system. Today Medicare pays doctors, hospitals, and other providers for every procedure, test, exam, or treatment given to a particular patient—the more tests and exams, the more money the hospital or physician is paid by Medicare. And there is abundant evidence that financial incentives do in fact influence treatment decisions that health-care providers make. In Japan, for example, physicians can own pharmacies, and those who do make a small profit each time they prescribe drugs. American doctors are not allowed to own pharmacies, which, it turns out, is a good thing. Japanese doctors prescribe twice as many drugs per person as do American doctors. Japanese doctors are also paid a flat fee for each office visit made by a patient; the average patient visit in Japan lasts only five minutes, and physicians there typically insist on a patient visit before they will renew a prescription. I suspect very few Japanese doctors let their financial incentives define the quality of care they give their patients, but that's one of the curious characteristics of financial incentives: Sometimes you aren't even aware that they are bending you toward a particular kind of behavior.

When the Congressional Budget Office studied Medicare spending by state and region, it discovered that the annual average cost per Medicare enrollee was $5,200 in one region and $14,000 in another, even after adjusting for a variety of demographic factors. The study found no significant differences in mortality rates or health outcomes for Medicare patients across those regions, but one disparity really jumped out. In the highest cost areas, there were significantly more specialists relative to the number of primary-care physicians. The CBO study offered no conclusion, but it's hard not to imagine that the *Field of Dreams* phenomenon applies: "If you build it, they will come," particularly if Medicare is paying the bills.

Migrating Medicare away from fee-for-service can reduce the rate of Medicare-spending growth. Under one approach, a health-care provider is paid a fixed amount for each patient with a specific condition—eliminating incentives to perform multiple tests or redundant procedures. Another so-called capitated plan pays the provider a flat fee for every person in the entire pool of enrollees—offering the provider an incentive to keep his or her patients healthy. Despite its detractors who charge that managed care is second-rate, it's actually preferred by large numbers of preretirement Americans as they choose the best way to meet their own health-insurance needs. In California, where managed care has been an option for many years, almost six million citizens are members of Kaiser Permanente's managed-care program, the nation's largest not-for-profit health organization, and it has consistently received top marks in reports by a variety of consumer surveys and consumer organizations.

Instituting an improved payment system will help solve the Medicare crisis, but to remain solvent over the long term, the system must undergo an even more fundamental alteration. When Medicare was created, it was envisioned as a plan to provide health care for the aged poor, but instead, it has grown into the nation's retirement health plan for all seniors. This evolution is an accomplished fact, and it doesn't matter whether it was a good or bad result, only that it is manifestly the result with which all of us must live and under which most of us must age. We need to make it work. As the baby-boom generation retires, the only way we can keep our children from being forced to pay our medical bills is for us to pay them ourselves—and a number of options would make that possible.

Medicare, for example, could offer each retiree a credit sufficient for a basic health plan, and individuals could opt to accept that plan or apply the credit toward a more comprehensive and higher-cost plan. Alternatively, co-payments, deductibles, and co-premiums could be adjusted upward for higher-income enrollees. As with Medicaid, there are many good ideas—we need to restart the process of arriving at a favorable mix of reforms, and soon. The bottom line is that there's simply no way to prevent Medicare from consuming our children's future if we baby boomers and our physicians can continue to order ever more expensive diagnostic procedures and treatments that we don't have to pay for. Very few grandparents who I know would ever consider ordering an extraordinarily expensive medical treatment and putting it on their granddaughter's charge card—at a high rate of interest—but that is exactly what we are doing, and it has to stop.

If health care is free to the patient and profitable for the provider, the only result can be runaway spending. And we need to acknowledge it's a result that has already arrived. We must recognize that the system is seriously ill, and that ignoring this truth will lead to even more grave consequences in the years to come.

Mountains of Debt

Entitlements comprise far and away the largest liability on our national balance sheet. Current estimates peg those obligations at over $42.9 trillion—more than three times the size of the entire American economy. But they aren't our sole liability; the debt we owe due to the federal government's deficit spending reached $6.8 trillion in 2008, and the Congressional Budget Office projects that President Obama's budget plans will add a staggering $9 trillion more in total deficits over the coming decade alone. During his first term, he plans to add more than a trillion dollars of debt each year. That amount is more than the total personal income taxes annually collected by the federal government. Under the Obama spending program, we will soon have accumulated more public debt than our entire GDP.

Consider the burden—or more aptly, the peril—associated with this debt. In 2009, the interest on the debt will consume *more than 40 percent* of our total individual income taxes! And that is with an average interest rate of 3.2 percent. Consider what would happen if lenders to the United States became worried about our ability to repay our debt and interest rates rose to Carter-era levels of 15 percent. In the words of Lawrence Kadish in *The Wall Street Journal:* "Left unchecked, this destructive deficit-debt cycle will leave the White House and Congress with either having to default on the national debt or instruct the Treasury to run the printing presses into a policy of hyperinflation." The consequences of either outcome for America and American families would exceed those of the Great Depression.

The fact that both parties have come to *accept* deficits and ever-higher levels of public debt is deeply troubling. There are times when deficit spending may be an appropriate bridge to finance a national emergency or to stimulate a depressed economy, but it should not be a permanent part of the budget. Almost half our public debt is financed by foreign entities, a circumstance that puts our currency at risk, threatens our annual budget, and makes our productive enterprises vulnerable to foreign ownership. Like most Americans, I recognize the need for government spending, but I cannot fathom the argument that it's fine to spend more than we earn year after year. Passing on ever-increasing debt to our children is not just bad policy, it is morally wrong.

There are people in both parties who see the budget as something of a game of chicken. Some Democrats are eager to spend so much that Republicans have to raise taxes, and some Republicans, on the other hand, are intent on lowering taxes so much that Democrats have to cut spending. Both sides take great satisfaction in their respective battle plans: the Democrats for spending more and the Republicans for taxing less. My vote is for the Republicans, but in either case, deficits cannot be accepted as part of political tactics; there is simply too much at stake.

Our big government debt problem is not a Democrat problem—it is a Democrat and Republican problem. When President Bush and Republicans were in charge, they grew government, grew spending, and grew debt just like the Democrats. Neither party has been willing to say no to the people who want more and more from government. Saying yes wins votes. Saying no means concession speeches. But what America faces today calls for truth, and having just experienced a brush with economic collapse, the American people are ready for truth. They know that if we go on borrowing, we will do to the country what was done to Lehman and AIG and General Motors and to millions of homeowners. Except in the country's case, there is no one that could bail us out.

If we wisely begin to reform entitlements and commit to live within our means, we will accomplish for our children what our parents did for us: Bestow upon them an America that is stronger and more prosperous even than what we have known. We do not have to become the "worst American generation." There is still time to correct our course—barely. And our example of admitting and remedying a critical error will be an example our children may find both informative and indispensable.

7

Healing Health Care

So there I was at Morristown Memorial Hospital in New Jersey. It was 1983. My job was to find millions of dollars in hospital savings, identify ways to improve patient care, convince doctors, nurses, and administrators to take the steps we suggested, and share what we learned with other hospitals around the country. But there was one small problem: I didn't know anything about health care—and that fact was more than a little unnerving for me and for the hospital's CEO.

This wasn't the first time I'd been hired as a consultant to do a job in a business I didn't know much about. One of my first senior assignments had been at the Morgan Knitting Mills in Tamaqua, Pennsylvania. Soon after our arrival, the junior consultant and I were ushered into the CEO's office, where John Morgan was behind his desk, catching up with *The Wall Street Journal*. As he put the paper down on his desk, he looked at us, let out a sigh, then stood and raised both hands above his head. He was about six feet, four inches tall—sufficiently imposing to attract my full attention. "Boys! Boys!" he bellowed. "They sent me boys when I needed men!"

Fortunately, we "boys" were able to understand and accurately present his business to potential acquirers. But John Morgan always had a way of putting people on their heels. One CEO asked him why he was selling his company. His answer: "That's a stupid question. I'm old, I have no kids, and they don't dig graves big enough to put it in with me!" I knew just how that CEO felt.

So Morristown, New Jersey, wasn't the first time I had felt a little apprehensive about an assignment. But over the years, I'd gained a measure of confidence about jumping into unfamiliar businesses and helping them find ways to improve. I'd performed well enough at companies that made farm tractors, glass bottles, pharmaceuticals, fiber optics, chlorine, and process-control valves. The analytical concepts and approach that I'd learned from my employers at Bain & Company, combined with hard work, help from smart people, and a little luck, got me up to speed and able to contribute in a variety of settings. We'd start by forming a team with the client's own people, who brought to the table the comprehensive industry expertise we sometimes lacked. We would add data—a lot of data, so much, in fact, that I wasn't comfortable until I had been fully immersed in it. We applied the proven concepts that Bill Bain liked to call "compressed experience." And then we would condense what we learned from the data, from the industry experts, and from our conceptual framework into the two or three issues we believed would make the biggest difference in helping an enterprise become more successful.

Morristown Memorial Hospital, however, was a different kind of challenge, and I wondered whether health care would be too dissimilar from the business world we knew for us to be successful. Just to add to the pressure, Morristown Memorial was one of four hospitals we were taking on at the same time.

After setting up our team at each of the hospitals, we began gathering data. We looked in minute detail at the costs of a number of procedures that we selected as examples, from triple-bypass surgery and gallbladder removal to suturing a minor laceration. We counted big things such as nursing hours, operating-room time, and pharmaceuticals, as well as little things such as Q-Tips, gauze pads, and the custodial time spent mopping the floors of patients' rooms.

We weren't the only ones surprised by what we discovered—the differences in cost for the same procedure done in separate hospitals were large, sometimes by as much as 100 percent. Quality and outcomes also differed.

One hospital, for example, had averaged much better recovery rates and half the length of stay for hip-replacement surgery than the other three. Differences like those pointed us toward changes that would yield meaningful cost and quality improvements. We also thought they might be of great interest to the patients getting hip replacements. We took those innovations we developed at Morristown Memorial nationwide. Bain & Company was ultimately engaged by nearly one hundred hospitals.

Really Helping People

I'm sure this experience was part of the reason why I didn't just dismiss my friend Tom Stemberg's admonition soon after I had been elected governor. He had a simple message for me. "Mitt, if you really want to help people, find a way to get everyone health insurance."

I told him that was impossible; I'd have to break my promise not to raise taxes, because after all, getting everyone insured would cost hundreds of millions of dollars, if not billions. "Yeah," he replied, "but if you really want to help people, you'll find a way."

I knew that he was right. Over the previous twenty years or so, I had served in various community and church service roles that gave me the opportunity to know quite a large number of people on a very personal basis. Some were poor, some were wealthy, and most were in between. Many were single; some were single parents.

Quite a few of the people I came to know and befriend were unable to afford health insurance, even if they had middle incomes. One was a young man who had been stricken with inoperable cancer. His doctor and hospital had provided the most basic care, but his hope for cure or longer life involved treatments that would be expensive and unaffordable to someone without insurance. Another was a single mom, a waitress. Her cancer, then in remission, had made it almost impossible for her to find work: employers didn't want someone with her health costs in their insurance pool. The number of people with these kinds of circumstances is far from small. And as governor, I was in a position to do something about it.

I've learned that when politicians say they want to help people, there is often cause for a good deal of skepticism. People are used to promises made and promises forgotten. Once when I was governor, I went to the scene of a flood in one of our cities. The first floor of a large nursing home was filled with water three to four feet deep. The patients were being carried out on stretchers by emergency workers and placed on buses to be taken to other facilities. I stepped into one of the buses to reassure the evacuees. I remember one very old, very small woman sitting with her health attendant in the front row. She looked so sweet and so worried. I smiled at her and proceeded with my promise to the people on the bus: "We will make sure that all of you are dry and warm and that you are taken to a facility where you will be well taken care of." That sweet old lady looked up and said, loud and clear, "Bullsh–!"

The hard-won wisdom of many decades had taught her what to think of men from the government arriving with promises of help.

I didn't want to overpromise and underdeliver on health care, so without fanfare or public announcement, we went to work to see if we could find a way to insure the uninsured and to make sure that no citizen in our state would ever need to worry about losing their health insurance. The group I formed wasn't made up of the usual political mix. Instead, it included a former investment banker, a Bain & Company partner, a Washington policy guru, an expert in federal health programs, and even some help from a professor at MIT and experts from the Heritage Foundation.

After about a year of looking at data—and not making much progress—we had a collective epiphany of sorts, an obvious one, as important observations often are: the people in Massachusetts who didn't have health insurance were, in fact, already receiving health care. Under federal law, hospitals had to stabilize and treat people who arrived at their emergency rooms with acute conditions. And our state's hospitals were offering even more assistance than the federal government required. That meant that someone was already paying for the cost of treating people who didn't have health insurance. If we could get our hands on that money, and therefore redirect it to help the uninsured *buy* insurance instead and obtain treatment in the way that the vast majority of individuals did—before acute conditions developed—the cost of insuring everyone in the state might not be as expensive as I had feared.

When we surveyed those who were uninsured, we became even more optimistic. About 40 percent of the uninsured were making enough money to buy insurance on their own and wouldn't need a subsidy at all. (The reasons for not buying insurance could be many and varied, including the typical young person's belief in their own invulnerability, even if they ski, parasail, ride motorcycles, or skydive.) Another 20 percent of the uninsured qualified for Medicaid, so half the cost of their care would be covered by the federal government. And most of the remaining 40 percent who were not making enough money to buy insurance could afford to pay for *some* portion of their premium. We envisioned the possibility of splitting the cost of health insurance with them. The subsidy would become smaller as their income grew, but not so much that we would create a disincentive for them to grow their income.

The survey of the uninsured also dispelled some of our misconceptions. A number of people had imagined that the largest group of the uninsured would be unemployed single moms. In fact, the survey showed that the largest cohort was white, employed, young single males. This group was not a population that private insurers would likely resist covering because they were healthier than the population as a whole.

Most of the uninsured young men were working, but they were employed by small businesses—such as restaurants, garages, and software developers—or they worked for themselves. They told the survey takers that when they went to buy insurance, the insurers weren't interested. First, insurance companies told them that it was simply too expensive for them to service an individual who was not part of a larger group, and second, the companies suspected that young males, for instance, would be interested in health insurance only if they believed they were likely to get sick or already had a preexisting condition. The companies called this "adverse selection."

Massachusetts insurance regulations also didn't help. The Commonwealth required insurers to offer only benefit-rich, low-deductible, limited co-pay policies—and consequently, such policies were very expensive. Further, the state didn't allow insurers to adequately discount policy premiums for young healthy people. As a result of all these regulations, premiums for individuals who were not part of a pool were excessively high, and young healthy people not surprisingly declined to pay them. When we asked the insurance companies what would happen to those premiums if we could solve the servicing problem, update our regulations, and get everyone insured—in effect, making the entire state their group pool—they calculated that premiums for an individual, nongroup young person could be cut roughly in half.

It began to appear that the cost of getting private health insurance for all our citizens would be much less than I had imagined. Many of the then-uninsured wouldn't need a state subsidy to buy health insurance, and the premiums we would subsidize would be less expensive because a good portion of the population pool would largely be relatively young and healthy.

The plan we ultimately constructed and proposed to the legislature relied on three basic components.

First, those who could afford insurance would either buy it or *pay their own health-care costs*—no more free riders showing up at the hospital expecting to get care at the taxpayers' expense. If they did not buy insurance or establish an account to pay for their medical expenses, they would forgo the benefit of a tax exemption.

Second, for those who couldn't afford health insurance on their own, the state would pay a portion of their premium with the amount of the subsidy determined on a sliding scale by income. Importantly, no one got health insurance for free—even the poor would pay some amount they could afford.

Finally, to make it easier for insurers to service individual customers, the state would create a "connector" or "exchange" that would collect premiums and pass them on to the insurers. The Heritage Foundation helped us construct an exchange that would make individual premium payments tax-advantaged, lowering cost even further.

The plan would work only if we could get our hands on the money that was then being used to pay for the health care of the uninsured, most of which came from the federal government. The U.S. Health and Human Services Department provides subsidies, known as DSH payments, directly to hospitals that have a disproportionate share of patients who are poor and without insurance. We wanted to redirect these monies from going to hospitals to go instead to individuals to help them buy their own health insurance from private insurance companies. Why would the feds agree to such a proposal? Our pitch was simple: if they agreed, we could get everyone in Massachusetts insured—an accomplishment never before achieved in that state or any other.

Our first stop in Washington in the winter of 2004 was the office of

Massachusetts's Senior Senator Ted Kennedy, a respected health-care advocate on Capitol Hill. The late Senator Kennedy and I disagreed on almost every major issue of public policy, and we had waged a knock-down battle for the Senate seat he held in 1994. Teddy was a tough, take-no-prisoners political opponent.

But to his credit he saw an opportunity to work in a bipartisan fashion to try an experiment that might become a model for other states. He quickly grasped the structure of our program, and following a few meetings, he agreed to support our approach. Together, we pitched former health and human services secretary Tommy Thompson. Our meeting was scheduled for the secretary's last day in office, and he agreed with our proposal in principle, but wanted to apply a number of qualifying benchmark provisions. We worked out a letter of agreement, and were on our way. Thompson's replacement, Mike Leavitt, was just as enthusiastic as his predecessor.

Back in Boston, I presented our plan to the Blue Cross Blue Shield Foundation and leaders from across the state. Massachusetts Senate President Robert Travaglini, a thoughtful and pragmatic Democrat, had made it a priority to get everyone insured. He liked our plan, and he liked the fact that Senator Kennedy had approved it. He agreed to support it with a few modifications, none of which I seriously objected to. The Democratic-controlled House, on the other hand, insisted on adding a number of features, a process that took an entire year. When it was finished, we had a bill that retained the original vision, plus added features. Their bill was projected to add just over 1 percent to the state budget; we had calculated that mine would not have added any cost. So I vetoed measures I felt were expensive or counterproductive, but these were overridden by the legislature.

At the April 2006 signing ceremony in Boston's famous Faneuil Hall, Senator Kennedy had the best line: "When Mitt Romney and Ted Kennedy are celebrating the same piece of legislation, it means only one thing: one of us didn't read it." It was a good joke, but this time there was no truth in the humor: We both had worked very hard to make the plan a reality. Beyond our personal collaboration, what was most noteworthy was that *every* interest group in the state supported the bill—business, labor, hospitals, and advocates for the poor. And the bill passed the 200-member houses of the legislature with only two dissenting votes.

All of us knew the bill wasn't perfect; nothing that groundbreaking could be. But it was a big improvement over what we had. It would need to be fine-tuned as it was implemented and it would undergo midcourse correction as time went on. From the outset, I and my team knew that some of the features the legislature had added would be expensive, including the full complement of coverage mandates such as unlimited in vitro fertilization treatments and dental care, a small fee paid by employers who didn't insure their employees, and no opt-out provision for people who wanted to forgo insurance and pay their own way. I was also concerned by the implementation decisions of the administration that followed my own: It decided to provide insurance entirely free to the lowest income people, whereas I had insisted that everyone should pay some portion of their premiums, even if only a small amount. I believed that the new administration set the state's share of premiums above the level I thought were affordable for the Commonwealth. It also provided for certain "hardship" individuals to receive free care without having to purchase insurance. Even the best written legislation is subject to rule-making and interpretation by political appointees, and it can be adjusted by subsequent administrations; their predisposition to grow or restrain spending has a major impact on cost.

Even with these added costs and policy choices by the legislature and the new governor, the plan is working. Of the 500,000 to 600,000 previously uninsured, approximately 440,000 have now obtained insurance—meaning that roughly 98 percent of Massachusetts citizens are insured. According to an independent analysis by the Massachusetts Taxpayers Foundation, a budget watchdog group, the cost of the health-care program has been "relatively modest" and "well within initial projections." Their estimate is that health-care reform increased state spending by less than one and one-half percent.

In the June 26, 2008 issue of the widely respected *New England Journal of Medicine*, Dr. Robert Steinbrook surveyed Massachusetts reforms and concluded:

> [T]he good news is that the new programs have ramped up rapidly, the number of people without health insurance has been substantially reduced, and overall public and political support remains broad. Early data suggest that access to care has improved, especially among low-income adults; there have also been "reductions in out-of-pocket health care spending, problems paying medical bills, and medical debt."

A 2009 comprehensive study by the Massachusetts Taxpayers Foundation—a think tank funded by business—determined that the plan's cost is "relatively modest" and "well within initial projections."

The board that manages the program has begun making the adjustments needed to keep the program on solid financial footing, and health insurance premiums for individual purchasers have declined, just as the companies predicted. The average reduction in the premium for individual purchasers has been approximately 20 percent; for young single persons, the premiums have declined by nearly half.

The Massachusetts Model

The success we achieved in Massachusetts proves that to get everyone insured, you don't have to create a government-run health-care system or government insurance. The basics for creating a workable, affordable system that insures everyone and keeps private insurance and personal choice intact are these: First, create incentives for those who can afford insurance to actually purchase it, which can be done by reducing tax deductions for people who don't buy insurance or by giving tax credits to all those who do. And it is important to allow people to opt out of buying insurance if they can demonstrate their ability to pay their own health-care bills.

Second, create an exchange to help make buying insurance easier for individual—as opposed to corporate—buyers. The exchange lowers premiums and enables individuals to buy health insurance in pretax dollars, just as companies are able to do.

Third, help the poor buy their own private insurance with a sliding-scale subsidy. The government's share of the cost comes from redirecting the federal funds that are currently sent to providers.

My own preference is to let each state fashion its own program to meet the distinct needs of its citizens. States could follow the Massachusetts model if they choose, or they could develop plans of their own. These plans, tested in the state "laboratories of democracy," could be evaluated, compared, improved upon, and adopted by others.

What we accomplished surprised us: 440,000 people who previously had no health insurance became insured, many paying their own way. We made it possible for each newly insured person to have better care, and ultimately healthier and longer lives. From now on, no one in Massachusetts has to worry about losing his or her health insurance if there is a job change or a loss in income; everyone is insured and pays only what he or she can afford. It's portable, affordable health insurance—something people have been talking about for decades. And it was done without government taking over health care.

It is too early to write a definitive evaluation of the Massachusetts reform, and as noted, much depends on the commitment of state officials to continuously monitor and improve the system. One early view is presented in the January 26, 2009 *New Yorker* by Dr. Atul Gawande, a respected author, a Rhodes scholar, a Harvard School of Public Health professor, and a practicing physician at Boston's esteemed Brigham and Women's Hospital. I quote Dr. Gawande's article at length because it was a balanced portrait from a moment in time before the debate became politicized:

> Massachusetts, where I live and work, recently became the first state to adopt a system of universal health coverage for its residents. It didn't organize a government takeover of the state's hospitals or insurance companies, or force people into a new system of state-run clinics. It built on what existed. On July 1, 2007, the state began offering an online choice of four private insurance plans for people without health coverage. The cost is zero for the poor; for the rest, it is limited to no more than about 8 percent of income. The vast majority of families, who had insurance through work, didn't notice a thing when the program was launched. But those who had no coverage had to enroll in a plan or incur a tax penalty.
>
> The results have been remarkable. After a year, 97.4 percent of Massachusetts residents had coverage, and the remaining gap continues to close. Despite the requirement that individuals buy insurance and that employers either provide coverage or pay a tax, the program has remained extremely popular. Repeated surveys have found that at least two-thirds of the state's residents support the reform.
>
> The Massachusetts plan didn't do anything about medical costs, however, and, with layoffs accelerating, more people require subsidized care than the state predicted. Insurance premiums continue to rise here, just as they do elsewhere in the country. Many residents also com-

plain that eight percent of their income is too much to pay for health insurance, even though, on average, premiums amount to twice that much. The experience has shown national policymakers that they will have to be serious about reducing costs.

For all that, the majority of state residents would not go back to the old system. I'm among them. For years, about one in ten of my patients—I specialize in cancer surgery—had no insurance. Even though I'd waive my fee, they struggled to pay for their tests, medications, and hospital stay.

I once took care of a nineteen-year-old college student who had maxed out her insurance coverage. She had a treatable but metastatic cancer. But neither she nor her parents could afford the radiation therapy that she required. I made calls to find state programs, charities—anything that could help her—to no avail. She put off the treatment for almost a year because she didn't want to force her parents to take out a second mortgage on their home. But eventually they had to choose between their daughter and their life's savings.

For the past year, I haven't had a single Massachusetts patient who has had to ask how much the necessary tests will cost; not one who has told me he needed to put off his cancer operation until he found a job that provided insurance coverage. And that's a remarkable change: a glimpse of American health care without the routine cruelty.

It will be no utopia. People will still face co-payments and premiums. There may still be agonizing disputes over coverage for nonstandard treatments. Whatever the system's contours, we will still find it exasperating, even disappointing. We're not going to get perfection. But we can have transformation—which is to say, a health-care system that works. And there are ways to get there that start from where we are.

Even with its successes, of course, Massachusetts health-care reform falls well short of Dr. Gawande's "perfection." When the bill was signed, we noted that as with any experiment, it would need mid-course corrections. In addition, we knew that the legislature had added a number of troublesome provisions to the program—subsequent data would prove that these would be among the necessary corrections.

I am often asked how I would make the program better. First, of course, I would reinstitute my vetoes of the legislature's additions. Among these, one of the most significant is my conviction that the state should not mandate which benefits must be included in health insurance policies: Consumers should be free to choose the benefits they want. Otherwise, the policies become too comprehensive and expensive. And further, when government decides what the insurance policies must include, the policies become subject to politics—medical providers lobby legislators to tack on their favored treatments.

I would also have rather provided a tax break for those who have health insurance rather than a tax penalty for those without health insurance. Both I would have provided the same mathematical incentive to become insured.

Among improvements to the plan, I would have made very different choices in the years since I left office than those that were made by the Democrats. When the reform was passed, for example, we required everyone who received subsidized insurance to pay a fair share of their premiums—the new liberal administration decided that some people should get their insurance *for nothing*. Imagine the additional cost to the state of such a decision. Imagine as well the incentive it creates for people—particularly unhealthy people—to move into the state. The new administration also set certain co-payments at too low a level. If, as has been reported, emergency rooms continue to be used for primary as well as for emergency care, then emergency room co-payments for routine treatment should have been sharply increased to curtail the misuse. There is no question in my mind that our program could be significantly improved if it were managed by a conservative administration. Elections have consequences.

Still, our health-care program has helped hundreds of thousands of people and probably saved lives. Had we not passed our program, it is probable that an expensive entitlement would have been imposed on Massachusetts taxpayers: a ballot initiative would have made government-provided health care for every resident a *constitutional right*—and that initiative was leading in the polls. And it has been an instructive experiment, teaching both the "do" and "don't."

Early in his term, President Obama and his Democrat supermajority passed a national health-care program. He claimed that it was like the reform I had signed in Massachusetts. There are similarities and differences. Here is why Obamacare will not work and should be repealed. First, the Massachusetts health-care plan was designed for Massachusetts, not for every state and not for the nation. From the outset, we cautioned that what worked in Massachusetts *would not work* in states like California and Texas, among others.

Second, Obamacare was a major departure from what we had crafted: It raised taxes, cut benefits for seniors, and imposed laborious burdens on small business—we did not. His bill was over two thousand pages and is intended as a step toward a government takeover of health care; our bill was seventy pages and was intended as a step toward market-driven health care. Our reform was constitutional; Obamacare is an unconstitutional federal incursion into the rights of states. And as Florida's Marco Rubio put it: "Even if Obamacare was a good program, which it is not, we simply cannot afford more federal spending."

Taming the Beast

The Massachusetts plan succeeded in getting our citizens insured without breaking the bank. It reduced health-care insurance costs for those who had been uninsured. And by removing the burden of free riders on everyone else, it lowered this health-care cost as well. But like all the measures that help to reduce health-care cost—malpractice reform, electronic medical records, transparency, etc.—achieving universal access alone cannot drive overall health-care costs for everyone to actually go down. That is the task that remains. As Michael J. Widmer of the Massachusetts Taxpayer Foundation said in *The Wall Street Journal*, "Virtually all stakeholders involved in the passage of the 2006 law understood that its principal intent was to achieve near universal access, and that the next chapter would be to deal with escalating health-care costs. . . . no informed observer ever said that the Massachusetts plan would lower health-care costs for everyone." It is the overall health-care cost for everyone that is the intractable problem in health care.

Over the last three decades, health-care spending per person has been growing 2.1 percent faster than the rest of the economy per capita. That's why health care has grown from 5 percent of the economy in 1960 to about 18 percent today. At this rate, the Council of Economic Advisers calculates that total health-care costs will constitute more than *a third* of the economy by 2040.

I do not believe America can remain the economic and military leader of the world if we approach that level of health spending. Even now, the fact that we spend far more per capita on health care than any other nation places an enormous burden on our employers and on the economy. Our current health spending is 6.3 percent of the GDP *greater* than the average developed nation. To put that in context, our *entire* defense budget is approximately 3.8 percent of the GDP.

The impact of runaway health-care spending is already being felt by families and employers. The average employer pays more than $12,000 annually for an employee's family coverage, almost double the cost of a decade ago, even after adjusting for inflation. Prior to its bankruptcy reorganization, General Motors was spending $1,400 per automobile on employee health insurance—more than the cost of steel. Not surprisingly, employers are dropping more and more employees from health-insurance plans in an attempt to stay competitive. And those employees who have been able to keep their insurance face ever higher copays, premiums, and deductibles. Most families are feeling a real squeeze and many are genuinely afraid and not just for themselves, but also for their children now and in the years ahead, when they are providing for themselves.

All levels of government are acutely aware of what health-care inflation is doing to their budgets as well. Medicare, Medicaid, and health-care coverage for the burgeoning number of government employees and retirees are ravaging federal, state, and local budgets. In thirty years, Medicare and Medicaid alone will grow from 6 percent of the GDP today to 15 percent, consuming three-quarters of all federal spending unless we dramatically change course.

If Americans enjoyed better health and longevity than people in other countries, it might be reasonable to argue that our excessive health-care spending is simply a rational consumer choice. But the life span of the average American is less than that of people in nations that spend far less. Japanese men outlive American men by five years; Frenchmen outlive us by three years. To put it bluntly, we spend more and die sooner. Most of the difference is explained by Americans' unhealthy lifestyles—we eat far too much of the wrong foods—but that's no excuse. We could be spending far more wisely if we worked hard to dissuade Americans from eating their way to an early grave.

New Methods, New Outcomes

The big-government politicians and bureaucrats haven't sat idly by in the midst of this crisis: they have been vigorously applying the tools that have been tried and tested time and again—and that have never worked. Price controls and regulations have been implemented in health care more than in any other sector of the economy. And the result over three decades? No improvement whatsoever in the rate of health-care cost inflation. Predictably, these politicians' prescription for the future is to apply more of the same. As Albert Einstein is reputed to have said, insanity is "doing the same thing over and over again and expecting different results."

Today's conventional wisdom adds some new tools to the fight. Information technology is one hot new idea: Politicians glibly calculate that if computers and electronic medical records replaced medical paperwork, they could save almost a third of our total health-care costs.

This is an idea with a big and very unrealistic if. Information technology is indeed critical to the future of health care, but it will not replace the time and cost of medical administration in our lifetimes. According to Dr. James J. Mongan, the president and CEO of Partners HealthCare, a multibillion-dollar hospital and health-care conglomerate in Massachusetts, his organization's cost savings have been modest despite spending over $100 million on electronic medical records. The same story comes from others who have made similar investments. Computers and digitalized data alone are not the panacea that many tout them to be.

There's a similar buzz surrounding the idea of "transparency"—the online reporting of the cost and quality of medical procedures performed at different hospitals or by different practitioners. As with the hype around information technology, so is the hope that transparency alone will drive down health-care costs. Thus far, even major efforts at such practices have had little impact on health spending. Transparency can lower costs only if people actually look at the data and are incentivized to act based on what they find.

By contrast, malpractice reform has made a significant difference in the few places where it has been tried because it removes an incentive for doctors to practice defensive medicine. There's a great deal more to be done, and not just because of the savings that will result. Patients actually injured by a doctor's negligence stand to benefit from genuine reform because to-day victims receive only 28 percent of all the money that goes into our malpractice system. Most of it goes to lawyers instead.

The burden of our broken tort law system on physicians is overwhelming. A Maryland study found that 70 percent of obstetricians have been sued at least once, with average awards topping $1 million; 50 percent of Maryland neurosurgeons are sued *every* year. The malpractice system actually causes doctors to exit badly needed practices: the American College of Obstetricians and Gynecologists reports that one in every ten obstetricians have stopped delivering babies due to the high cost of malpractice insurance. Professor Christopher Conover at Duke University estimates that in addition to the direct costs of our current malpractice-award system, $70 billion is spent annually on defensive medicine—tests, procedures, and treatments that are medically unnecessary, but which reduce the physician's likelihood of being sued. The American Medical Association puts the number for defensive medicine at $200 billion. This is staggering waste. Defensive medicine also leads to unnecessary treatments that carry risk to the patient. Reforms that limit non-economic damages, assign malpractice cases to special health courts, and provide awards or indemnity according to a predetermined schedule can reduce the burden and ought to be widely implemented; states like Mississippi, Texas, and California are models. What prevents the adoption of malpractice reform, of course, is the massive financial contribution of the trial lawyers to the Democratic Party. This truly is an example of putting profits ahead of people.

Confronted by the sheer magnitude of the health-care cost problem—our overspending compared to the Organisation for Economic Co-operation and Development (OECD) average is about $750 *billion* a year—an increasing number of observers recognize that small measures simply will not get the job done. Robert Samuelson, a left-of-center columnist at *Newsweek* and *The Washington Post,* framed our predicament well. "President Obama's health care 'reform' is naive, hypocritical, or simply dishonest," Samuelson wrote. "[W]hat's being promoted as health care 'reform' almost certainly won't suppress spending and, quite probably, will do the opposite." He continued, "In the past, scattershot measures have barely affected health spending. What's needed is a fundamental remaking of the health care sector—a sweeping restructuring."

For some liberals, the answer to Samuelson's searing critique is simply to apply more government. They favor a single-payer system, where government and its taxpayers become the single payer. Government takes over the entire health-care industry. These big-government advocates once pointed to Canada and the United Kingdom as models, but a closer look at these two countries has revealed downsides these supporters would like us to forget. Rationing is at the center of the cost-control approach of a single-payer system. By limiting the availability of new technologies and physicians, costs are held down by effectively denying care to certain terminal or elderly patients. And in some cases, explicit cost-benefit calculations are applied to deny treatment.

My son Josh lived in England for two years, during which time his primary-care physician there became concerned that Josh might have colon cancer. The waiting time for his colonoscopy was six weeks—enough time to make an operable, curable cancer become an inoperable terminal condition. We were fortunate that our relationship with physicians in Massachusetts enabled Josh to go to a private practice, where he received a timely examination and a very welcome clean bill of health. Most of the British are not so fortunate.

According to a Cato Institute analysis, delays for treating colon cancer in the United Kingdom mean that 20 percent of those who are diagnosed with treatable disease become incurable by the time they receive care. Among all types of cancer patients in Britain's island-length queues, 40 percent are never seen by an oncologist. Approximately 750,000 people are currently waiting to be admitted to British hospitals. In Canada, patients face similar kinds of waiting times for MRI procedures. There are *one-quarter* as many MRI machines per capita in Canada as in the United States.

In addition to the poor performance of these single-payer systems in other countries, we can look at the less-than-stellar track records of the non-health-care entities already run by government here at home—Amtrak, the U.S. Postal Service (particularly before it received competition from FedEx and UPS), Fannie Mae, Freddie Mac, as well as Medicare and Medicaid themselves. Even the U.S. military is a poor example of efficiency and cost management, though its performance as a sword and shield is unmatched in human history. Wherever a private sector alternative is unavailable, such as with the national defense, police, and the courts, the need to monitor and manage costs is critical because of government's natural tendency toward inefficiency, low productivity, and excessive cost.

The biggest reason why government isn't as efficient and productive as the private sector is that businesses have to please their customers or those customers will go elsewhere. Government, on the other hand, has to please politicians who want to please voters, contributors, and lobbyists. Businesses that are unproductive inevitably encounter competition, which can put them out of business. But government that is unproductive is often heralded for "creating jobs," and without competition, government never goes out of business. Business rewards innovation and risk. Government rewards the status quo and the avoidance of risk.

When General Motors collapsed, we saw all too clearly what happens when government runs something. Massachusetts Congressman Barney Frank, chairman of the House Financial Services Committee, called on the company to change its plans to close a distribution facility in his home district—and GM relented. It's not that Congressman Frank wasn't doing his job; in fact, he was doing exactly what the voters expect him to do. But that's precisely why government, which must respond to voters, is a poor manager of businesses, which must respond to consumers and the marketplace.

Of course, a number of economists and health-care analysts see the data on U.S. health care in a different light and conclude that a government-managed single-payer health-care system is the solution to the crisis. But there is another argument that I believe is irrefutable: putting government in control of nearly one-fifth of the economy would necessarily create a government that is far larger and much more powerful than it is already. Such a massively larger government would strike at the very premise of the American experiment. It would demand that we accept the belief that free people, pursuing happiness as they see fit, are less able to build and guide the national economy than politicians and bureaucrats.

Free-Market Health Care

Cost containment measures haven't worked to rein in our skyrocketing health-care spending, and a single-payer system would do no better. There is, however, another alternative: rather than trying to make health care less and less like a consumer-driven market, do the opposite. Apply the principles of a market guided by consumer choice. In such a market, consumers purchase a product when they decide that they need or want it. They care how much it will cost because they are paying for it. In fact, they trade off the cost and the value of the product, making the choice that best meets their needs. This is the system that governs the American marketplace, and governs it very well.

In purchasing health care, however, the choice of the insurance plan is to a significant extent made by the employer, not the consumer. The consumer doesn't really care how much a medical treatment costs because, for the most part, he or she won't be paying for it. And the product—in this case, the treatment—is largely chosen by the doctor who provides it. It's a bit like a hypothetical broadband market in which someone other than you chooses your provider. Let's say the provider they choose is AT&T; a third party pays your AT&T bill . . . and AT&T gets to decide which of its services you need. Obviously, because AT&T makes more money if it gives you more services, you can expect your broadband service will be chock-full of features. Clearly, under this kind of "market," AT&T and the broadband industry itself would grow uncontrollably.

Unfortunately, this AT&T hypothetical is more like the health-care industry than some would like to admit. Employers select your health-insurance options for you, motivated by factors that are important to them, but not necessarily to you. Not surprisingly, then, individuals are often dissatisfied with their health-insurance plans. These people may resent the coverage limits, practitioners, and procedures of a plan they didn't select. And if they change jobs, they are likely to be forced to change health plans, often meaning new doctors, new coverages, and new complaints.

Consumers don't pay for the medical treatment they receive. Once copays and deductibles have been met, any further care or treatment is "free" to the consumer. An orthopedist explained to me that he had a patient schedule a knee replacement as soon as he found out he had appendicitis: the appendicitis meant that the patient would exceed his deductible, so anything after that would cost him nothing.

I once asked a friend whether he had compared the cost of cardiac-bypass surgery at different hospitals in the Boston area before choosing where to have his operation. "Why would I?" he responded. "It costs me the same [deductible] wherever I go." I knew of two hospitals in the region with virtually identical cardiac-surgery success rates, but the cost at one was almost twice that of the other. Yet my friend, like patients across the country, doesn't care because the cost to him is the same.

Consider as well the doctors and hospitals. The more services they provide the patient, the more they are paid—just like AT&T in my hypothetical example. This is true whether they are paid by private insurance, Medicare, or Medicaid. Money doesn't enter into the thinking of most doctors when they consider what tests, procedures, and treatments to give a patient. But some providers' decisions are very much influenced by money. In a recent *New Yorker* article, Dr. Atul Gawande wrote of his visit to McAllen, Texas, one of the most expensive health-care markets in the country, where he found that the "medical community came to treat patients the way subprime-mortgage lenders treated home buyers: as profit centers."

Fifteen years ago in McAllen, Dr. Gawande explained, a one-time chest-pain incident for a woman with no family history of heart disease would have meant an EKG and, if normal, instructions to return home and report any further pain. But today, a McAllen cardiologist and an internist admitted to Gawande that the same woman would also receive a stress test, an echocardiogram, a mobile Holter monitor, and a cardiac catheterization.

"The primary cause of McAllen's extreme costs was, very simply, the across-the-board overuse of medicine," he wrote. Not only are doctors paid more for doing more, they've also found ways to make more money by owning blood-analysis equipment, surgery centers, imaging centers, gastrointestinal labs and sophisticated diagnostic centers. Some even earn rewards for referring patients to a particular hospital or home-care provider. As one doctor told Dr. Gawande, "It's a machine."

The Incentives of a Consumer Market

America's health care is expensive because the incentives are all wrong—for the patient, the doctor, the hospital, and the insurer. Health care can't function like a market if it doesn't have incentives like a market. Fixing health care begins with fixing incentives.

For consumers, copays and deductibles do indeed discourage unnecessary visits and treatments, but once a threshold is crossed, the motivational effect vanishes—the patient's cost is the same for a $20,000 hip replacement as for a $50,000 hip replacement. In an attempt to align incentives, France and Switzerland have instituted "co-insurance systems" in which individuals pay a portion of their *entire* bill. The French, for example, pay 20 percent of each hospital bill, 30 percent of their physician's charges, and 35 percent of their prescription charges. The system places upper limits on the amount an individual must pay, of course, and a number of conditions and nonelective surgeries are exempt. But the incentive features of co-insurance remain, giving the patient a vital financial interest in how much physicians and hospitals charge for his care. If two hospitals offer care of comparable quality, the patient-consumer will almost always choose the less expensive one because he or she pays a share of the entire bill. Because he or she is a paying partner with the health insurer, the patient is also resistant to unnecessary tests, diagnostics, and procedures.

There are a number of potential problems with co-insurance, of course—you certainly don't want to discourage someone from getting an important diagnostic test, for example. But high deductibles create the same or a greater problem. And if an upper limit is placed on the amount of co-insurance and certain tests, procedures, and health conditions are exempted, much of the downside can be eliminated. France and Switzerland are not models for our own health system, but their co-insurance provisions have much to commend them.

Some Americans pay for all their health-care costs with health savings accounts (HSAs), except for the extraordinary costs of catastrophic care. Like co-insurance, health savings accounts discourage overuse of medical treatment and promote the patient's selection of low-cost, high-quality providers. This in turn leads physicians and providers to compete on the basis of both cost and quality. If HSAs and co-insurance made up a large share of the market in the United States, the consumer incentives would go a long way toward aligning patient interest with the national interest. HSAs would get health care working like a market.

In addition to aligning consumer incentives, we will fix our health-care cost problem only if we also fix the incentives for doctors, hospitals, and other providers. As long as the people who provide medical care make more money when we are given more treatments and use more facilities, the growth of health-care costs will continue to outstrip the rest of the economy.

Excessive medical treatment is not only expensive, it is unhealthy. Almost every prescription drug has counterindications and side effects. Unnecessary surgeries, catheterizations, and invasive procedures also come with their own risks. According to a 2007 study by the Association for Professionals in Infection Control and Epidemiology, at least 5 percent of those admitted to U.S. hospitals annually— about 30,000 people—become infected with hospital-borne superbacteria. Any patients who were there unnecessarily not only incurred unnecessary costs but also were exposed to completely avoidable infections, including fatal infections.

Health maintenance organizations (HMOs) were originally designed to hold down medical costs by, among other things, requiring that tests, treatments, and procedures be preauthorized. But this new layer of controls did not alter the fact that doctor and patient incentives remained the same as they had always been. Understandably, every denial by HMO accountants was met with frustration, even anger, by the patient and by the doctor. HMOs correctly identified the overuse of medical treatment as a major problem, but they incorrectly thought they could fix the problem from the top down—just as big-government proponents think they can do today. Experience proves again and again that incentives are more effective than controls.

The best incentive for doctors and providers is to pay them for the quality of their work rather than the quantity of their work. Imagine, for example, a system in which doctors and hospitals are paid a single all-inclusive amount for treating a patient who requires bypass surgery, one in which they receive a single amount for everything from tests and pre-operative procedures to surgery and postoperative care. Imagine, as well, a group practice receiving a single all-inclusive payment for each patient's primary care—from physicals and prescriptions to flu treatment and suturing a cut. Imagine a system in which an entity is paid a fixed amount to meet the health needs of an individual rather than being paid a fee for every activity that's carried out to meet those needs. It may be possible for us to create a system in which we pay doctors and hospitals for what they do *for* a patient rather than what they do *to* a patient. Rather than promoting a single-*payer* system, we should design and test a single-*fee* system.

Instituting the right incentives for both individuals and providers will have a dramatic effect on the quality and cost of health care in this country. The health-care entities that have instituted these kinds of incentives are now offering higher quality medical care at much lower costs. Intermountain Healthcare, a health insurer and provider in Utah and Idaho, has achieved per-patient health-care costs that are *one-third* less than the national average, a level that compares favorably with the best of the OECD nations. An analysis by Dartmouth Medical School professor Dr. John Wennberg of the cost of treating patients in the last two years of their lives found that if every health provider practiced medicine like Intermountain Healthcare, their costs would drop by 43 percent, on average.

The Mayo Clinic in Minnesota and Arizona has also lowered its overall costs to a level well below the national average. In several states around the country, Kaiser Permanente achieves cost and quality performance by aligning incentives through a staff model—its doctors are employees of the system. Others, like Intermountain, have succeeded in aligning incentives with independent physicians. These providers and a number of others across the country have implemented incentives that reward *quality* patient care, not the *quantity* of treatments provided.

Once incentives have been aligned, other health-care management tools will come into their own. Electronic medical records are an important innovation, not only allowing doctors and care facilities to transfer records smoothly, but also providing evidence of best practices that can lower costs and improve care. Instituting electronic medical records *alone* will not have a dramatic effect on cost, but if we *combine* these with aligned incentives, we should expect to see much greater savings.

Technology will also have an impact on the quality of care. Dr. Mongan of Partners HealthCare quoted one of his physicians as saying that while she "can't stand" electronic medical records, she "couldn't live without them." Another health-care-system CEO admitted to me that his coronary surgeons have long been aware that one of the greatest reasons that heart-surgery patients have to be readmitted to the hospital is because they were not given three essential exit medications for use at home—a statin, a beta-blocker, and aspirin. Nationwide, he explained, only 50 percent of discharged heart patients leave the hospital with these drugs. But by employing an electronic medical record system's ability to monitor practices, his coronary physicians successfully implemented a discharge procedure and feedback report that boosted their own system's exit-prescription compliance from 69 percent to 95 percent, resulting in a sharp reduction in readmissions and over a hundred fewer deaths systemwide.

Data from electronic records and properly aligned incentives led a panel of obstetricians to successfully reform their rules for inducing births. Their previous practice had been to agree to induce birth at the mother's request as long as the pregnancy had reached thirty-seven weeks or more. But the new data showed that if births were only induced after thirty-nine weeks, the number of babies requiring a ventilator and ICU care was cut by two-thirds. Once this information was provided to doctors and expectant mothers, the proportion of births induced at thirty-seven weeks dropped from 29 percent to 5 percent. As an obstetrician described these results to me, he also noted that under the prevailing American reimbursement system, reducing ICU and ventilator care would have meant lower revenue for both the doctor and the hospital. Better incentives and better information mean better medicine as well as lower cost.

Reshaping incentives does not require a complete reconstruction of our health-care-provider system. We will never see genuine reform arrive if it can't be implemented by the providers and networks that already exist. Fortunately, variations like those I described on the single-fee approach can readily be applied to much of our current health-care system. Realigned incentives will lead to changes in provider networks. Real, effective changes will have to be driven by a desire to provide better quality care at lower cost, not by bureaucratic dictates from government authorities. That, after all, is how consumer-driven markets work: competitors who innovate in quality and cost attract customers and grow. And as the best and most efficient competitors grow, the industry and the economy become more productive.

The suggestions I have made here for aligning incentives will undoubtedly give way to new ideas that are developed as states promote more market-oriented, consumer-driven health care. Some are already working—like HSAs. These should be heavily promoted. Others should be the subject of experiment. But this much is clear: it is possible and necessary to align incentives, and once we do, we can expect the power of the marketplace to tame runaway costs and to foster ever-improving quality of care.

Americans Living Better Lives

No serious participant in the health-care debates denies this obvious truth: America's health-care costs would also be far lower if all of us lived healthier lifestyles. According to Dr. Majid Ezzati at the Harvard School of Public Health, the twelve leading behavioral risk factors account for over a million deaths in the country every year—about 40 percent of all deaths.

One of the biggest behavioral contributors to sickness and death is our big waistlines, and the cascading negative health impacts of that excess weight. In the 1960s, 15 percent of people aged twenty to seventy-four were obese. Today that figure tops 35 percent. And if you combine the obese and the overweight, it reaches a shocking 68 percent of Americans. And the problem extends to the youngest Americans as well. In the 1960s, 4 percent of six- to eleven-year-olds were obese. Today, over 15 percent are obese and an alarming number of kids are affected by the type of diabetes that just a few years ago appeared only in adults.

The obese are six times more likely to develop diabetes and almost four times more likely to develop hypertension. The World Bank estimates that 12 percent of our national health-care spending can be directly attributed to obesity—that's $250 billion a year. According to an Institute of Medicine study, if the obesity trend continues for our children, the average life span of American adults will be cut by at least two to five years, which would mark the first time in history that our children didn't live as long as their parents.

We know what causes obesity, and it's not genetics. Our gene pool didn't somehow suddenly gain weight. Almost everyone knows that obesity isn't healthy, yet that hasn't slowed the trend. Until someone invents a miracle pill, we're going to have to solve the problem the authentic and realistic way—by eating less, eating better, and exercising more. And like most complex issues, solving our obesity crisis begins at home.

The good news is that the reforms I've described will help foster healthier living. With everyone insured, every citizen will have a doctor. And with doctors and providers paid a fixed fee for the primary care of each individual, they will at last have a big incentive to keep their patients *healthy*. As more and more individuals have their own permanent and portable health-insurance policies, they will be more likely to stay with the same insurer and provider system over an extended period of time, making it very much in the insurer's and the provider's interest to invest in their wellness. Pediatricians will be far less tolerant of parents who let a child become obese. Training and intervention systems will be developed to help guide and support parents. Providers and doctors will partner with schools and churches to encourage exercise and smart diet choices. A number of companies may well begin to offer discounted premiums to individuals and families who are not obese, just as they do today for nonsmokers. In fact, some already do. Perrigo Company, an employer of 7,500 people, provides health-insurance discounts to those who choose to make healthy choices such as having annual physicals and, for those who are overweight, getting into a program to take off the pounds. After implementing the discounts, the company's health-care costs actually *declined*. Perrigo's former CEO said that more than one employee has told him that the company's healthy-living program had saved his life.

As we endeavor to reform health care in ways that will lower cost and improve patient care, we should not lose sight of the fact that America has the best health care in the world. Sometimes statistics are trotted out to attempt to refute that reality, but they are invariably incomplete, distorted, or tortured. When, for example, statistics show that the survival rate for our newborns may not be higher than for another single-payer nation, remember that our singularly advanced, extensive, and enormously expensive neonatal care system means that babies are born alive in America that could never have been born alive in other nations. These very high-risk newborns are in our statistics but not in theirs.

My own experience is a personal testament to our health-care professionals. My boys, being boys, were in the emergency room so often that the nurses at Mt. Auburn Hospital knew their names on sight. One day Matt and Tagg climbed up on the counter in the kitchen to open the cabinet where the cookies were hiding. Matt hadn't calculated that when he opened the door, it would send Tagg flying. That fall required only a few stitches. But many and more serious accidents and illnesses were treated with care and competence.

The fact that my wife Ann is still here to bless my life is because of America's health-care professionals. A gangrenous cyst would have taken her had she not received emergency surgery. She has survived breast cancer, thanks to early detection by attentive radiologists, surgery by a skilled surgeon, and radiation by highly competent technicians. The pain from a herniated disc has repeatedly been kept in check by creative and caring physicians. And in 1998, we got our greatest scare and felt our greatest appreciation for caregivers. Ann felt numbness in her leg. She lost balance. And she felt unusually tired. Her condition was diagnosed by a neurologist with the help of an MRI—she had multiple sclerosis. In the years that have followed since her diagnosis, she has been helped immeasurably by traditional and nontraditional medicine, by pharmaceuticals and treatments invented by American innovators, and by people who are true healers. There is no other country on earth that could have done for Ann what America has done. It is one more reason why I love America.

Whatever we do to reform medicine, we must make sure that we "do no harm."

Health-care legislation may be passed by Congress in 2010, but the battle over the direction of health care in America is ongoing. Some believe that Obamacare is a good first step. Others, like me, believe Obamacare should be repealed and replaced. At its core of this debate is the question of what creates better patient outcomes and more efficiency: free enterprise and consumer-driven markets, or government management and regulation? The proponents of a government solution point to the obvious failures of our current health-care system. But our current system is *far* from being a consumer-driven free market. In my view, the failures we encounter virtually every day are the result of features imposed on the health-care system that have distorted market incentives—tax benefits only for those who receive insurance through their employer, fee-for-service payments to providers, the monolithic scale of Medicaid and Medicare, and an oppressive malpractice liability system, to name a few.

Before we go the way of socialized medicine, let's bring to the health-care crisis the tools the American economy has perfected—innovation, productivity, cost efficiency, and quality through a consumer-driven free market.

8

An American Education

I didn't give my education much thought back when I was a child—it just seemed to unfold on its own. I guess I presumed that all mothers read to their children because that's what my mom did with me. In retrospect, some of what she read *was* a bit out of the ordinary, like Alfred, Lord Tennyson's *Idylls of the King,* which went on for hundreds of pages in iambic pentameter blank verse. The King Arthur legends claimed so much of my attention that I wasn't aware that my mother was educating me as she read them—stretching my imagination and tuning my ear to the cadences of great writing.

I got two turns at kindergarten, first at Hampton School in Detroit and then, after we moved, at Vaughn School in Bloomfield Hills, so I had a solid head start. I still clearly remember Mrs. Vandenberg, who taught second grade. She liked me, or made me think she did, and from then on, that was my test for what it meant to be a good teacher. The following year, Miss Clark liked me a good deal less, but in the fourth grade, Mrs. Clouse made up for it by making me believe that I could learn anything.

I left public school in seventh grade to attend a nearby private school, just as my sisters and brother had. Of all the things my attendance at Cranbrook School did for me, the most important was to teach me to read well and to write with a degree of confidence. Virtually every weekend, each of us was required to write a theme: a poem, an autobiographical sketch, a brief television script, a short story, a one-act play, etc. Our teachers critically analyzed them, graded them, and sent the best of the lot to the *Detroit News*'s writing contest, in which Cranbrook students often won the lion's share of the honors. Pushing nouns against verbs made the student at Cranbrook. If I could wave a wand over American education and get one result, it would be a national rededication to the practice of writing. (Those who read this book may quarrel with the success of the Cranbrook writing program in my case. But at least I gained the confidence to give it a try.)

I didn't get serious about my college education until I left it for a while. After my first year of college, I went to France to serve a two-and-a-half-year mission for my church, a custom in my Mormon faith and a long tradition in my family. A mission is about serving others, of course, but in my experience, it shaped the missionary as well. Like my fellow missionaries, I lived on a hundred dollars a month—about six hundred of today's dollars—and that had to cover rent, food, transportation, and clothing. Accordingly, I lived quite differently than I had as the son of an American auto executive. Spending my days with French people in every sort of economic circumstance, I quickly came to recognize the value of a good education. Several years later, when I walked across a stage to collect my diploma, I understood that my parents and teachers had given me a gift of incomparable worth.

After Ann and I became parents, our highest priority became the education of our five sons, Tagg, Matt, Josh, Ben, and Craig. When I became a governor many years later, I wasn't so much looking to *find* good schools as I was trying to help *create* good schools for the children of Massachusetts. In my life, education had evolved from being about me to being about my children and ultimately to being about bettering the lives of hundreds of thousands of children.

As I toured schools and spoke to students in Massachusetts, I often told them about a television show I watched as a boy called *Let's Make a Deal*. Contestants were given a small sum of money, then offered the chance to trade it for the unknown contents inside a box. If the contestant opted to make the trade—and if the trade went well—she was given the opportunity to make another trade, such as for what was behind a curtain on the stage.

Sometimes the hidden objects proved to be valuable—a car, appliances, dream vacations. Other times they were not—a crate of carrots or a box of balloons. People in the audience shouted for the contestant to go for the trade, because there wasn't a downside for the spectators either way. Some contestants walked away overjoyed at their good fortune, and others saw the winnings in their hands evaporate when a booby prize was behind the curtain they chose.

Over and over again, I explained to audiences of Massachusetts students that life was a little like that television show of my youth. All of us necessarily make "deals" that have either fortunate or unfortunate consequences. But in life, you often know what lies behind the curtain before you have to make your choice. If you choose to stay in school and get a high-school diploma, for example, your lifetime income will be $400,000 greater than if you drop out. If you choose to go to college and get a bachelor's degree, your income will be $1,700,000 greater. In fact, the average college graduate earns 2.7 times more over her lifetime than a high-school dropout. And there's much more to education than money. A high-school dropout is more likely to go on welfare, become divorced, and spend time in prison. Of course, many million Americans overcome the disadvantage of having dropped out, but the effort and sacrifice to do so may be substantial.

Choosing education is a very good decision, not only good for the student, but also for our country. The United States was the first nation in history to recognize that public education for every citizen, regardless of class or station, was vital to its future, and over the centuries, we have devoted enormous resources and effort toward enrolling each successive generation in high school and college.

In 1940, less than one quarter of American adults had completed high school, but today 84 percent have a high-school diploma. Immediately following World War II, only 6 percent of adult Americans had a college degree, but the G.I. Bill propelled hundreds of thousands of returning soldiers into higher education, and today almost 30 percent of all Americans are college graduates. "There is little doubt from our research that education and training are *decisive* in national competitive advantage [emphasis added]," writes Michael Porter in his book *The Competitive Advantage of Nations*. America's commitment to education helped build a base of human capital that was broader than any other nation's. That human capital propelled our productivity, which in turn generated higher standards of living, economic growth, and world leadership. Without Americans' collective commitment to education, America would not have reached the heights we have achieved.

There are serious warning signs about where education will take us in the future. "The educational foundations of our society are presently being eroded by a rising tide of mediocrity that threatens our very future as a nation and a people," the National Commission on Excellence in Education reported *in 1983*. Now, more than twenty-five years later, scholars and think tanks are in unfortunate agreement that we've made virtually no progress in stemming that tide. And when it comes to our ability to compete around the world, the National Academy of Sciences goes so far as to conclude that America is on a losing path. Never have so many alarms been sounded to so little effect.

A recent education report commissioned by the OECD ranked American fifteen-year-olds as being twenty-fifth in math skills and twenty-first in science among the group's thirty-plus developed nations. The cause of the low ranking was not because low-income, immigrant, or at-risk student scores pulled down the average. When the study compared only the wealthiest students among OECD member nations, our rank rose no higher than eighteenth. Stanford economist Eric Hanushek calculates that when the comparative tests over the last decade are combined, American students still rank no better than seventeenth out of the twenty-five OECD nations he examined. Having led the world in public education and human capital during the first three-quarters of the twentieth century, we have fallen dramatically below average in the twenty-first.

We still tie other nations in the percentage of students who obtain bachelor degrees, but others far surpass us in the proportion of advanced degrees awarded in science and engineering. In 2005, just 6.4 percent of advanced degrees awarded by American universities were in engineering, while in Japan and South Korea, the percentages were 38.5 percent and 32.3 percent respectively. That same year, advanced degrees in science accounted for 13.7 percent of the total in the United States, 38.5 percent in Japan, and 45.6 percent in South Korea. The lead we once held in science and engineering has long since vanished, and the consequences for an economy driven by innovation are sobering. The impact ominously extends to our national security—the Pentagon recently reported that our severe shortage of engineers and scientists will soon jeopardize our lead in military technology.

If Michael Porter is correct that human capital created via education and training is *decisive,* America's economic future, military edge, and prospects as the world's leader throughout the twenty-first century are in jeopardy.

Several years ago, I spoke with a prominent venture capitalist who argued that the quality of education of our brightest students is what matters most to America's economic future, not the education level of the general population. He cited a study of manufacturing that showed that workers with limited education can be given on-the-job training that lifts their productivity to near world-class levels.

I deeply disagree with him. First, manufacturing is a smaller and smaller portion of our economy. And even in manufacturing, there has been a shift toward technical, managerial, and professional jobs that require higher education levels. In the economy at large, the trend has moved even more decidedly to positions that require greater education and literacy. In a "flat world," as *New York Times* columnist Thomas Friedman observes in his books, the product of labor moves easily across national borders. If the American workforce receives inferior education and skills, it will necessarily be confined to inferior tasks that pay inferior wages, producing, in turn, an inferior GDP. Education matters, not just for the few, but for the many.

Education Is a Civil Right

What's been labeled the "achievement gap" has been lamented for decades, but distressingly little has been done to combat it. African American and Hispanic American achievement in primary and secondary schools falls far below that of Anglo or Asian American students—and that's among those students who stay in school. About half of African American and Hispanic American students drop out before receiving a high-school degree. The result is that we are virtually assuring the creation of a permanent underclass. It is an inexplicable human tragedy when millions of American children barely attain a third-world education in the most prosperous nation in the world, one that offers all its citizens access to free public schooling. Our current failure to educate our minority populations is the foremost civil-rights issue of our generation.

The combined African American and Hispanic American proportion of the U.S. population is projected to rise from 26 percent today to 34 percent by 2030, and if the achievement gap and dropout rate among minorities continues, the average educational level of the nation's entire workforce will continue to decline dramatically at the very time when increased educational skills are in critical demand. In addition to the ruinous human and societal costs, we therefore face a significant economic cost as well.

Our inexcusable national dropout rate isn't limited to minorities. In absolute numbers, in fact, more Anglo students drop out of school than do minorities, and *nearly 29 percent* of all American children currently do not complete high school. For that 29 percent, it becomes nearly impossible to break out of poverty during their lifetimes. As the Educational Testing Service warns, "Unless we are willing to make substantial changes, the next generation of Americans, on average, will be less literate and have a harder time sustaining existing standards of living." States and municipalities should launch emergency efforts to keep kids in school at least until they receive their diploma. These could include programs to better match a student's interests with his or her curriculum, bonus compensation for teachers who are successful in keeping their students in school, and drawing on community heroes and mentors to counsel young people.

Even among students who receive high-school diplomas, their average educational aptitude is woefully lacking. On the most recently available National Assessment of Educational Progress tests, the averages of all eighth-grade American students scoring "proficient" were a mere 27 percent in science, 17 percent in history, 31 percent in reading, and 22 percent in civics. What does such a level mean in practice? Here's one telling example: when the same eighth graders were asked what organ a human being *cannot* live without—an appendix, the liver, a lung, or a kidney?—only 42 percent correctly chose the liver. The majority thought you couldn't live if you lost your appendix, or one of your two kidneys, or one of your two lungs.

There is no greater indictment of American government than the sorry state of American education. It is an epic failure.

The consequences of a failing educational system reach to the foundations of our democracy. During the 1960s, the idea set associated with progressivism gained ascendancy in educational circles. Our classical education tradition had held for decades that we should imbue each generation with the wisdom of the ages and the discoveries of modernity. Progressives, on the other hand, rejected the notion of universal truths, objective judgments, and, ironically, progress itself, embracing neutrality among competing belief sets and rejecting the primacy of Western civilization, the great thinkers of the ages, and the principles espoused by the Founding Parents of the nation. In their view, all cultures are of equal value.

Progressives de-emphasized the subjects that had previously been considered essential. Rather than teach the history of Western and American civilization, for example, they presented all the world's cultures to our children and insisted that none was superior to the others. Presidents, generals, founding patriots, and "heroes proved in liberating strife" were less important than the champions of social causes. If our children do not learn about and come to cherish America's heritage, history, culture, and founding principles, how can they be expected to defend the freedoms on which their country is based? How can young citizens become adult citizens equipped to critically examine contemporary political ideas in the light of history, or become informed about matters of public policy, or even simply understand the value of voting? Even in 2008, a year in which record numbers of young people were engaged in the presidential election, still only 52 percent of eligible voters under thirty bothered to vote. The abysmal voting patterns of young Americans are ample evidence that our education system has not equipped our children with the requisites of citizenship that sustain a democratic republic.

The 1983 warnings by the National Commission on Excellence in Education did not go entirely unheeded. Politicians set out to significantly increase education spending and to shrink the average number of students in public school classrooms. The average amount spent per pupil, adjusted for inflation, *rose by 73 percent* between 1980 and 2005, and the average class size was *reduced by 18 percent*. But during that same period, the educational performance of our children has hardly budged. Why not? Why have we failed at this most essential task? And how do we repair public education in America?

Studying How We Teach

Following my election as governor of Massachusetts, and knowing that I now shared responsibility for the education of hundreds of thousands of young people, I studied the education literature to gain perspective. What I found was a virtual quicksand of differing opinion in which it would be easy to sink, but what was missing was an examination of data. Instead, most writers sought to convince their readers by appealing to their inherent prejudices and by recounting anecdotes that supported their particular policy preferences. But as R. Glenn Hubbard of Columbia Business School has observed, real data is the collection and processing of anecdotes into reliable information. Anecdotes are illustrative but data is compelling—particularly if it is comprehensive and presented by an unbiased source. Far too often, I found that neither of these conditions prevailed when it came to discussions of education policy.

During my four years in office, several education policy debates emerged in Massachusetts. A requirement that students pass the statewide assessment exam as a condition of receiving a high-school diploma was scheduled to go into effect. Parents, teachers, education-union leaders, and politicians wanted to see that provision relaxed, if not eliminated outright.

In addition, bilingual education was slated to be replaced by English immersion, a move vigorously opposed by nearly all of the loudest voices in the education establishment.

And, of course, there were the perennial education debates—how much more funding should we allocate for schools, colleges, and universities, and by how much should we shrink our average class size. A large revenue shortfall in Massachusetts made these latter two issues particularly emotionally charged.

In 1993, the state was ordered by the Massachusetts Supreme Judicial Court to raise education funding levels in low-income school districts to a minimum acceptable level. The increased funding would have to come from the state. A negotiated agreement on the new funding was reached between then Governor Bill Weld, a Republican, and the Democratic Party leaders in the legislature. Funding in low-income school districts would be dramatically increased, but all students would be regularly tested in math and English. And the agreement provided that in 2003—my first year as governor— students would have to pass a test in order to graduate from high school. Further, schools where students consistently fell below agreed-upon levels of achievement would be subject to remedial actions—including the possibility of being taken over by the state Department of Education and being subject to the cancellation of any union contract provision that was deemed to interfere with student achievement. And finally, the state opened the door to the creation of charter schools. People on both sides of the aisle deserved credit for enacting such bold reforms. It was the sort of meaningful and practical reform agenda that is needed across the United States.

Objections to the graduation requirement became increasingly intense as the first school year of my administration was drawing to a close. Ninety-two percent of our seniors had passed the test by the end of their senior year, and those who had not would be entitled to summer school and another try. The parents of the 8 percent of students who failed to pass the test were vocal and angry. Despite the program's apparent early success, the Massachusetts teachers' union launched a $600,000 advertising campaign, calling the graduation requirement "flawed and unfair."

As the issue continued to heat up, Mayor Scott Lang of New Bedford announced that he would direct his local high school to give diplomas to *all* seniors, regardless of whether they had passed the state test. My powers of persuasion were unable to dissuade him, but when I announced that I would enforce powers given the governor under the legislation and cut off all state education aid to his school district—an amount of tens of millions of dollars—he came around to my point of view.

Elsewhere, the city of Springfield, the third largest in Massachusetts, was on the verge of bankruptcy. I obtained emergency powers from the legislature to appoint a finance control board to take over the management of the city. The board's focus was on the city's fiscal health, but the failure of its schools emerged as a critical priority. Student outcomes were far behind state standards. And there was an even more immediate crisis. Many of the city's best teachers were opting to abandon the inner-city schools. In fact, we couldn't find teachers to fill Springfield's most severe shortages in math and science classes. The teachers' union refused to allow the city to either assign teachers to the schools where they were needed most or pay a bonus to those willing to teach in the inner city or give higher pay to science and math teachers. The union was, in my view, putting the interests of its members—narrowly defined—ahead of those of the students.

Armed with the club of a potential bankruptcy filing, we finally got the teachers' union to budge. An agreement was struck that allowed us to assign teachers where they were needed most, to pay more to those who accepted difficult assignments, and to boost salaries for new math and science teachers. When I spoke with the head of the state teachers' union, I recognized that he and his members had made very significant concessions, and we agreed that it was an encouraging sign that we had found consensus on an experiment to remedy a broken school system.

Even the provision for new charter schools came under attack during my term. The legislature passed a bill that put a moratorium on any new charter schools—a law that went into effect immediately. Yet because the bill was enacted at the beginning of summer, it would force the abandonment of three new charter schools only recently constructed and scheduled to open in the fall. The teachers for these schools had already been hired. The students had applied, been accepted, and had notified their regular public schools of their decision to attend the new charter schools. It was an egregious exercise in special-interest-driven legislation, and evidence of how fervently the teachers' unions oppose school choice. I vetoed the bill. And while Republicans made up only 15 percent of the legislature, enough Democrats joined with me to uphold my veto, and the new schools opened as planned.

There was another education success during my time as governor that was the product of collaboration with the legislature. As noted, Governor Weld had successfully championed a testing requirement for high-school graduation, and I had defended it at every turn, so there was a "stick" to get our kids to learn enough to pass the exam. But we wanted to create an incentive for more students not just to pass the test but also to excel. I proposed offering a scholarship to our best-performing students. We agreed that the those who scored among the top 25 percent in their school on the graduation exam would be entitled to receive a four-year tuition-free scholarship at any of our state institutions of higher learning—a savings of about $2,000 per year. I called it the John and Abigail Adams Scholarship because

I had just read David McCullough's biography of the president and was moved by the Adamses' intellect, education, and erudition. And after all, they had been Massachusetts citizens and among the country's greatest patriots.

Some of my favorite moments as governor came on the day each year when we announced the scholarship recipients. I asked the school principal of a high school I had selected to invite all those who had scored in the top 25 percent to come to a special assembly. Of course, they did not yet know that they had placed in the top quarter of their peers, nor were they told why they were coming together. David Driscoll, the head of our state Department of Education, and I then addressed the students. At one point I asked them to reach under their seat, remove the envelope that had been taped there, and open the enclosed letter. The letter broke the news: they had scored in the top 25 percent and had been awarded an Adams Scholarship. The cheers were deafening. I got more hugs than I get around the tree at Christmas. Kids had me talk to parents on their cell phone—by special dispensation, they had been allowed to bring phones to school. More than once, parents told me that they had not thought they could afford college for their child before, and that the scholarship would make the difference.

Massachusetts once took pride in pioneering bilingual education, creating a system in which elementary school students were taught in their native language, often for a number of years. Like smaller classes, the concept made sense—many feared that foreign-language-speaking immigrant children would be left behind if they were thrust into a standard English-speaking classroom. Yet I also had heard about students graduating from Massachusetts high schools who were not fluent in English, and I could not imagine how they could successfully make their way in our English-speaking society. Solid, reliable data comparing student achievement in bilingual programs with the results of those in immersion programs was scant, so I called principals in California, where bilingual education had been replaced with English immersion programs. The administrators I spoke with were very supportive of immersion.

Not surprisingly, there were a number of advocates that remained fierce defenders of bilingual education. In Massachusetts alone, the bilingual program had required that we employ hundreds of teachers to instruct youngsters in Cambodian, Vietnamese, Spanish, and Portuguese—teachers who in many cases would be otherwise unemployed in teaching because they weren't proficient in English. In speaking to immigrant parents, I was surprised to learn that many of them had wanted their child to attend regular English-speaking classes, yet despite this often expressed preference, school officials had shuttled them into bilingual classes instead. For me, that was a warning sign.

One morning, I visited an elementary school in Boston where most of the school's students were taught in bilingual classes. At a student-body assembly I asked how many youngsters were born outside the United States. Only a few hands went up. Surprised, I asked my next question: "How many of you are in bilingual education classes?" This time, the great majority of hands shot skyward, and the truth became obvious. Kids who were born in America, who watched television in America and played video games in America—thoroughly *American* kids—were being assigned to bilingual classes only to allow bilingual teachers to keep their jobs. The result that these students would be *less* fluent in English didn't seem to bother anybody! From that morning on, I became an even more ardent proponent of English immersion and sought to rapidly implement it throughout the state. Under the immersion program, recent immigrant children who spoke no or little English would initially receive instruction in their native tongue, but would be moved into English instruction as soon as possible. Time and again, I heard from parents in the immigrant community who applauded the decision to scrap bilingual education in favor of English.

The National Assessment of Educational Progress exams—known as the Nation's Report Card—test fourth and eighth graders from every state in math and language skills.

During my third year in office, Massachusetts fourth graders scored first in math out of all fifty states. And they scored first in English.

Our eighth graders were also number one in math. And they were ranked first in English.

This was the first time any state had been ranked number one in all four measures. What Massachusetts was doing right during those years under

Governors Weld, Cellucci, Swift, and Romney and the collaboration of an overwhelmingly Democrat legislature—measuring student progress, establishing high-school graduation standards, providing for school choice, and rewarding excellence—was consistent with the lessons we had learned from educational studies and data around the world. These results have helped to inform my beliefs about what we must do to regain our country's tradition of educational excellence, to close the achievement gap both within America and with other countries around the globe, and to prepare coming generations for the economy of the future and the demands of a democratic republic.

At the outset of my term as governor, my perspectives were shaped by the writings and studies by education experts, by discussions with teachers, principals, parents, and students, and by my study of statewide data on student achievement that was mined, collected, and carefully analyzed. What I learned was in large measure confirmed by data collected at the national and international levels, but even so, I did my best not to close the door entirely on alternative views.

When it comes to the question of class size, there was and still remains a near-consensus among the general public that the smaller the class, the better the education the student will receive—a view that's also widely promoted by teachers' unions and a number of education experts. Parents especially love the idea of smaller class sizes.

The data in Massachusetts told a different and surprising story. Because the state had a long history of testing its students' math and verbal skills, we were able to determine the average education score for students in nearly all of our 351 cities and towns. We then matched a municipality's test scores with its average class size, expecting to see what common sense told us: that towns with smaller class sizes would evince higher average student scores.

The data revealed that there was no relationship between class size and the performance of students. None. Cambridge, the city with the smallest class size, ranked in the bottom 10 percent in student achievement, for example, and its average classes had just half the number of students as the state's largest classes.

The data at the national level told the same story. When the average

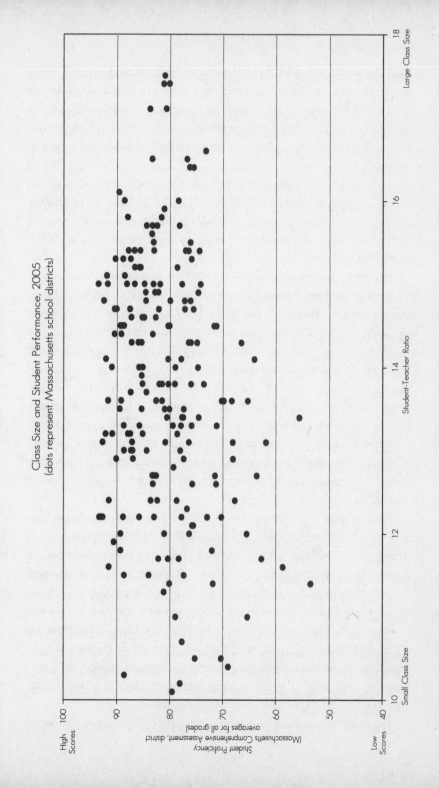

Class Size and Student Performance, 2005
(dots represent Massachusetts school districts)

class size across the nation had been reduced to its smallest level in history, the performance of America's students had failed to appreciably improve. It goes without saying that the data doesn't endorse unlimited class sizes—a class full of a hundred first graders would be unimaginable, of course. But within the range of most school systems nationwide, class size has very little impact.

McKinsey & Company analyzed a total of 112 studies evaluating the effect of class size on student achievement, fully 103 of which found no relationship whatsoever or a negative one. Only *nine* studies found a positive relationship, and in none of these was the positive relationship statistically significant.

Internationally, some nations whose students far outperform our own go to school in much more packed classrooms than ours. South Korea's student-teacher ratio, for instance, is thirty to one—almost twice ours at sixteen to one and well above the seventeen-to-one average of OECD nations.

Given the very persuasive data, why do politicians continue to promote and fund the massive investment required to reduce class size? To a certain degree, they are playing to the pervasive public perception that smaller classes mean better education. Politicians may also wish to curry favor with teachers' unions. Smaller classes mean more teachers, more union dues, and more power, so teachers' unions are almost always supportive of the idea, claiming that small classes are an educational reform they can support. Embracing such a "nonreform reform" also spares many the hard choices involved in making real productive change in our classrooms.

Because most of the funding we've added to education over the past decades has been used to reduce class size, it isn't surprising that simply increasing spending does *not* correlate with higher educational outcomes. As national per-student spending has risen by 73 percent, student achievement has barely improved, something we affirmed in Massachusetts when we conducted the same kind of town-by-town analysis of spending per student that we had for class size. Once more, there was no relationship whatsoever. Cambridge again—spending more than any other city in the state at more than $16,000 per student—showed student outcomes in the bottom 10 percent statewide. Simply spending more money, particularly absent fundamental reform, did not create better-educated students.

International results mirrored ours. Singapore, for example, has one of

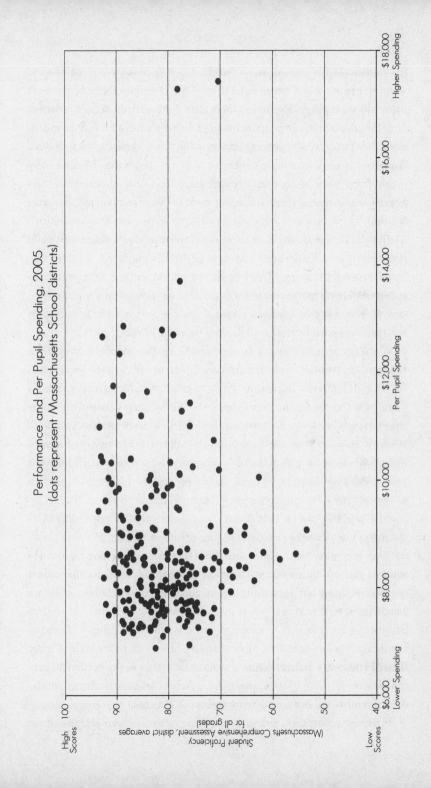

Performance and Per Pupil Spending, 2005
(dots represent Massachusetts School districts)

the best education systems in the world, but it spends less on per-student education than all but three of the thirty OECD nations. Spending doesn't drive education results abroad any more than it drives them here in America.

The usual coterie of proponents of ever-higher levels of school spending is, of course, ready with explanations for this undeniable data. Today's American students are more expensive to teach, they argue, because more come from poor economic circumstances, because children are less healthy, and because there are more special-education students than ever before.

But the data does not bear them out. Over the past few decades, child poverty has actually declined and child health has improved. It is true that more children today are placed in special education than in previous decades, but interestingly, this is not because of an increase in severe disabilities. The number of students classified by the government as "mentally retarded" dropped by nearly 40 percent between 1976 and 2000.

A study conducted by Jay Greene and Greg Forster of the Manhattan Institute determined that almost two-thirds of the growth in special-education enrollment during the 1990s "was attributable to funding incentives." Of the remaining third, much of the increase was due to better detection and diagnoses—learning-disabled kids were present in overall student groups at contemporary levels during the 1970s; they just weren't diagnosed. If more money actually improved education, then "spending more money on the same students should produce better results regardless of the categories into which we put students," Greene observes. "Rearranging the labels we put on kids doesn't provide an excuse for spending ever-greater amounts on them without seeing any improvement."

Simply putting more money into the system we already have has not and will not give our kids a better education. Neither reduced class size nor increased spending will repair our broken education system. There are much better answers.

The Home of Education

Education begins at home. My mother's early reading to me undoubtedly gave me an understanding and fluency with language that stimulated my young mind and fueled my lifelong love of learning. I once asked a group of teachers in Boston if they could determine at the beginning of a school year those students who will succeed and those who will fall behind. To my surprise, they agreed that there absolutely was a way, one that was a virtual litmus test for every public-school teacher.

"If a child's parents come to school on the first day of school or reliably come to parent-teacher meetings, we know that that child will do just fine."

This is a very simple standard to observe, and all it measured was whether a student's parents cared enough about his or her education to show up at school. Teachers rarely, if ever, saw the parents of a chronically failing student. Children with parents who show up fail much less frequently than children with parents or guardians who can't make it.

I endeavored to find out something about those absent parents, the ones who didn't come to school to learn about and support their child's education. Some were addicts, and others were in entirely dysfunctional settings. But by far the largest number were simply single parents who were so busy with work, other children, meals, and housekeeping that they literally didn't have time to be involved with their child's education. They weren't home when their kids got out of school, so video games, television, the Internet, and the street took the place of help with homework from a mother or father, activities at home, or sports in the community.

I knew as a matter of general knowledge that there were a lot of young single parents. But I was shocked when I learned the actual figures.

Among all children currently born to mothers age thirty or younger, 44 percent are born outside of marriage. Among African Americans, the figure is 77 percent. Forty-six percent of Hispanic American births to mothers under thirty are unmarried, and 34 percent of those to Anglo moms are. The percentage is lower for Anglo mothers, but the absolute number of out-of-wedlock births is far larger—there are 420,000 out-of-wedlock births by under-thirty Anglo moms each year compared with 292,000 for same-age African American moms. Among all moms who do not have a high-school degree, of all ethnic groups, 62 percent of their children are born outside of marriage. That figure is only 13 percent to mothers with a bachelor's degree. Among young, African American moms without a high-school degree, 90 percent of the births are out of wedlock.

It is very difficult for a poor, undereducated single mother to devote sufficient attention to her child's education. Study after study demonstrates that these children are far more likely to perform poorly at school, drop out of school, end up on welfare, use drugs, and commit crimes that send them to prison.

I believe it's time for all Americans to be honest with ourselves. We will never be able to truly address the achievement gap until we eliminate the high rate of out-of-wedlock births in our country. It is not a coincidence that student achievement scores by ethnicity mirror the rates of out-of-wedlock births.

This is not solely or predominantly an issue for minorities—remember, most out-of-wedlock children are born to white mothers. We must engage in a national campaign much like the one waged against smoking beginning in the 1960s and against drunk driving in the 1970s and 1980s. Kids must be taught in school about the advantages of marriage. Welfare and safety-net programs must be reshaped to ensure that they do not facilitate or encourage out-of-wedlock births. Media and advertising executives must be held to account if they tacitly encourage the choice to conceive babies with no intention of bringing them up in two-parent families. It would make an enormous difference if film, music, and athletic role models around the country began to take their influence on millions of young people seriously. Unlike them, single parents in real America can't afford a phalanx of nannies.

Any discussion of out-of-wedlock births must exercise extreme care and compassion to make sure that we in no way appear to judge or condemn these moms or their children. These moms are some of the best people we know. They work hard and sacrifice much to raise their children. But given the enormous human and national implications of nearly half our children being raised without the benefit of two parents, it is long past time to tell the truth: a *marriage between one man and one woman* is one of the best things a parent can do for a child.

It's the Teachers

The best thing that can happen to a child once he or she arrives at school is to have a great teacher. Every one of us remembers the teachers who had the biggest impact on us—like Mr. Wonnberger, who taught my tenth-grade English class. He could barely see and, as a result, was the target of a lot of teenage humor, but despite the fact that he was nearly blind, he understood how to get the most out of all of us—and he did. He tore our papers apart paragraph by paragraph and line by line with critiques that sharpened our skills without crushing our confidence. He insisted that my classmates and I push our thinking and our writing beyond the superficial. I don't remember what grades he gave me, but I do remember what he taught me.

When Bain & Company carried out an exhaustive study of education in Boston, the consultants followed individual students and their test results as they moved from class to class and from school to school. The study demonstrated the obvious truth that the quality of the teacher was the educational variable that mattered most. Some excellent teachers were able to move their students ahead by a full grade level, while other, less gifted educators simply could not. The best teachers were consistently the best, year after year, and the worst were consistently the worst. Classroom size, school-building quality, community income levels, access to computers, and the ethnicity of the students—all these factors paled in comparison with the individual capabilities of the teacher. These findings do not surprise us, but the Bain study confirmed with data what each of us knows from experience.

In 2009, McKinsey & Company carried out an exhaustive global study of education systems at both the international and the city level, analyzing student assessment scores, interviewing more than one hundred experts, policy makers, and practitioners, and visiting schools around the world. The best national performers, such as Singapore, Korea, Japan, and Finland, and the best city performers, such as Boston and Chicago, were studied in depth and were compared with underperforming systems. This study again confirmed what by now had become clear to anyone willing to immerse themselves in the data about educational achievement: "The available evidence suggests that the main driver of the variation in student learning at school is the quality of the teachers," it concluded. "[E]ven in good systems, students [who] do not progress quickly during their first years at school, because they are not exposed to teachers of sufficient caliber, stand very little chance of recovering the lost years."

This study also concluded that neither the level of education spending nor the size of the average class had any significant effect on student

achievement—it all came down to the caliber of the teachers. The best education systems, the study determined, did at least three things to guarantee
quality teachers: they hired only the best and brightest; they worked to develop and improve their teachers' skills; and they monitored the performance of each child, teacher, and school, intervening when needed to ensure
the best possible education for every student.

If hiring among the brightest of our graduates is key to creating schools
with great teachers, then we have some serious work to do. McKinsey
noted that the top-performing systems around the world recruit new teachers from the top third of their graduating classes. In Finland, they are recruited from the top 10 percent; in South Korea from the top 5 percent.
But in the United States, McKinsey reported, our teachers are generally
drawn from the *bottom* third of graduates. In too many cases, we send our
weakest students to teacher-training colleges, and then expect that studying education theory and teaching pedagogy will transform them into
great teachers.

Another key finding from the McKinsey study was this: "A teacher's
level of literacy, as measured by vocabulary and other standardized tests,
affects student achievement more than any other measurable teacher attri-
bute." Consider the implications of that finding. If our goal is to have great
teachers for our children, we have to recruit from among the best to produce the best. Boston, Chicago, and New York, for example, have begun to
absorb this lesson and have established programs that seek to recruit top
university graduates to the teaching profession. These three cities are now
among the most rapidly improving education systems in the nation. The
education writer for *The Washington Post,* Jay Matthews, recently authored
Work Hard, Be Nice, which explains the success of KIPP—"Knowledge Is
Power Program"—in charter schools. It is clear that talented, motivated,
high-achieving teachers are at the core of KIPP's success, and at the core of
the success of schools that consistently outperform national averages.

Of course, removing the least effective teachers from the classroom is
also an important way to improve overall teacher quality. My own boys had
great teachers in the Belmont, Massachusetts, public schools, with a couple
of glaring exceptions. In elementary school, one of our sons began to show
some of the classic signs of trouble at school, and Ann called a few other
parents with kids in the same class to see if their children were having dif-

ficulty as well. Some reported that their child loved the teacher, and others reported real trouble. After a bit more investigation, what Ann discovered was that most of the girls in the class were happy, and that most of the boys were miserable. One parent told Ann that her son had been called to the front of the class, and the teacher had held up his paper, said it was sloppily written, and had torn it up in front of the entire class. This, in elementary school.

Ann and I went to see the school's principal. He quickly acknowledged that we were not imagining things, that this teacher had a real problem with boys, and that the situation was clearly becoming worse. However, the principal's hands were tied because the teacher's years of seniority had secured her an assignment to our school. We asked whether there wasn't some way she could be removed from the classroom. He explained that under the school district's contract with the teachers, that was virtually impossible. This was one reason why, when the option of private school became available to us, we took it. But most parents are not in a position to place a child in a private, a charter, or a parochial school. If we truly want better public schools, we will have to insist on contract provisions that allow for removing the few teachers who should not be working with children.

There are several lessons we can learn from other nations about creating great teachers. First, make the application process to our teaching programs highly selective at the outset. Don't admit from the bottom third academically. The "winnowing" process cannot wait until graduates have made it to the front of a classroom.

Second, select only those teacher candidates who have demonstrated high levels of intellect, literacy, and numeracy.

Third, open alternative pathways into teaching, particularly for individuals who have excelled in other fields. The experience of the best-performing education systems is that nontraditional teachers tend to be of high caliber.

And fourth, raise the base salaries of teachers who are beginning their careers. We spend much more than other countries on education, but in the United States, starting teacher salaries lag far behind the comparable starting salaries of other nations. When recent graduates are often faced with six-figure student loans, starting salary is a very significant issue in their choice of career. Further, as salaries increase over time, they should not be capped by adherence to a lockstep seniority-based salary grid. Teachers should be treated like the professionals they are—and low starting salaries and fixed salary progression dissuade some of our best students from choosing this essential and valuable profession.

The McKinsey study to which I've referred found that "South Korea and Singapore employ fewer teachers than other systems: in effect, this ensures that they can spend more money on each teacher at an equivalent funding level." In the United States, then, the effort to reduce classroom size may actually hurt education more than it helps.

There are other reasons why we spend so much on education and still pay starting teachers less than comparable nations: we employ too many administrators and nonteaching staff, who drain dollars away from the pool available for teacher salaries. The political movement aimed at directing at least two-thirds of every education dollar to the classroom is motivated by this reality.

Obstacles to Better Schools

In addition to improving the quality of new teachers, we need to do a much better job building the skills of teachers throughout their careers. Too often, the undergraduate training our teachers receive does not significantly enhance their effectiveness in the classroom. In other professions like medicine, law, investment banking, consulting, and accounting, the most effective training occurs in the workplace. Similarly, teachers need mentors and coaches in the classroom, particularly in their early years. They need to see how their students' progress stacks up against their fellow teachers' classes. And young teachers especially need to be motivated to improve by viewing and adopting the best practices of others, to receive the kind of motivation that isn't helped by a compensation system that pays the same amount to every teacher, regardless of ability. Better teachers deserve *better* pay, and they should have access to a teaching-career track that provides higher status and greater rewards, such as in programs that create "mentor" or "master" teachers who supervise and support other teachers.

Teachers' unions often oppose compensation differences among teachers, whether for different levels of accomplishment, or for qualifying to teach subjects in which there are teacher shortages, such as math and science.

They often also oppose using student achievement data to evaluate individual teachers. If these measures continue to be blocked, our public schools will remain uncompetitive.

Accountability is one of those things we expect from others but would prefer not to submit to ourselves. Most of us would rather be rewarded regardless of whether we excel, yet we know that if that were the case for everyone, our society would falter. Teachers' unions do their very best to secure these insulations from performance for their members, and the results are lack of accountability, rising pay as a simple function of years on the job, and near-absolute job security. These have a deadening impact on student achievement. I don't blame teachers' unions for asking for such gold-plated benefits; the unions' job is to work for their members. I blame administrators, school boards, and parents for saying yes, even when schools are manifestly failing their students.

It is not the unions' job to fight for our children. That is our job, and it's the task of the people we elect to represent us. Our elected representatives' role is to sit across the table from the unions and bargain in good faith in the interest of children and parents. But the teachers' unions long ago discovered that they could wield influence—and, in some cases, overwhelming influence—over the selection of our representatives on school boards and in state legislatures. In states like Massachusetts and in many others, it's almost impossible to be elected a city mayor if you are opposed by the local teachers' union, and the same is true for candidates for state representative in many legislative districts. As a result, candidates for office woo the teachers' unions. If they secure their endorsement and are elected, the official sitting across the table from the union at bargaining time is the very person the union campaigned for and helped get into office. All too often, no one at that bargaining table is there solely to represent the interests of children and parents. Of course, there are always the requisite public nods to education reform, accountability, performance pay, and all the potential education reforms that are currently in vogue. But meaningful change is seldom accomplished. Instead, the priority almost always remains more education funding and creating smaller classes—the two measures with the *least* positive impact on the quality of education, but the *most* impact on teacher pay and union dues. When citizens vote to reduce education revenues or the state cuts back on funds, the education officials typically make the cuts where the voters will feel them most—in sports, music, arts, libraries, and computers. You simply don't see administrators being fired or salaries being cut across the board.

The teachers' unions have secured their greatest influence within the Democratic Party, of course, and while both parties have their respective positive attributes, the teachers' union power in the Democratic Party isn't one of them. My Democrat friends, in turn, point to influence groups in my party that they find objectionable, but I believe there's a key difference. In the case of the teachers' unions, the deleterious impact of undue influence is felt by *millions* of our children. The unions' influence directly affects policies that lie at the foundation of our nation's economy, the core of our ability to preserve freedom, and the heart of our children's future prosperity. The reform and improvement of our failing schools is a priority that is simply too important to be shaped by such a powerful and self-interested special interest.

Beginning in the 1960s, states began to allow collective bargaining for public employees, and at the time, people plainly didn't see the future implications for education. So-called campaign-finance reform only strengthened the relative power of the teachers' unions by allowing them to collect dues from their millions of members and devote them to political causes and candidates. Today, the two major teachers' unions in the United States have over 6,000 employees and annual revenues in excess of $1.5 billion, more than both political parties combined. The political power they wield to block education reforms is considerable. Even the proposed education reforms proposed by the California "Governator" were defeated by the massive money-power of the teachers' unions. "It is a fact that [teachers' unions] are more powerful—by far—than any other groups involved in the politics of education," write Terry Moe and John Chubb in *Liberating Learning.* "To recognize as much is not to launch ideological attacks against unions. It is simply to recognize the political world as it is." Whether you agree with the teachers' unions' perspectives on specific reforms or not, it's difficult to claim that it's healthy for education policy to be controlled by such a self-interested player.

Are there any realistic hopes for change? Well, a Democratic president or Democratic governors could, at long last, put children ahead of the unions and champion essential reforms. Or the public could vote out of office those politicians who blindly adhere to the union playbook. In fact, I believe it's entirely possible that one key demographic within the Democratic Party, the African-American community, will see the negative effects the party's bonds to the teachers' unions have on their children. They will demand action that brings genuine reform to the schools that are failing their community. When I vetoed the bill that would have put a moratorium on new charter schools in Massachusetts, the Black Caucus of state senators and representatives was one of the groups that came to my defense and to the defense of the charter-school movement.

Change also may come when data about teacher and school performance becomes increasingly available to parents and communities, leaving the unions unable to staunch swelling public demand for accountability and reform. Former president George W. Bush was right to champion the No Child Left Behind legislation, which requires states to test student progress and to evaluate school performance—it was the only way to ensure that critical information reached the public. Only the federal government had the clout to force testing through the barricade mounted by the national teachers' unions.

Those who object that national testing is too expensive are falling for one of the unions' most specious arguments. While costs vary by state, testing generally costs less than $50 per student per year, a tiny fraction of the massive amount of funding that federal and state governments send to local schools. The unions also claim that the result of No Child Left Behind is that teachers are now simply "teaching to the test." Yet when I went online and personally took the exam that Massachusetts now administers to prospective high-school graduates, I discovered that "teaching to the test" can only mean teaching the fundamentals of math, algebra, geometry, calculus, reading comprehension, and English composition. If giving student these skills is "teaching to the test," then I'm all for it—our kids can't succeed in life without these basic literacy and numeracy skills.

In an ideal world, all parents would be able to send their children to the schools of their choice, something those with high incomes can do today by selecting the city or town in which they live or by enrolling their children in private schools. Yet for average Americans, the choice is limited, or nonexistent. Some parents with modest incomes still have access to excellent parochial schools. I know, for example, that Boston's public-school system is highly successful in part because a very large Catholic school system sits alongside it. Over 40 percent of Boston's children attend Catholic schools, where they receive an excellent education, and the public schools feel community pressure to perform to the same standard. While vouchers that would help middle-income and moderate-income families send their children to private school are, for the most part, politically infeasible, charter schools have become a viable and very promising alternative for school choice in a number of states like Massachusetts.

Reliable studies like the one recently conducted by the Rand Corporation indicate that, on average, charter-school students do not outperform their regular public-school counterparts in math and English scores, even when adjusted for income and background disparities. But even if the results of that study are replicated in other places by other researchers, it's possible that those literacy and numeracy scores parallel the general results from public schools because charter schools often are designed to emphasize disciplines like music, art, science, or history, and to excel in those areas of study to the satisfaction of both students and parents. Charter schools also succeed when they demonstrate new practices and stimulate innovation in the neighboring regular schools and in other public-school districts. And underperforming charter schools can have their charters revoked. If a charter school fails, it can and should be closed, something that's hard to do with regular public schools. And, crucially, parents can choose or reject a charter school for their children, a choice that is an expression of parental right on a matter of paramount importance to them. It's the American way to provide an American education.

Education and Innovation

Parents and students in Washington, D.C., recently got a taste of school choice, when 1,700 families received $7,500 vouchers per student to help them attend private schools under the Opportunity Scholarship Program. The recipients, 99 percent of whom were black or Hispanic, liked what they saw—there were four applicants for every opening. And the student outcomes were encouraging as well. Early participants in the program developed reading skills that were nineteen months ahead of their public-school peers, and an evaluation by the Department of Education confirmed that the students had made big gains. But under intense pressure from opponents of school choice, Congress and the Obama administration passed legislation that terminated the program. It reminded me of my experience with the legislature's attempt to impose a charter-school moratorium in Massachusetts, although in the District of Columbia, children and parents did not have a happy ending. (There are still efforts under way at this writing to restore the program. The intense criticism of the presidential and congressional indifference to these students may yet win the day, or at least a reprieve.)

In Detroit, students in the city's public schools were offered a lifeline by a philanthropist who pledged to personally fund $200 million to establish fifteen charter schools. Unbelievably, the teachers' union successfully persuaded their friends in the Michigan state legislature to turn down the gift. As those experiences in Washington, D.C., and Michigan attest, the political forces thwarting education reform are extremely powerful, and their exercise of that power is often very discouraging.

There is, however, a burgeoning new type of reform that likely will be far more difficult for the special interests to defeat. As Moe and Chubb describe in *Liberating Learning,* a company called Advanced Academics currently provides classes over the Internet for 60,000 students in twenty-nine states, and each of their courses is supervised by a teacher who federal regulations certify as "highly qualified." A number of other companies offer varieties of supervised Internet learning as well, and now nearly a million public-school students a year complete courses online. At two public schools in Dayton, Ohio, children spend several hours online each day in classes that have twice the average number of students and are taught by teachers who receive higher pay for the innovative teaching they do. The state of Wisconsin has chartered a "virtual academy" from a private company that pioneered distance learning, "providing a rigorous, customized curriculum to students who 'attend' from locations all over the state . . . [and] whose needs were not being met by their own districts." At Pennsylvania Cyber, the largest "virtual" charter school in the country, eight thousand students receive textbooks and are assigned individual teachers who work with them online and in real time. A faculty adviser is required to e-mail each student's parents every week and speak with them by phone every two weeks, providing feedback and counseling. The results are impressive—Pennsylvania Cyber students have posted SAT scores 97 points above the average for the state.

At least thirty-eight states have now established so-called cyber-schools, with Florida boasting the largest enrollment—100,000 students. This new learning technology is a far cry from the computer labs of the 1990s. Students today are presented with materials that are tailored to match their capabilities and progress. Teachers monitor each student's advancement, intervening to help guide them through whatever learning challenges arise.

These and other technology-driven innovations are bringing to education something that has long been available in the private sector. Some years ago, the CEO of a firm that provides software for computer-assisted engineering around the world explained to me that his company's system determines the level of proficiency of each of its users, which it then matches with the tools, tutorials, and prompts that can best help that user perform his or her work. Education software has now made the same transition, from one size fits all to individually crafted and individually guided materials and mentoring. Students with different learning abilities can now attend the same class without some being held back and others being left behind. And teachers can be far more effective, applying their guidance where and when it is needed most.

These new technologies also enhance the education experience of kids that are homeschooled. My sister-in-law Becky Davies has homeschooled four of her children. My hat is off to her and to other parents like her. Having the kids at home for most of the day, preparing and providing daily instruction, arranging for social interactions with other kids, and simply knowing that your child's education is wholly in your hands—this is a burden many of us would find overwhelming. I admire such parents a great deal and applaud every innovation that assists them in their efforts. As cyber-tools become even more available, I expect that the number of homeschoolers will grow exponentially.

The teachers' unions oppose a good deal of this computer-learning revolution, and the homeschooling movement drives many of them to near apoplexy. They have gone to court to close cyber-schools across the country, including Wisconsin's virtual academy. They may well prove to be just as successful in blocking technology innovations as they have been in blocking other education reforms. But Clayton Christensen, Harvard Business School's eminent innovation scholar, is more optimistic. In his *Disrupting Class*, he argues that technology will penetrate education just as it has private enterprise, pointing to rates of technology adoption in public education that closely parallel those that have occurred in the private sector. As parents are increasingly exposed to performance data, I'm convinced that the resistance to specious arguments for limiting technology will grow. And I sense that enough political support is building to overcome resistance to effective reform generally. I simply cannot believe that the teachers' unions and the Democratic Party can successfully persist in opposing the very fundamentals that have propelled America's leadership in every other dimension of our economy— competition, innovation, and higher rewards for better performance.

Far too much is at stake for America to stand by as yet another generation falls behind. The solution begins with doing everything we can to support stable marriages and families, but it goes well beyond that enormous challenge. Even students from the most disadvantaged homes can achieve, something that's been proven in highly innovative programs around the country. The key to successful schools is providing students with excellent teachers. We must recruit teachers from among our brightest students, pay them well, and provide them with excellent mentors. Accountability and school choice matter, whereas class size and spending levels do not, at least up to a certain point. Plus, innovation and technology are critically important as we move forward. They moved our nation's economy out of heavy industry into the information age, and they can similarly help restore American public education to the heights it once achieved. I am convinced that the barricades to competitive, high-quality education have begun to tumble.

There are so many outstanding and passionate people in education—as governor, I felt that not a week went by without my meeting a number of them. They know the system desperately needs to change and they want to be a part of a brighter future for our children. What we need is leadership at the higher levels of government to free education from the grip of forces that are keeping our schools and our kids from realizing their potential.

9

Running Low

There wasn't much about having a Rambler in the driveway that qualified as cool to a ten-year-old. My friends' parents drove Buicks, Pontiacs, Plymouths, Chevys, or Fords, cars that were bigger, faster, better looking, and more popular. Yet there was one thing going for my parents' car: Rambler, the plain-Jane car my dad built, was the television sponsor of *Disneyland*, the predecessor to *The Wonderful World of Disney*, and my friends certainly thought *that* was cool. At home every Sunday night, we would gather around the television set as Walt Disney introduced episodes of classic features like *Lady and the Tramp*, or my favorite series, *Davy Crockett*. Each show was sponsored by Rambler, and everyone in the Romney family was proud of it.

My father chose to advertise on the Disney program because he viewed Rambler as a family car, and *Disneyland* was the preeminent family show of the era. Ramblers were inexpensive, easy to service, and most important, they were fuel efficient. One of the most anticipated announcements at our house every year was the winner of the Mobil Economy Run, and Rambler often won because it achieved thirty miles a gallon or more—not bad even by today's standards. Dad called his competitors' cars "gas-guzzling dinosaurs," a term that he helped make popular. He wore a tie with a dinosaur print on it, and there were two brontosaurus sculptures in his study. My friends may have been cool, but their parents drove around in fat, giant, extinct reptiles. Our car got great mileage, and even with relatively inexpensive gas prices at that time, good mileage meant less pressure on a family's budget.

In the 1950s, good mileage wasn't about reducing reliance on oil imports—the U.S. produced 90 percent or more of the oil we needed. The threat of global climate change didn't concern anyone yet, either. In fact, some scientists were predicting a return of the Ice Age. Gasoline cost about thirty cents a gallon—the equivalent of about $2.10 today—and people wanted good mileage simply to save money. Then things began to change.

By the early 1970s, America's oil production had sharply declined and its import of oil had risen dramatically. Oil went from being a pocketbook issue to a strategic one. By 1975, we were importing almost as much oil as we were producing, and President Gerald Ford declared that our oil trade imbalance threatened our national security. All six presidents since then have repeated that same warning, yet today we import about 50 percent more oil than we produce.

"America's dependence on oil for transportation and consumer products is huge and dangerous," insists Thomas Friedman. "It limits military and foreign policy options, handcuffs the economy, and generates a steady stream of revenue that helps finance Muslim terrorism." He is absolutely right. From a foreign policy perspective, our addiction to imported oil necessitates a massive military presence in the Middle East, and it has contributed to involving us, whether we like it or not, in ancient and seemingly intractable conflicts. Oil profits fund global violence against America and Americans. Oil finances the development of weapons of mass destruction. Our thirst for oil has led us to sell advanced weapons technology to states like Iran, which then saw revolution turn a former ally into an enemy, a transformation that could happen again in other oil-exporting states to which we sell advanced armaments. And of course oil and the profits it promises have led to war in the past, most memorably when Saddam Hussein invaded Kuwait in order to seize his neighbor's oil wealth, triggering the first Gulf War.

Our reliance on imported oil weakens our hand outside the Middle East as well. Venezuelan president Hugo Chávez's verbal buffoonery is exceeded only by his persistent desire to supplant democracy throughout Latin America, an effort financed through the sale of Venezuelan oil. Chávez is fast becoming a menace to freedom across his continent, and his instability is exactly the sort of megalomania that has plunged other states like Zimbabwe into cycles of crushing violence and destruction. Chávez could become our hemisphere's Mugabe, all because of the wealth his exploitation of oil provides him.

Our efforts to end genocide in Sudan are frustrated by China's reticence to interfere with the flow of oil from its Sudanese wells. Intensified geopolitical rivalries with nations like China, and even allies like India, are the by-products of the search by modern economies for the energy they need to run. The demand for oil could draw those nations into closer alliance with the increasingly hostile Russia of Vladimir Putin.

The global addiction to oil promotes corruption, autocracy, terrorism, and repression; conflicts in Iraq, Nigeria, Sudan, Indonesia, Yemen, Algeria, the Congo, Georgia, and Chechnya all have been sparked or fueled by oil. Freedom House reports that only 9 percent of the world's marketable oil lies in countries that it considers free. Oil brings wealth, but it also has been a curse for many of the countries under which it pools.

One of best things that could happen for the advancement of American foreign policy and world peace would be an end to the global dependence on oil. Our oil gluttony is not good for the American economy. We spend over $200 billion a year buying oil from other nations—a staggering amount that accounts for a third of our current account deficit. Economists note that buying something for less than it costs you to produce is generally a good thing. It isn't bad economics for American companies to use oil imported from abroad when energy produced at home costs more. But we have better options than producing energy here at higher cost: We can dramatically reduce our appetite for oil and over time transition to cost-efficient alternative sources of energy. Spending our energy dollars here for domestically produced energy while also funding research, development, and production of new sources of energy creates jobs, strengthens the dollar, and reduces our exposure to supply risks and volatility.

We must vigorously embrace and develop all of our domestic energy sources. One of the great disappointments of the so-called stimulus package of 2009 was that we spent nearly a trillion dollars and have no new energy production facilities to show for it. These dollars could have funded dozens of clean and safe nuclear plants, hundreds of offshore or onshore wells, and natural gas pipelines that could have provided low emissions fuel to electric utilities. Instead, just as much foreign oil arrives in American ports as before.

The Question of Climate Change

It's impossible not to take a look at our current energy policies without considering the question of climate change. I believe that climate change is occurring—the reduction in the size of global ice caps is hard to ignore. I also believe that human activity is a contributing factor.

I am uncertain how much of the warming, however, is attributable to man and how much is attributable to factors out of our control. I do not support radical feel-good policies like a unilateral U.S. cap-and-trade mandate. Such policies would have little effect on the climate but could cripple economic growth with devastating results for people across the planet, as I will discuss later in this chapter.

Oil is purported to be one of the primary contributors to rising global temperatures. If in fact global warming is importantly caused by our energy appetite, it's yet one more reason for going on an energy diet. As we have seen, it is hardly the only reason for doing so.

Scientists are nearly unanimous in laying the blame for rising temperatures on greenhouse gas emissions. Of course there are also reasons for skepticism. The earth may be getting warmer, but there have been numerous times in the earth's history when temperatures have been warmer than they are now. Climate cycles with great variations in temperature predate the greenhouse gas emissions of the past three centuries, and they even predate the rise of human populations. In fact, climate change has been going on from the beginning of the world; it is certainly not a new phenomenon.

Even the apparent unity among scientists is not a sure indicator of scientific fact. The idea that earthquakes are caused by the movement of tectonic plates, for example, was roundly rejected in the scientific community well into the twentieth century but is now accepted as scientific fact.

Whether or not you agree that the climate is changing and that human beings have something to do with it, assume for the sake of argument that both positions are accurate. What then should be done? Here the unity among scientists tends to splinter. Most argue for extreme measures to limit greenhouse gas emissions, citing catastrophic consequences if global temperatures rise. In addition to severe impacts on agriculture and freshwater, some estimate that the seas will rise between one and three feet by the end of this century, devastating low-lying cities and their populations. While no credible voice predicts that the polar ice caps will melt entirely in this century, the threat is truly alarming. If the Greenland ice cap disappeared, oceans would rise about twenty-four feet. They would rise an additional two hundred feet if the Antarctic ice cap melted.

Yet even given these disastrous scenarios, and even accepting that there is some possibility of their occurrence, not everyone argues for draconian measures to curb greenhouse gases. Some, in fact, believe the most responsible action is to reduce emissions where economically reasonable on the one hand, and to prepare to mediate the effects of sea level changes on affected populations on the other.

In 2004, Danish economist Bjørn Lomborg gathered ten of the world's leading economists, including three Nobel laureates, in what he called the Copenhagen Consensus. He asked them to prioritize the greatest problems faced by humankind. They were not asked to determine which problems were the most severe, but rather to rank the most severe global challenges according to the cost and benefit of overcoming them. They were asked to determine the benefit of remediating each problem in terms of saving human life and reducing human suffering and then comparing that with the cost of doing so. Given the worldwide attention given to global warming by politicians, the media, and scientists, it presumably would be at the top of the list. It was not. Instead, HIV, the economists agreed, was number one: $27 billion spent over eight years to prevent AIDS would save 28 million people from contracting the disease. This choice would be the most effective in sparing human life. Eliminating micronutrient malnutrition by distributing vitamin A, iron, zinc, and iodine was second. Preventing malaria was high on their list: at a cost of $13 billion per year, the 500,000 malaria deaths that occur annually would be cut in half. Remarkably, promoting free trade by reducing tariffs and removing protective subsidies was also high on their list. The economists determined that doing so would add $2.4 trillion to the world economy, lifting two to three hundred million people out of poverty.

Astonishingly, spending money to prevent global warming came in last. Why? To reduce global temperature even by a very small amount requires enormous investment. Achieving the Kyoto objectives, they reasoned, would cost $150 billion a year and only delay the global temperature that would otherwise have been reached in the year 2100 by six years. For just half that amount of money, in fact, all of the other global problems they had considered could be solved. Therefore, if human life and well-being is the measure, they concluded, money would be better spent on other global problems.

Lomborg's own view is that planning for and addressing the remediation of the effects of global warming are far more economic and more humane than massive spending to reduce emissions. British zoologist and author Matt Ridley agrees. "Bjørn Lomborg's rational and compassionate suggestions would save more lives, preserve more wilderness, and have a better chance of eventually halting man-made warming than hysterical catastrophism, global treaties, and high-minded energy rationing," Ridley writes.

My own visits to China convince me that there is at least one more significant reason to pause before we engage in extreme and expensive measures aimed at cooling the planet: the thorny issue of feasibility. China emits more carbon dioxide than does the United States. It accounted for *two-thirds* of the entire world's increase of greenhouse gases in 2007, the latest year in which the figures have been reported. By 2030, China will emit more greenhouse gases than North America and Western Europe combined. In fact, China and other developing nations will be the source of over 80 percent of the worldwide growth in emissions. At present, China and other developing nations are focused on improving the standard of living for their populations. These governments have mouths to feed and famines to prevent. This is a higher priority for them than making meaningful reductions in greenhouse gas emissions. In one respect, their position is compelling—the prospect of malnutrition or starvation of large numbers of people must necessarily engage their primary attention. The sometimes catastrophic events of the here and now take precedence over the far-off and potential disasters brought about by climate change.

Even if developing nations' food, water, and basic medicines are secure, they also want to obtain for their people the basic standard of living that we in the West take for granted. Before they reduce energy consumption, they argue, shouldn't they be entitled to enjoy the benefits that the burning of fossil fuels makes possible in developed nations? In contemporary China, for example, there is one automobile for every forty people, compared with one car for every two people in the United States. As nations like China and India make available to their citizens the automobiles, home heaters, air conditioners, and appliances that we take for granted in the West, their energy demands—and their emissions—will rise dramatically. As they build better housing, more hospitals, and the sort of minimum amenities that rural America considers outdated, these emissions will rise again.

If developing nations won't curb emissions, even extreme mitigation measures taken by the United States and other developed nations will have no appreciable effect on slowing the rate of greenhouse gas emissions. Massive spending—or even worse, borrowing for emission reduction—would only make us less able to remediate the effects of warming later.

These considerations lead me to this: We should pursue a no-regrets policy at home, and we should continue to engage in global efforts—not just U.S. and European efforts—to reduce global greenhouse gas emissions. By no regrets, I mean that we ought to take unilateral action on emissions when doing so is also consistent with our objective of reducing our dependence on foreign sources of oil. In that way, if the human contribution to global warming turns out not to be the problem most consider it to be today, we will have no regrets for having taken action; these actions will have reduced our dependence on fossil fuels.

Internationally, we should work to limit the increase in emissions in global greenhouse gases, but in doing so, we shouldn't put ourselves in a disadvantageous economic position that penalizes American jobs and economic growth.

The notion that if we spend trillions to reduce emissions then China will feel morally obligated to follow suit is folly. "The world is littered with instances where American moral leadership has been ignored or actively defied by the People's Republic of China," the Heritage Foundation's Derek Scissors points out, including "the Sudan genocide, Iranian and North Korean nuclear programs, Burmese human rights repression, and so forth."

At least until China's jobs crisis recedes during the coming decades, it's unimaginable that the country will do anything that would risk slowing its economic growth. The Chinese believe in economic growth in a way that few in the West can grasp—a belief powered by the almost desperate need to keep up with their own population. We simply cannot blind ourselves to that reality.

Our Energy Legacy

If the economy, geopolitics, and potential repercussions of climate change aren't enough to cause us to dramatically reshape our energy habits, I hope that our collective concern for the legacy we leave our children will bring us to our senses. Will the next American generations have sufficient clean, safe domestic energy, or will our children and grandchildren be economically captive to some of the world's most unstable nations and the tyrants who lead them? Today, we produce just 42 percent of our own oil, and production is on a downward trend that is likely to continue. Crude oil production peaked in 1970 in our lower forty-eight states and peaked in 1988 in Alaska. Since 1972, the amount of crude oil produced per well in the United States has declined from 18.6 barrels a day to about 10 per day.

We consume roughly 24 percent of the world's oil but possess only 2.4 percent of the world's oil reserves. Even if we were to begin to drill in the Arctic National Wildlife Refuge and on the continental shelf, it wouldn't be enough to appreciably have an impact on our dependence on other nations for oil. And if we were to open the domestic oil spigot too wide and drain our last fields, we would risk leaving America even more vulnerable twenty-five years from now than it is today. But there should be no objection to preparing the energy infrastructure to tap known reserves and to discover more reserves: This is a vitally important insurance policy against future energy shocks or threats to national security. And it is always possible that new, very large discoveries could surprise us.

With all that is at stake, the time has come for America to adopt a proactive energy strategy, one that will generate a dramatic change in our energy habits instead of waiting for change to be thrust upon us by others. Some believe that our goal should be energy independence. Other very credible energy experts explain that energy independence is impossible or impractical and therefore that "energy security" is a more realistic objective. I think both camps actually mean the same thing: We need to become independent of oil geopolitics and oil-state blackmail so that our citizens and our economy will never be hostage to price manipulation by the oil oligopoly. And in addition to achieving energy security for ourselves, we should make sure that we provide for future generations of Americans as well.

In recent years, there's been a view in Washington that we should simply "let the market work" by taking a hands-off approach, rather than adopt a proactive and comprehensive set of energy policies. That prescription is exactly the right one in most economic sectors, but it falls short when it comes to energy. And it ignores the fact that we have policies in place right now that distort how the energy markets function.

Markets can't be expected to work their unique magic when they're controlled by oligopolies, as the oil market currently is—free markets simply don't exist when sellers collude. When an aspiring superpower like Russia seeks to dominate the energy market with monopolistic and militaristic measures, "letting the market work" could obviously pave the way to a very bad outcome indeed. If the energy market were truly free, it long ago would have attracted global investors to develop alternative sources of energy, but the oligopolists have intentionally manipulated production and prices to dissuade investors from making long-term commitments. "The aim of the OPEC cartel is to constrain supply," note the authors of *Winning the Oil Endgame*, "and thereby force others to produce high-cost oil first, then sell the cartel's cheap oil for that higher price—and by depleting others' oil first, make buyers even more dependent on the cartel later."

Our own policies interfere with free-market mechanisms. We subsidize domestic oil and gas production with generous tax breaks, penalize sugar-based ethanol from Brazil, and block investment in nuclear energy. Our navy assumes the prime responsibility for securing the oil routes from the Middle East, effectively subsidizing its cost. Thus, we don't pay the full cost of Middle East oil, either at the oil-company level or at the pump.

Market economists also identify a number of externalities—real costs that aren't captured in the price of fuel—the most frequently cited of which are the health-care costs of pollution and the climate costs of greenhouse gases. There is a further externality: potentially leaving the next generations in the lurch by using so much oil and energy ourselves—domestic and imported—that our children face severe oil shortages, prohibitively expensive fuel, a crippled economy, and dominion of energy by Russia and other oil-rich states. No matter how you price it, oil is expensive to use; we should be encouraging our citizens to use less of it, our scientists to find alternatives for it, and our producers to find more of it here at home.

Many analysts predict that the world's production of oil will peak in the next ten to twenty years, but the late oil expert Matt Simmons, author of *Twilight in the Desert: The Coming Saudi Oil Shock and the World Economy*, presented a compelling case that Middle Eastern oil production may have already reached its peak. Simmons based his contention on his investigation into the highly secretive matter of the level of reserves in the Saudi oil fields. But whether the peak is already past or will be reached within a few years, world oil supply *will* decline at some point, and no one predicts a corresponding decline in demand. If we want America to remain strong and wish to ensure that future generations have secure and prosperous lives, we must consider our current energy policies in the light of how these policies will affect our grandchildren.

An argument can be made that by the time we would experience a severe shortage of crude oil, we will have found new energy sources to replace it, so we should continue to consume oil just as fast as we want. Hydrogen, for example, is frequently touted as an energy panacea; my greenest friends have assured me that we can expect widely commercialized hydrogen cars within ten years. But I remind them that they've been saying that for more than a decade. Energy Secretary Steven Chu has decided to shift federal research funding from hydrogen to other energy sources because the lead time on hydrogen is so great.

Cold fusion looked like it was the answer . . . for a couple of weeks in 1989. And today, many are enthusiastic that we will soon be powering our automobiles with cellulosic ethanol—liquid fuel derived from trees, woody plants, and switchgrass. I fully agree that we need to pursue every promising new source of clean energy, but it is irresponsible to act as if one or more energy miracles wait around the corner. After all, we've been looking for replacements for oil, coal, and nuclear fuel for decades. It would be unwise to rest our future security on the blithe assumption that we will be more successful in the next thirty years than we have been in the last thirty.

Addressing Demand and Supply

Our energy strategy must address both the demand and the supply sides of the equation. We need to lower the amount of energy we use and increase the supply of domestic energy sources.

Americans use a lot of energy. We own more cars per capita than any other country in the world. Many are fuel inefficient. And in part because ours is a big country, we drive our cars long distances. Our homes are large, and we heat and cool them to keep the temperature within a narrow range. Televisions, computers, home appliances, and lighting account for another big portion of our overall energy use, and there are many indirect uses as well—the energy required to produce our food, homes, clothing, entertainment, and communications among them. When it's added up, each of us uses about twice as much energy as a European or Japanese citizen, and *seven* times as much as the average Chinese. One would expect, therefore, that we could find ample opportunities for greater efficiency and reduction in use.

Better auto mileage is where most people look first. In 1975, Congress enacted Corporate Average Fuel Economy (CAFE) standards for new cars and light trucks, and a decade later, new auto mileage had more than doubled, from 12.9 miles per gallon (mpg) to 27.5. But in the twenty-five years since, there's been virtually no improvement. In fact, with the big growth in SUVs and pickups, the average mileage of all new passenger vehicles has *declined* over the last two decades. Early in 2008, as the price of a gallon of gasoline exceeded four dollars a gallon, average mileage statistics spiked as consumers fled from SUVs and other low-mileage vehicles, but it remains important for us to improve mileage standards without depending on oil-nation profiteering.

The National Petroleum Institute calculates that the national average mpg can double in twenty years simply by applying today's proven and nearly proven technologies—with no need to reduce automobile weight, power, or accessories. Because cars in general have grown heavier and more powerful over the past two decades, if consumers support modest changes in vehicle size and acceleration levels, average auto mileage of 50 mpg appears entirely within reach. Japan already mandates that average new car mileage reach 46.9 mpg in just six years, and Europe mandates 48.9 mpg even sooner.

Some energy experts believe that even mileage targets like these are too conservative. Amory Lovins is one of them. When I was governor, he and I met in my office in Boston. Lovins, head of the Rocky Mountain Institute, shared his vision of a 75 mpg hybrid automobile built with high strength steel and composites. Further, he described a car with aerodynamic design features that would reduce its weight enough to make hydrogen fuel cells practical as its power source. At the heart of his analysis were his calculations of the efficiency of our current automobiles. About 85 percent of an auto's energy is lost as heat and friction in the engine and transmission, he explained. The remaining 15 percent moves the car, which weighs about three thousand pounds, and most often transports only a single occupant. Doing the math, Lovins concluded that only *1 percent* of the car's energy moves the driver down the road—the rest is inefficiently consumed in moving the car.

I shared my own dream for a super-efficient commuter vehicle. It would be a lightweight, two-passenger car in which the occupants rode tandem— one behind the other instead of side by side. These much narrower vehicles would allow for the addition of more highway lanes at very little cost, reducing traffic and commuting times. I tried out my idea on Brian Schweitzer, Montana's no-nonsense governor. "Mitt, you'd be real smart not to ever mention that again," he said to me with a slight smile. "People will think you've lost it."

But putting aside the fanciful, the issue isn't whether our current technologies can produce cars with very high mileage—it's how to get them to market and out on the road. The oil shocks of 1973 and 2008 demonstrated that Americans will quickly and dramatically change buying and driving behavior when gasoline is scarce or prohibitively expensive. But sudden shocks devastate family budgets and can trigger job-destroying recessions. We need predictability and gradual change, not a roller-coaster ride.

The approach government has employed to date is to impose federal fuel economy standards on auto manufacturers. CAFE requirements did indeed improve mileage, but they led to some harmful side effects as well. Asian manufacturers that were already producing a full line of smaller, fuel-efficient vehicles suddenly had a significant advantage over U.S. automakers. Both foreign and domestic companies also gamed the system, shifting the mix of vehicles in their fleets to produce more minivans, pickups, and SUVs, which carried less stringent standards. While the revised CAFE standards passed in 2009 will eliminate much of the gaming, they will give foreign companies the same kind of boost they got when CAFE was first introduced, and they will impose a large financial burden on domestic automakers at a time when they are least able to afford it. My guess is that taxpayers will end up with the bill for government subsidies to the industry, probably totaling $100 billion.

Doug Foy, former president of the Conservation Law Foundation and recipient of the President's Environmental and Conservation Challenge Award, is a proponent of an idea he calls a "feebate." Under his plan, auto buyers who choose to purchase a fuel-efficient car would get a significant government rebate check. But conversely, buyers who chose a fuel-*inefficient* auto would pay a fee. Since the rebates the government paid out would equal the fees collected, government spending would be unaffected and incentives would be put in place that favored greater fuel efficiency. The amount of each feebate would vary from a few hundred dollars to a few thousand, based on the vehicle's mileage compared with others cars in its class. And the feebates would also be adjusted for size, so you wouldn't be penalized for buying a seven-passenger van, only for buying a seven-passenger van that was less fuel-efficient than its in-class competition.

I liked Foy's idea enough that I proposed a similar but more palatable plan during my tenure as governor. Instead of adding fees, I proposed lowering or eliminating the sales tax when an individual purchased a fuel-efficient vehicle in a given class. I also proposed an additional tax break based on how much of the vehicle's labor and materials came from the United States. Under my plan, the sales tax savings on a new car purchase could amount to $2,000 or more. The measure didn't pass, but it should have.

It's Not Just Cars

Automotive fuel economy can be dramatically improved and doing so will reduce our vulnerability to foreign sources of oil. The bad news is that automobiles and light trucks account for well less than half of our overall oil consumption. When you consider the energy we consume from all sources—coal, gas, oil, and alternatives—passenger vehicles are responsible for only 16 percent of the total. If we want to achieve energy security, we can't look just to our cars.

The majority of U.S. oil consumption is by heavy trucks, airplanes, homeowners, manufacturers, and companies that produce products such as plastics, cement, and chemicals. The list of the consumers of all types of energy is as broad as the economy is diverse. So how can we achieve substantially greater energy efficiency if it means changing the habits of thousands of types of users in thousands of settings rather than just those of automobile drivers?

McKinsey & Company conducted a study in 2009 to determine how much the emission of global greenhouse gases could be reduced worldwide and at what cost. Because greenhouse gas emissions are highly correlated with energy consumption, the study provides a window on the opportunities for energy efficiency and fuel substitution as well. The firm set out to determine whether enough greenhouse-gas-reduction opportunities exist to limit the increase in the world's average temperature to two degrees Celsius. They evaluated the abatement potential and the costs for more than two hundred different abatement opportunities. On page 238 is a bar chart illustrating the summary findings of the study, with each bar representing one, or in some cases, a group of opportunities. The width of each bar indicates the potential greenhouse gas emissions reduction that each opportunity can achieve by 2030 if exploited to its fullest—the wider the bar, the higher the impact. The height of the bar indicates whether, over its lifetime, the opportunity will result in annual savings (bars below the baseline) or annual costs (bars above it).

Like the authors of the study, I was struck by a number of its findings; foremost is that achieving the study's temperature objective would require a very wide range of measures and investments—none of which is so large that we could afford to concentrate on it alone. Second, the opportunities that save money (the bars below the line) tend to involve energy efficiency measures while fuel-substitution measures like nuclear and particularly wind and solar power are much more costly. The same holds true for a no-regrets policy for energy security: it will require actions from a multitude of

Global greenhouse gas abatement cost curve beyond business as usual—2030

Abatement cost
€ per tCO₂e

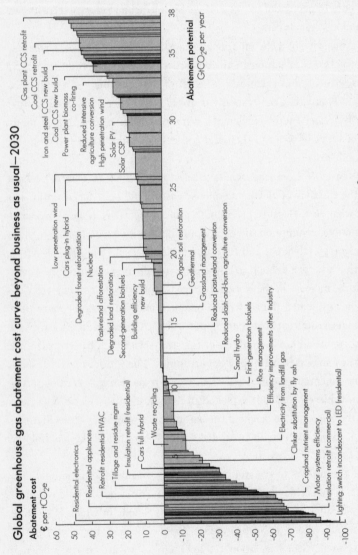

Abatement potential
GtCO₂e per year

Note: The curve presents an estimate of the maximum potential of all technical GHG abatement measures below €60 per tCO₂ if each lever was pursued aggressively. It is not a forecast of what role different abatement measures and technologies will play.

Source: McKinsey & Company

users and a multitude of technologies, some that will pay for themselves and some that will not. There is no one silver bullet.

As part of its effort to stimulate energy efficiency and fuel substitution, the federal government to date has employed mandates like CAFE, product energy standards for home appliances, and subsidies such as home-insulation tax credits. While all of these measures do in fact stimulate energy savings, they are far from sufficient for us to reach the goal of energy security. Government simply can't identify—let alone effectively regulate, mandate, and subsidize—all the energy consumption and energy users in the American economy. True energy security will require game-changing measures that will lead users of all kinds to voluntarily and independently make energy-investment and energy-consumption modifications based upon their individual economic self-interest. Determining which measures are needed depends in part on the extent of the opportunities for replacing foreign oil with domestic sources and for exploiting new fuels and energy sources.

Alternatives to Foreign Oil

Whether global warming or energy security is one's primary concern, everyone agrees that finding substitute fuels for oil is a good thing. Oil is what makes us most vulnerable economically and oil accounts for 44 percent of our carbon dioxide emissions. Both camps also agree that we should exploit renewable energy sources like wind, solar, and agriculture-based fuels, as well as maximize energy opportunities from cogeneration—which is the simultaneous production of heat and electricity from a single-fuel source. When it comes to nuclear power, coal, and increased domestic drilling, the agreement disappears.

Nuclear power is a win-win; it's a domestic energy source with *zero* greenhouse gas emissions. The McKinsey analysis determined that nuclear power poses the single largest opportunity to reduce global greenhouse gas emissions. Without increased nuclear generation, the same study predicts global temperatures cannot achieve the two-degree Celsius goal. So if you're serious about global warming, you have to say yes to nuclear; and if like me you're serious about energy security, you get to the same place.

I confess that I don't understand why some environmental activists still consider nuclear power such a boogeyman. They should consider the contemporary evidence—the United States now has 104 trouble-free nuclear reactors at sixty-five power plants. France gets 80 percent of its electrical power from nuclear generations. Nations all over the world are currently building new plants, and scores of naval vessels have been safely and efficiently running on nuclear power for decades. Vermont, the state which many consider to be the "greenest" in the country, gets 73 percent of its power from nuclear power. Nuclear generation has a safe and economic track record, and it is here to stay.

Some argue that "nuclear power has no prospects in market-driven energy systems for a simple reason: nuclear plants cost too much to build . . . electricity from new light-water reactors will cost twice as much as from new wind-farms." This argument would be more persuasive if Argentina, Canada, China, Finland, France, India, Japan, Pakistan, Russia, South Korea, the United Kingdom, and other nations didn't have a total of forty-eight new nuclear reactors under construction as of the summer of 2009. Can all of those countries be pursuing energy solutions that make no economic sense?

Here in the United States, governments insist on interminable permitting, regulatory, and legal delays to deter the construction of new nuclear power plants; that's what has made them economically infeasible. Update the regulations and nuclear will take off. "The potential market for new nuclear reactors and the services necessary to keep them running is so large that the private sector is already beginning to expand," argue the Heritage Foundation's Jack Spencer and Nicolas Loris, who are convinced that government subsidies of nuclear generation aren't needed to make nuclear energy viable in this country again. They believe nuclear power makes economic sense right now and does so entirely on its own.

I think there is actually a simple way to resolve this disagreement. Why don't we retool governmental regulatory processes so that they solely provide for safety rather than giving professional anti-nuclear activists a set of labyrinthine regulations and tools with which to block new construction? If nuclear power proves to be economically viable, new plants will be built.

I don't dismiss the concerns of people who object to nuclear power out of a concern for a terrorist attack or accident—even given the industry's track record in the United States and around the world. Each of us must make our own calculations of acceptable risk as we line up for or against nuclear power. But in my view, the risk to liberty, prosperity, and human life is greater due to our dependence on foreign oil than it is when we build nuclear power plants.

Neither can we ignore coal as a substitute for foreign oil. Coal currently provides 48 percent of our electricity and 23 percent of our total energy. The United States has the largest coal reserves in the world, reserves that we can count on for the next 200 to 300 years. In addition to being used to generate electricity, coal can be liquefied and used as a transportation fuel. For those who see energy security as the primary goal of our energy policy, coal is an obvious answer. For those who are also concerned about warming, the challenge is that coal is one of the largest emitters of greenhouse gases of all energy sources.

We could overcome the challenge if we were able to capture the carbon dioxide from coal and store it away. Technology to do so already exists—the coal capture and storage process is currently being employed in a small coal gasification plant in Beulah, North Dakota, which sends the carbon dioxide it emits not into the air but into a pipeline that travels north to Canada, where some of it is used for enhanced oil recovery and the rest is stored underground. Whether carbon dioxide from coal can be captured and stored by larger commercial facilities remains to be seen, but surely research and development of this technology should become a high priority for us and for other nations with large coal reserves like China, Russia, and the United Kingdom.

Natural gas is an energy source everyone can love. It is abundant domestically, it can substitute for oil in a number of applications, and it emits very little greenhouse gas. Recently developed horizontal-drilling technology has transformed the natural gas industry by multiplying the amount of gas that can be extracted from old and new wells. Shale gas that is abundant in North America is less costly to produce than oil, coal, and most other forms of energy. As vast new reserves are being opened, natural gas has suddenly become the most promising immediate oil substitute, as well as a much larger contributor to our overall energy requirements. America should be building gas pipelines as quickly as possible.

Expanding the domestic drilling for oil is a highly charged issue largely because of its environmental implications. The best opportunities for finding important new fields are in pristine areas off our coasts, mountain-state wilderness areas, and in Alaska's Arctic National Wildlife Refuge. The U.S. Department of the Interior estimates the nation's total volume of undiscovered, technically recoverable oil at about 134 billion barrels, compared with proven reserves of 21.3 billion barrels. Oil discoveries during 2009 got off to a strong start, prompting *The New York Times* to report that "people in the industry say there is plenty of oil in the ground, especially beneath the ocean floor, even if finding and extracting it is becoming harder." Until 2010, there had never been a major oil spill from a U.S. offshore platform. With the massive BP oil spill in the Gulf, many Americans are understandably reticent to resume deepwater drilling. But once the oil companies can demonstrate that they have implemented and vastly improved their safeguard provisions, we will reinstitute the drilling—the long record of safety prior to the BP disaster suggests that properly managed offshore drilling can be safe. Alaskans and Rocky Mountain residents overwhelmingly support increased oil drilling in their regions. Opposition to drilling comes not from neighbors to the potential platforms, but from environmental activists in other states who oppose it on general grounds, regardless of how sensitively the oil extraction can be carried out.

I have a different concern. If we drill and pump the last available drop of oil from every domestic source, we may walk into a trap set by the oil oligopolists who would like nothing better than to watch us exhaust our own oil supplies now so we'll become entirely beholden to them in the future. On the other hand, if we don't drill, we risk aiding the oil cartels by increasing demand for their oil today and watching helplessly as that demand drives world prices skyward—filling their coffers and emptying ours.

The solution to this dilemma may be to explore and develop oil from these new domestic locations, but also to carefully meter the amount of oil we actually produce from them in order to moderate the pricing power of the foreign cartels and to safeguard our long-term supply. In effect, the oil produced from these new sources would serve as a kind of supersize strategic oil reserve. And if very large oil reserves were discovered or if oil substitutes showed greater and earlier potential, we could open the spigot.

Given the decade or longer lead times that are often required to produce oil, it would take years to significantly expand actual production, but in the near term, the presence and potential of these reserves—and America's willingness to exploit them—would have a stabilizing effect on world oil prices. The more difficult production environment, enormous investment, and long lead times to bring new wells into production would make this course difficult, but not impossible. The right step is to get started by authorizing exploration and infrastructure construction.

The Game Changers

Nuclear, natural gas, coal, and additional drilling for oil will help a great deal in moving us toward energy security. If major discoveries are made or if new technologies for energy extraction are achieved, they may take us to our goal. But barring a truly massive discovery, they alone can't get us there. Wind, ethanol, and solar help, too, but their impact on reducing foreign-sourced oil is relatively small. We can hope that hydrogen or some new energy source will emerge, but we can't stake America's future on them. So to become energy secure, we may need to turn to those game-changing incentives that will lead individuals and businesses of all kinds to invest in efficiency and to reduce their use of oil and energy.

Four game-changing approaches are currently in broad debate, each with distinct advantages and disadvantages. Simply pointing out the problems with each is a luxury we cannot indefinitely afford—we will need to choose the best alternative among those we currently know, or develop a new one.

A so-called carbon cap-and-trade mandate is widely supported, even by some Republicans, including Senator John McCain, the Republicans' 2008 presidential nominee. Once a national cap on greenhouse gas emissions is set, each emitter is given or acquires credits that allow it to continue to emit these gases. If it wants to emit more of the gases, say to grow its business, it can acquire credits from others—at the price set by supply and demand in the marketplace. Or if it finds ways to reduce its emissions and thus doesn't need all the credits it already owns, it can sell its excess credits to others.

In many ways, cap-and-trade seems market-oriented, and it has worked reasonably well as it has been applied to other pollutants when it has been limited to a narrow group of players and geographies. For example, emissions of sulfur dioxide from electric power plants have been successfully reduced in the United States through a cap-and-trade strategy. But that success was achieved among only a few hundred entities, all of whom are in the same highly regulated industry in the same country. Most important, those utilities had ready options that would help them eliminate their sulfur-dioxide problem—they could invest in scrubbers that remove pollutants from coal, or switch to alternative fuels like natural gas. Even with those advantages in place, the price of sulfur-dioxide emission credits has swung by as much as 80 percent a year. A healthy market cannot sustain that kind of unpredictability.

A cap-and-trade mandate for carbon dioxide emissions would be even more complex. Most entities that emit carbon dioxide have no alternative to reduce their emissions other than shrinking their production or closing down—there aren't any current commercial-scale technologies that scrub carbon dioxide from coal or from oil. And a carbon dioxide cap-and-trade system would involve thousands of industries across the full spectrum of the economy. The oversight and regulatory requirements alone would be daunting, and how would credits be fairly allocated? Lobbyists are already having a field day on the various proposals moving through Congress—the special-interest carve-outs and set-asides have already destroyed the credibility of the bill. Further, it would be virtually impossible to predict the price of permits and credits. European attempts to use a cap-and-trade program to help meet Kyoto Treaty emissions standards have been hit hard by these drawbacks, and current estimates are that the European Union will achieve less than half of targeted carbon dioxide reductions with little environmental benefit.

As governor, I explored joining with other New England states to create a carbon dioxide cap-and-trade program for our electric utilities. I was assured by its proponents that it would raise electric rates by only 3 to 5 percent. But when I met with the state's major manufacturers, they produced estimates of 30 percent increases in rates. One of the state's largest employers insisted that if we implemented the plan without a "safety valve" to limit the cost and volatility, his company would not be able to locate any new facilities in our state. I didn't sign on.

A national program that included not just the electric-utility industry but all industries would likely spark unmanaged volatility. It would depress industrial investment in America, leading to job losses in a wide array of industries. An international cap-and-trade treaty would entail even greater and perhaps insurmountable problems with measurement, price volatility, allocation of credits, and enforceability.

Perhaps the greatest weakness of an international cap-and-trade program would be the fact that the largest and the fastest-growing carbon dioxide emitters, China and India, have no interest whatsoever in joining. Absent their participation, our cap-and-trade program would disadvantage our employers with higher and more volatile costs. Those that are large energy users would likely move their activities to countries that were not part of the cap-and-trade treaty, costing more American jobs, and incidentally, emitting the same or more greenhouse gases in their new location. Besides losing jobs, American consumers would ultimately shoulder the cost of the credits in the form of higher prices for products, services, and electricity.

Cap-and-trade is an energy tax, disguised in the sheep's clothing of market terminology. And it is an energy tax that would have little or no effect on global warming.

As bad as a well-crafted cap-and-trade program may be, what was passed in 2009 by the House of Representatives was worse. Even cap-and-trade proponents like Senator McCain voted against it.

An alternative to cap-and-trade is the imposition of a wide array of government mandates, standards, and subsidies—something that again would be a lobbyist's delight. The automotive CAFE mandates are the most familiar, and they have in fact improved fuel economy while also depressing the auto industry and its employment. But as discussed above, automobiles are just one part of our oil and energy picture. Given the number and extent of energy consumers and carbon dioxide emitters in our economy, it would be literally impossible to impose enough mandates to make a meaningful difference. We might feel good about ourselves for doing something constructive, and we might win a bit of approbation in Europe, but we would remain dependent on foreign oil, just like the Europeans.

Subsidies do in fact stimulate private investment, and they may be effective in building an industry from its infancy. For that reason, I have supported ethanol subsidies, which have encouraged its relatively rapid development. But we should acknowledge that subsidies for one form of energy also *discourage* investment in alternatives that don't receive subsidies, which may undermine innovation. And because taxpayers ultimately have to pick up the tab for government spending, subsidies are in fact a hidden form of energy tax. Once an industry is up and running, the disadvantages of subsidies outweigh their benefits.

The third alternative is a direct oil or carbon tax. This would indeed stimulate oil efficiencies and investments in oil substitutes, but it would also fatten government, harm employers and employees, and hurt consumers. It's a regressive form of taxation that would penalize those least able to shoulder the burden. It's a nonstarter.

The fourth incentive system, a tax swap, has been proposed by conservatives such as Greg Mankiw, Harvard economist, author, and former chairman of the Council of Economic Advisers under President George W. Bush, and by Charles Krauthammer, the accomplished author, commentator, and columnist, among others. Under this approach, a gas or carbon tax would be paired with a coinciding reduction in another tax, such as the payroll tax, creating no greater burden for taxpayers and no new revenues for government. The higher energy prices would encourage energy efficiency across the full array of American businesses and citizens. It would provide industries of all kinds with a predictable outlook for energy costs, allowing them to confidently invest in growth. And profit incentives— rather than government subsidies—would stimulate the development of oil substitutes and carbon-reducing technologies.

Comparative analyses of the tax-swap plan with a cap-and-trade system have demonstrated that the tax swap is likely to be *five times* as effective in reducing carbon dioxide emissions and presumably, about five times as effective in reducing energy consumption. A major drawback of a tax-swap program, however, is that some energy consumers would be disproportionately affected, particularly those in certain energy-intensive industries, those who must travel long distances, and those who rely on fixed incomes. Americans who have worked their entire lives under one set of expectations shouldn't find their retirement years shaken by a radical switch in government policy. While the tax swap may be the best among the four alternatives currently under consideration, a great deal of work remains to be done if it is to become a viable option. (And we may hear of entirely new alternatives—as Ross Perot said, "I'm all ears.")

In the final analysis, we should aggressively pursue domestic energy sources such as oil, gas, coal, nuclear, wind, and solar. And as we also consider game-changing measures and incentives, we should make our choice with three things in mind: Will it actually achieve energy security? Will it strengthen the economy? Will it avoid unfairly creating winners and losers?

Energy is a far more complex subject than it was back when my father was building fuel-efficient if uncool cars and berating the gas-guzzling dinosaurs. And it has become much more important in the half-century since—economically, environmentally, and geopolitically. Most of us don't give a thought about how dramatic a role energy plays in our everyday lives—even as we begin each day by switching on lights, showering with hot water, toasting a slice of bread, and catching a bit of news on television in the minutes before we drive our car off to work. It's time for that to change. The moment is long past due for us to recognize that we will inexorably run low on oil and that we must replace it with substitute fuels that make us more secure, free us from unfavorable foreign entanglements, make our economy stronger, and don't endanger the health of our planet. It's an enormous challenge—yet it's the kind Americans have proven time and again that we can meet head-on.

10

The Culture of Citizenship

My jobs required travel. Consultant, venture capitalist, Olympic manager, and even governor—each put me on the road. I hated being away from Ann and the boys, so while I was away I focused on my work as much as possible, completing projects as quickly as I could so I could head home. Yet, in the end, what I learned about the places where I traveled and the people there was often greater than what I learned about my projects.

The differences between the places I visited were startling. I had seen the countries and their citizens on television, of course, but *being* there and experiencing life there—driving, shopping, eating, holding meetings, telephoning, conversing, and simply observing the daily events of people's lives—offered new perspectives and raised questions I wouldn't otherwise have considered. I wondered how such vast differences could exist between countries that were literally next door to each other. How could Americans be so rich and Mexicans so poor? How could Israelis have created a highly developed, technology-based economy while their Palestinian neighbors had not yet even begun to move to an industrial economy? As I traveled to Africa, Asia, the Middle East, South America, and to both halves of Europe that had previously been divided by the Iron Curtain, I discovered that the prosperity gap is really a canyon. Why is that?

In his best-selling book *Guns, Germs, and Steel*, Jared Diamond notes that long ago, the availability of minerals like iron ore meant that some nations could fashion weapons and conquer their neighbors while others without those minerals could not. The complex geography of germs and disease could cripple the economy of one nation while opening new possibilities for another. A nation's rivers, mountains, and deserts dramatically shaped the transportation network essential for trade and economic development. For scholars like Diamond and many others, the relative differences between nations and people are largely the result of these kinds of inherent natural features. To a degree, there is truth in that perspective, but it simply doesn't fully account for the great differences between nations and civilizations.

Harvard professor David Landes's *Wealth and Poverty of Nations* adds crucial insight as to why some nations prosper and others do not. His examination concludes that "culture makes all the difference," not only when it comes to understanding why great civilizations failed in the past, as described earlier, but also in explaining why differences between nations exist today. What people believe, value, strive for, and sacrifice for profoundly shape the nature of their society and affect its prosperity and security. So while America's abundant natural resources certainly facilitated its ascent, it is America's culture that enabled the nation to become and remain the most powerful and beneficent country in the history of humankind.

Many aspects of America's culture are today in question, in decline, or even under attack. Before the essentials of American culture are replaced or weakened, we should explicitly acknowledge the values that got us where we are, ask whether they are important to our national strength, and if so, take urgent measures to strengthen and in some cases to restore them.

A Nation of Hard Workers

What is it about America's culture that propelled us to world leadership? What elements of our culture are essential to our future strength? The list is long, but among them is the fact that Americans like to work. After forty hours a week on the job—and many more for a lot of us—we head out to wash the car, weed the garden, mow the lawn, tackle household chores, and taxi the kids.

And when Americans recreate, many do so with a kind of dedication and gusto that *looks* a lot like work; even when we relax, many prefer to quietly work on a project rather than sit in a lawn chair. When my father-in-law retired after a career as an engineer, the first thing he did was buy a drafting table and secondhand machine tools so that he could make things in his garage. His retirement move to Florida changed his climate but didn't change his occupation. He spent more time in his retirement garage in Florida than he had at his workplace back in Michigan.

Almost everyone who agreed to come to America as an immigrant surely understood that the new life would entail back-breaking work. Essential tasks in the early settlements were brutal, unrelenting, and sometimes matters of life or death. Recent immigrants, too, have known that driving a taxi, washing dishes, cleaning construction sites, or picking vegetables might very well be part of their future. Whether we learned our work ethic from our parents or it was passed to us in their genes, we are hard workers. And it's an element of our culture critical to our economy.

Creative destruction closes the doors to hundreds of thousands of businesses a year, putting millions of Americans out of work. Entrepreneurs open the new businesses that put the temporarily unemployed back to work again. Few undertakings require more work than starting a business from scratch. The grueling demands of getting a business up and running, the inevitable setbacks and roadblocks, and the fear of losing one's savings and the investments of friends and family, drive these people to work a hundred hours a week or more. I've never met a successful entrepreneur who didn't like to work.

Our collective ability to be focused, smart, and accurate over long hours of work are a big part of our productivity. Over centuries, these attributes helped create America's productivity lead, our high standard of living, and our national wealth. Americans continue to know how to work—on average we're on the job 25 percent more than the Germans, 15 percent more than the French, and even slightly longer hours than the famously industrious Japanese.

During my campaign for governor, I decided to spend a day every few weeks doing the jobs of other people in Massachusetts. Among other jobs, I cooked sausages at Fenway Park, worked on an asphalt paving crew, stacked bales of hay on a farm, volunteered in an emergency room, served food at a nursing home, and worked as a child-care assistant. I'm often asked which was the hardest job—it's child care, by a mile.

One day I gathered trash as a garbage collector. I stood on that little platform at the back of the truck, holding on as the driver navigated his way through the narrow streets of Boston. As we pulled up to traffic lights, I noticed that the shoppers and businesspeople who were standing only a few feet from me didn't even see me. It was as if I was invisible. Perhaps it was because a lot of us don't think garbagemen are worthy of notice; I disagree— anyone who works that hard deserves our respect.

I wasn't a particularly good garbage collector: at one point, after filling the trough at the back of the truck, I pulled the wrong hydraulic lever. Instead of pushing the load into the truck, I dumped it onto the street. Maybe the suits didn't notice me, but the guys at the construction site sure did: "Nice job, Mitt," they called. "Why don't you find an easier job?" And then they good-naturedly came down and helped me pick up my mess.

Over the years, I've seen a lot of Americans at work. The work on a farm is unrelenting. Work at service jobs in places like restaurants, airports, and retail stores means being on your feet for hours on end, and smiling about it. Nurses, caregivers, dentists, vets, and doctors regularly go about some of the most difficult tasks, often with little recognition. Manufacturing jobs can be numbingly repetitive. Taxi and truck drivers put in long and lonely hours. Even the men and women in business suits and skirts often experience a level of stress that more than makes up for their air-conditioned environment. Americans work hard.

In some quarters, however, the American work ethic is waning. Some people devote themselves to finding ways *not* to work. Some seem to take a perverse kind of pride in being slipshod and lackadaisical. In many cases where our work culture has deteriorated, shortsighted government policies share a good part of the blame.

Welfare without work erodes the spirit and the sense of self-worth of the recipient. And it conditions the children of nonworking parents to an indolent and unproductive life. Hardworking parents raise hardworking kids; we should recognize that the opposite is also true. The influence of the work habits of our parents and other adults around us as we grow up has lasting impact.

Despite all the evidence of their harm, advocates and politicians continue to promote safety-net policies that strip out the requirement for work—and too often they are succeeding. During my tenure in the Massachusetts statehouse, the majority of people on welfare qualified for an exemption from the state's work mandate. For example, welfare recipients with a child two years old or younger were exempted. Before you applaud that policy, think of the incentive that creates for having an out-of-wedlock child.

One of the largest groups receiving government support was for those with disabilities. While people with incapacitating disabilities shouldn't be required to work, abuse of that exemption and outright fraud is not uncommon.

When the Merrimack River overflowed its banks and flooded a large trailer park, I stopped by the motel where the park's evacuees were temporarily housed to make sure they were well cared for and to assure them that the state would help them get on their feet again. As we gathered in the motel lobby, I went around the room asking people about their personal circumstances, and to my surprise, most reported that they were on disability. One fellow complained that he had lost three cars in the flood—automobiles that he was restoring in his driveway. It was not the right moment to ask him, but I certainly would have been fascinated to know how he was physically able to repair cars but not to work at a job—any job. There are plausible answers, of course, and some of those in the room may have had health conditions I couldn't see, but most appeared to be healthy and able-bodied.

Back at my office, I learned that disability exemptions regularly followed diagnoses of conditions like chronic back pain or mental distress—conditions that can lend to malingering and abuse of the system. Proving deceit in those kinds of cases was difficult, but occasionally the cheaters themselves inadvertently assisted the fraud investigators—as happened when a city worker who had been on disability for some time was pictured in the newspaper for winning a bodybuilding contest.

My administration proposed programs such as child care and training for single parents of young children, which were designed to get people who were on welfare or disability back to work. The legislature turned us down, intimating that we were heartless. But what's truly heartless is to deny someone the dignity of work. Because my proposed program was built on training and child care, it would have actually cost the state more than simply keeping people on welfare—it wasn't cost savings we were looking for. We wanted to help save people from a culture of indolence and an endless cycle of poverty.

In some cases, even the conditions in the workplace can affect our culture of hard work. Many years ago, I toured an American Motors assembly plant in Kenosha, Wisconsin, with one of the plant's managers. When we neared a group of two hundred or so workers who were punching out for the day, the manager stopped and waited for them to disperse before we continued. When I asked why he was reluctant to walk through the assembled workers, he said, "Because we would be hurt." I couldn't believe it, but he insisted that it really would be dangerous.

American Motors was on the ropes at the time, and rather than pull together in an effort to turn things around, some employees considered management to be the enemy. Without question, that sentiment was translated into sloppy workmanship, poor concentration on the job, and at times even vindictiveness—a dealership once discovered that a rattle in a car door was caused by a tool a worker had placed inside it. This was not the American Motors that my dad helped build with a dedicated group of autoworkers. Over the years, the workplace had become a battle zone, and the consequences were that everyone lost—shareholders, managers, workers, and consumers.

Whenever an us-versus-them attitude pervades an enterprise, resentment and disengagement are the inevitable result, and workers lose the sense of commonality of purpose with their employer. This in turn can lead to enterprise-penalizing work rules and excessive demands that threaten the viability of the company.

At American Motors before my dad became CEO, for example, the workers had set up a barbershop in the men's room, run by company employees, on company time. The ladies' room was being used as a part-time restaurant, preparing breakfast for workers and take-out dinners for home. When my father headed the company, he had a private meeting with Walter Reuther, then the head of the UAW, about the direction of the labor movement. During their conversation, Reuther candidly admitted that "doing less and less work for more and more money is a dead-end street." With the financial collapse of Chrysler and General Motors in 2009, his words finally proved true. My dad and Reuther were somewhat famous antagonists, but neither disrespected the other, and both were convinced of the necessity of hard work to sustain a growing enterprise.

Not all unions adopt counterproductive attitudes. The United Brotherhood of Carpenters, for example, works hard to instill pride and professionalism in its membership, and provides extensive training aimed at making its members more productive. And it remains true that in some cases, unions are a necessary check on excessively demanding, insensitive, or thoughtless employers.

Poor corporate management and excessive CEO compensation are capable of causing the kind of worker resentment that undermines hard, smart, effective work. While governor, I met with union workers at a plant in western Massachusetts that manufactured socket sets. These workers had been informed by their management that they had to agree to a pay cut or the facility would be closed. The union leaders understood that it was in their best interest to agree to the cuts rather than risk unemployment in a weak job market. But the fact that the company's CEO had received a reported $20 million bonus the prior year outraged these workers as it would have me had I been in their shoes. It was all they could talk about. The rank and file simply wouldn't surrender a large share of their wages when the CEO had been so selfish. In the end, the workers refused to give in, and the plant was closed—and the cost of management excess fell on the workforce.

In my experience, most successful corporate managers, on the other hand, have a way with people and demonstrate their concern and appreciation for their employees. For many years, as a friend and as a Marriott International board member, I've watched J. W. "Bill" Marriott lead his company. He personally visits as many as 250 hotels a year and knows a remarkable number of his longest-serving employees by name—and not just hotel managers, but doormen, telephone operators, and cleaning staff as well. He doesn't just call them associates, he *considers* them such, and among the company's corporate management ranks are people who began their Marriott careers as hourly workers. The company is regularly ranked high on the lists of best places to work, best places for the disabled to work, and best places for minorities to work. These awards, though earned and richly deserved, may be less telling about the company than the experience and reviews of its customers. I'm a bit biased, of course, but I stay in a range of hotels, and Marriott people simply seem more attentive to the guests than do most of their competitors.

Across the workplace spectrum, if America is going to continue to lead the world, we must reinvigorate our national work ethic. Government safety-net programs must be reshaped to reward work if we are to help make every person a productive citizen. Labor leaders and corporate managers need to be evaluated and rewarded at least, in part, on their effectiveness in encouraging teamwork, productivity, and engagement on the job. Let's rate, rank, and publish surveys and assessments of labor leaders and corporate managers based on such criteria. And we need to remind parents that teaching their children to work is even more important than soccer, video games, or music lessons.

Our work ethic has been a critical part of America's success, and our national strength depends in part on retaining this distinct cultural advantage. Stories we hear about the value placed on work and the commonality of purpose of teams of workers in nations like China and Japan are real— and we cannot afford to fall behind.

An Education Culture

Only sixteen years after the Pilgrims arrived at Plymouth and were still enduring terrible hardship, they voted to establish a university. When it opened, the school had an enrollment of nine students and employed only a single faculty member. The institution was later named Harvard in honor of a minister who left it his library and one half of his estate. The rigors of Harvard's early curriculum are evident in the writings of its early graduates like John Adams, who were arguably far more proficient in Latin, modern languages, classical history, political science, and philosophy than are students today.

We continue to esteem education. Bumper stickers proclaim that a child has made the honor roll. Window decals note a son or daughter's attendance at a respected college or university; and caps and sweatshirts you see parents proudly wear are often reminders that they have sacrificed a great deal to ensure that their children are able to attend the best schools possible.

Parents accurately believe that the more education their children receive, the better their lifelong opportunities.

In addition to the failures in schools and homes I described in Chapter 8, the weakening of America's *education culture* also contributes to the deterioration of our educational standing and excellence. Many of America's chronically poor believe that education *doesn't* make a difference. New generations come of age presuming that their lives will mirror those of their parents—with welfare, crime, and menial jobs as a way of life. They believe that education cannot alter those realities. Among immigrants, however, there characteristically has been a far greater appreciation of education. In fact, it's often been the concern for a child's educational opportunity that has led immigrant families to America. I think many people are surprised when they look at the *Boston Globe*'s annual profile of each year's valedictorians from our high schools: almost one quarter were born outside the United States.

In some cases, however, new immigrants fail to understand or appreciate the critical role education plays in the lives of their children in this country. Some don't know what colleges and universities actually do, and others even fail to see why high school is important. In their home countries, manual labor may have been the only provident path to secure a decent life, and people believed that the sooner you went to work, the better.

Among some chronically poor young people, there is an even more troubling development. While parents may encourage their children to study and achieve, friends or gang members may belittle these children for being studious. In these situations, education is not just underappreciated, it is disparaged, and though this attitude is far from pervasive, destructive behaviors and ideas do have a way of spreading.

As governor, I proposed a Parental Preparation Program in Massachusetts for every underperforming school district. In order for parents in these districts to enroll their children in public school, the parents would have been required to attend classes themselves, where they would learn about the value of education as well as ways in which they could support their children's educational experience. The American Civil Liberties Union objected to the proposal—which convinced me I was on to something.

From classes designed to change parental attitudes to sermons in churches and conversations at family dinner tables, we must all make a renewed and active effort to expand our education culture. If we don't, we risk wasting precious young lives and the diminishment of our nation.

Risk and Its Rewards

More than any other people in the world, Americans accept risk in order to venture for reward. We're a nation of entrepreneurs. Many fail, of course—that's the nature of risk—but a few succeed magnificently. In the late 1970s, in addition to my consulting work at Bain & Company, I was asked to help recruit bright, recently graduated MBAs to join the firm. At the time, Bain was a very attractive place to land for recent business school graduates—we were a cutting-edge company, we paid high starting salaries, and we usually landed the cream of the crop. After a series of interviews with a particularly impressive MBA, we made an offer to the young man. But he confessed that he was leaning toward turning us down in favor of joining a start-up business with a friend from college. I pointed out that if he did, he'd make far less money and be committed to a tiny company that could easily fail. But, in the end, he rejected the bird in the hand we offered him in favor of birds in the bush.

I saw Steve Ballmer twenty-five years later at the home of Microsoft cofounder Bill Gates. He reminded me of my long-ago effort to recruit him. I joked that if he'd taken my offer instead of joining Microsoft, he'd likely be doing pretty well by now. It was a pretty good joke—at the time, Steve was worth an estimated $15 billion.

Most entrepreneurs don't dream of reaching the Microsoft heights. They want to own their own taxi medallion, pizza shop, or automotive repair garage. And when they reach their goals, I suspect that most are as happy as Steve Ballmer, perhaps more so. Taking a risk and succeeding is enormously gratifying, no matter the scale. In fact, many Americans agree that taking a risk and *failing* is more rewarding than never having ventured at all. Remember Teddy Roosevelt's famous assertion: "The credit belongs to the man who is actually in the arena . . . who at the best knows in the end the triumph of high achievement and who at the worst, if he fails, at least he fails while daring greatly, so that his place shall never be with those cold and timid souls who know neither victory nor defeat."

Yet while we esteem risk and opportunity, most of us also harbor a desire for security and stability. As a nation, when we salve our collective need for security by regulating and burdening the risk-taker and heavily taxing the reward they receive for risk and innovation, we deaden the entrepreneurial spirit and imperil the American economic engine. Columnist George Will recounted the warning of the renowned nineteenth-century observer of the American life and the American character, Alexis de Tocqueville. As George Will tells it, he foresaw our government becoming:

> "an immense, tutelary power" determined to take "sole charge of assuring their enjoyment and of watching over their fate." It would be a power "absolute, attentive to detail, regular, provident, and gentle," aiming for our happiness but wanting "to be the only agent and the sole arbiter of that happiness." It would, Tocqueville said, provide people security, anticipate their needs, direct their industries, and divide their inheritances. It would envelop society in "a network of petty regulations—complicated, minute, and uniform." But softly: "It does not break wills; it softens them, bends them, and directs them" until people resemble "a herd of timid and industrious animals, of which the government is the shepherd."

Will was not quoting Tocqueville as a matter of historical curiosity but because what he warned about is almost here.

The monarchists of the eighteenth century found the kind of security Tocqueville described in a "shepherd" king, believing that an all-knowing, all-powerful government was better able to provide for the well-being of the public than could the citizens themselves in an inherently unruly democratic system. But the American revolutionaries disagreed. They held faith in the individual, not only as a voter, but as a responsible actor in all aspects of life. For them, guaranteeing that people could pursue happiness according to their own dictates was not just good politics, it was good economics. And they have been proven correct.

Today's monarchists-in-spirit—those people who envision massive government control of virtually every aspect of our lives—are relentless. The economic crisis that befell the nation beginning in the fall of 2008 was just another opening in their endless campaign to promote their agenda, to play on public fears and the resentment of the successful, and to amass to government—and thus often to themselves—the power they could not win in a free economy. If allowed to go far enough, these modern-day neo-monarchists could replace our culture of opportunity with a culture of dependency. The consequence of a cultural shift of that magnitude would take decades to recognize, but it would ultimately be catastrophic for our national prosperity and strength.

Belief and Purpose

Americans are a religious people. According to a 2006 Harris poll, 73 percent of us believe in a Supreme Being, more than twice the percent of believers in either the United Kingdom or France. In a 2009 *Newsweek* poll, almost 90 percent of respondents said they believed in a "spiritual being," and 78 percent said that prayer was an important part of their daily life—larger percentages by far than any other developed nation. Per capita, Americans donate more of their resources to churches than the French donate to churches, universities, and all other charities combined. Our founding document, the Declaration of Independence, cites the role of the Almighty in validating our revolutionary course, and our currency declares our trust in God.

Not all Americans believe in a Creator, yet in my experience, even most of those who don't nevertheless believe in a purpose greater than ourselves—perhaps our family, our community, or the nation itself. People who have purpose in their lives are more willing to sacrifice for others, and many choose service over personal comforts, often in ways that strengthen our nation. People with purpose-driven lives invest in activities that often have lasting and beneficial impact on the society as a whole. When people raise children, promote their education, endow them with enduring values, and set them on a productive life course, the nation as a whole is the beneficiary. The same is true for those who volunteer as scoutmasters, coaches, teachers' aides, and mentors.

It is of particular value to the nation when men and women volunteer to serve in the military. Those who have served in any of the uniforms of the United States military have sacrificed for a cause greater than themselves, and they are heroes. As a boy, Bill McCaffrey was my hero. The son of a neighbor who lived just down the street and brother to my best friend, Bill was handsome, humorous, smart, and athletic—he played end on West Point's football team and was its undefeated heavyweight boxing champ. Rather than join his dad's highly successful business, he served for twenty years in the army, often away from his wife and four children on long tours of duty, undoubtedly missing baptisms and birthdays. He was laid to rest in 2006, surrounded by family and framed by medals of honor from his country.

For other men and women in the military, the sacrifice that Providence requires of them is even greater. When Ann and I were given a tour of the Walter Reed Army Medical Center in 2007, we were ushered into a large hall where combat amputees were being given occupational therapy, learning how to care for themselves without the use of one or more limbs. One soldier, originally from a farm in Iowa, had lost both arms. Ann had to quietly step out into the hall, as her tears were not what the soldier needed.

I have also visited the new home of Peter Damon in Massachusetts. An Army National Guard sergeant, he, too, had lost both arms in combat in Iraq. Few of us even consider the reality of such injuries throughout an entire lifetime by men and women like Peter. A group called Homes for our Troops had constructed the home for him and his wife, specifically adapting it to his now-limited capabilities. Previously, Peter had attended my State of the State address in the Capitol. When he was introduced, the legislators and audience erupted in cheers and an ovation that lasted over ten minutes. The applause was so vigorous that it dislodged a large glass ceiling fixture, causing it to fall to the floor below. We cannot do too much to honor our men and women in uniform, even when it causes fixtures to fall. The heroic members of our military protect America and allow it to continue to be the power and force for good in the world that it is.

America has many heroes, including many whose service is quiet, private, and primarily devoted to family. We all know these heroes. My sister Lynn raised eight terrific kids, one of whom has Down's syndrome. Jeffrey is now almost forty, and his mother still cares for him at home. My uncle Miles worked hard in construction throughout his life to help pay debts that his father, my grandfather, left behind when he died. My mother Lenore often took troubled kids into our home, trying to love them back onto the right track—and sometimes she succeeded. My cousin Joan took in more than fifty foster children during her lifetime. What's remarkable about America is that so many heroes surround us—and the vast majority of them are not rich, famous, or athletic. Most are ordinary Americans by almost every measure except their willingness to surrender self for service, and in doing so they make us a stronger and a better nation.

There was a time when many worried out loud that we would lose this American commitment to service. The celebration of the "Me Generation," the advent of the sexual revolution, and the emergence of the drug culture startled my parents' generation and persuaded some that a new culture of selfishness was rising. But for the most part, that generation of 1960s-era rebels became service-oriented citizens. Some of the battles of the sixties still linger, however, as with the current push to legalize marijuana, which reflects the passion and zeal of those members of the pleasure-seeking generation that never grew up. Their arguments are elaborate but empty—a great nation has never been built on hedonism.

Faith, purpose greater than self, and willingness to sacrifice are part of what makes America, America.

My Country 'Tis of Thee

We love our country. At the completion of the Olympic Winter Games in Salt Lake City in 2002, former vice president Dick Cheney attended the Closing Ceremonies. He asked me to choose one American athlete to join him in the president's box, someone who would represent all our athletes. I chose Derek Para.

Derek is an Hispanic American, born and raised in Los Angeles. As a young man, he became an accomplished in-line skater, successfully winning many competitions. With news that the Winter Olympics were coming to the United States, one of Derek's teammates suggested that he take up speed skating. Derek had never skated on ice before, but in-line skating wasn't an Olympic event, and he wanted to compete.

Speed skating is a sport that's usually dominated by strapping young men and women from northern climes—Johann Olav Koss of Norway, Eric Heiden of Minnesota, and Dan Jansen and Bonnie Blair of Wisconsin are its Olympic legends. Derek, on the other hand, is five feet four inches tall and slightly built. He was also utterly inexperienced at skating. Nevertheless, he began to train and prepared to face the best skaters in America. Lots of heads were shaking when Derek made the U.S. Olympic team, yet in the 500-meter event in Salt Lake City, he won a silver medal. A day later, he broke the world record in the 1,000-meter event, winning a *gold* medal.

As Derek walked into the box at Closing Ceremonies, I asked him what had been the most memorable part of his Olympics. "What I will never forget," he explained, "was carrying the American flag that had flown above the World Trade Center on September 11, 2001, into the Opening Ceremonies."

Derek had been one of eight U.S. athletes chosen by their teammates to carry that most symbolic of American flags. Because it was tattered and burned, it could not be raised and flown from a pole, but had to be held horizontally.

Derek explained that when the flag was introduced—"Ladies and gentlemen, the flag that flew above the World Trade Center on September 11 is now entering the stadium"—he expected the audience to erupt in cheers. Instead, total silence. Complete reverence. They carried the flag to a position in front of the Mormon Tabernacle Choir, which then sang our national anthem.

"It was hard holding on to my emotions as they sang *that* song and as I was holding *that* flag," Derek said. "But then, the choir did something I hadn't expected. They sang a reprise of the last line—'O, say does that star-spangled banner yet wave/O'er the land of the free and the home of the brave?'—and just as they did, a gust of wind filled the flag, and lifted it in our hands.

"For me," Derek continued, "it was as if all those who had died for America's liberty had just blown into the flag—and the tears began to run down my face." As Derek related his experience to me, tears welled in my eyes as well.

I remembered some months before, hearing Mike Eruzione—the captain of the famed "Miracle on Ice" Olympic hockey team—describe to an audience his experiences at the 1980 Winter Games in Lake Placid, New York. His most memorable experience, he said, was not scoring the winning goal that beat the Russian team or winning the gold-medal game against

the Finnish team. "It was carrying the American flag into Opening Ceremonies, representing the nation that is the greatest country on earth," he
said. The audience burst into applause.

At an event in Utah leading up to the Olympics, I learned from an
elementary-school teacher that Americans are the only people in the world
who place their hand over their hearts when their national anthem is played,
and so I paid particular attention to the medals ceremonies to see if that really was the case. Every gold medalist stood tall and immensely proud as his
or her nation's flag was raised and the national anthem was played, but what
I had been told held true throughout the ceremonies: Only the American
gold-medal winners held their hands over their hearts.

I believe that we instinctively place our hand over our hearts in memory of those who shed their blood for America. It is fitting that we do so
during the playing of "The Star-Spangled Banner," as that song—written
during battle in the War of 1812—commemorates the sacrifice that won
our liberty.

Former education secretary Bill Bennett has reported in his books and
on his radio program that American schools are failing to teach our children about America's greatness. America's contribution to liberty around
the world and our past and present sacrifice in treasure and life is simply
not taught as it once was. While every child rightly has been instructed in
the heroes of social movements, Bennett has observed, very few are taught
of the patriots of the wars fought for freedom, particularly those of the
twentieth century. Instead, he explains, some educators are smitten with a
devotion to multiculturalism, not merely as an appreciation of the cultures
and customs of other peoples, but out of a conviction that no single system
of values is superior to another, including our own. This reorientation away
from a celebration of American exceptionalism is misguided and bankrupt.

National testing bears out Secretary Bennett's concern. Among eighth
graders, for example, only 1 percent were able to explain how the fall of the
Berlin Wall affected foreign policy. Think about that: fully 99 percent of
America's eighth graders didn't understand why President Reagan made
the bold call to tear the wall down, didn't understand what life had been
like behind the Iron Curtain, and didn't appreciate the freedom that was
won for hundreds of millions of people, thanks to American resolve in the
face of communism's once limitless ambitions and vast military strength.

Among *seniors* in high school, only 14 percent could offer even one reason for America's involvement in the Korean War, yet 67 percent could identify an "important idea" stemming from President Johnson's Great Society programs. Orlando Sanchez, formerly a mayoral candidate in Houston, Texas, recounted that when he came to America in 1962, his schoolteachers taught him things that made him a patriot. But today, he said, millions of immigrants are given little if any appreciation for America's greatness. And it is not just immigrants from foreign shores; it is native-born children as well. My young friend Theresa Eaton recounted that in 1990, she had a small American flag patch sewn on her San Francisco high-school backpack, and she was frequently asked by other students why she would do that.

I'm convinced the time has come for American schools to once again systematically teach our children about the heroes of the battles that won our freedom and about the heroes that fought in the wars that gained liberty for millions of people around the world. The multiculturalism movement must be unmasked for the fraud that it is. There *are* superior cultures, and ours is one of them. As David Landes observed, "Culture makes all the difference."

The Respect for Life

There are cultures where life is cheap, but thankfully, ours is not one of them. The marines' pledge to "leave no soldier behind" is emblematic of our entire military's common commitment to their brothers and sisters in arms. Who can forget the heroism of posthumous Medal of Honor recipients Gary Gordon and Randy Shughart, army snipers in Somalia in 1993, who insisted on being lowered to the wreckage of a Blackhawk helicopter in an effort to save the lives of four of their fellow soldiers? Ours is a far cry from the kind of culture in which strapping on a bomb and blowing up a bus filled with schoolchildren is considered an act of honor.

We have long respected life, at its beginning and at its end. In part, this is the product of our Judeo-Christian heritage, which teaches that we are created in the image of God. And while almost all Americans profess respect for life, the subject of abortion has been a difficult issue for our country, for a variety of reasons. The debate over abortion puts two of our fundamental values in conflict: our respect for life and our love of personal freedom. Arguments in support of abortion generally revolve around the right of a mother to make decisions about her own body. But in any decision about whether to end a pregnancy, we must remember that *two* lives are involved, and on this point, courts have been long and conspicuously silent. Because the fact is that two lives, not one, are involved, I am unapologetically pro-life. Both mother and child are human beings, but only one does not yet have a voice to defend itself.

There are, of course, heartfelt and passionate convictions on both sides of the abortion question. Many women considering abortions face terrible pressures, hurts, and fears, and we should come to their aid with all the resourcefulness and empathy we can offer. At the same time, the starting point should be the innocence and vulnerability of the child waiting to be born. For all the conflicting views on this issue, it speaks well of our country that we recognize abortion as a problem. The law may call it a right, but no one ever called it *good*, and in the quiet of conscience, people of both political parties know that more than a million abortions a year cannot be squared with the good heart of America.

It Takes a Family

Consistent with our European religious heritage, ever since the founding of the nation, most Americans have expected men and women to marry and raise children. They also recognized that a number of circumstances could alter the typical pattern, as with divorce, the death of a spouse, or personal considerations.

Regardless of what one's moral or religious beliefs may be about marriage, most will admit that the societal benefits of a marriage commitment between a man and a woman are well documented. Two parents are more able than one to raise, nurture, and financially provide for their children. The traditional family unit promotes economic productivity and enhances the opportunities of succeeding generations. Marriage and family are good for America.

If marriage remains in ruins among African Americans, we risk that they become a permanent underclass. If other ethnic minorities follow the same downhill path, they could suffer the same tragic outcome. And what of the nation? If marriage and family persist in a weakened state, or continue their decline, it is hard to imagine that we can remain the world's leader. We cannot lead the family of nations if we fail the family here at home.

These conclusions are neither new, nor are they exclusive to conservatives. Thirty years ago, New York senator Daniel Patrick Moynihan, a giant among liberals who was also respected across the aisle, predicted the same calamities. In the 1960s, when the War on Poverty was launched, 7 percent of American children were born out of wedlock. Today, almost *40 percent* of our children are born to unwed mothers. As noted earlier, among African Americans, that figure is almost *70 percent*, a deep concern to almost every African American pastor I know. The collapse of marriage and the resultant epidemic of out-of-wedlock births may be America's most critical social problem. More than that, it's a human tragedy. Compared with children living with married parents, children living with single mothers are ten times more likely to be physically abused, five times more likely to be poor, three times more likely to use cocaine, twice as likely to end up in jail, and twice as likely to be in the bottom half of their class at school and to suffer emotional and behavioral problems. Single mothers themselves are twice as likely to be victims of domestic violence.

Of course, most children who are born to out-of-wedlock mothers also grow up in homes without a father. "When fatherless young people are encouraged to write about their lives," writes author and National Public Radio and Fox news analyst Juan Williams, "they tell heartbreaking stories about feeling like 'throwaway people.'" Best-selling author Walter Dean Myers says that this is because "they don't have a father to push them, discipline them, and they give up trying to succeed . . . they don't see themselves as wanted."

We have failed to take even the most elementary steps to reduce out-of-wedlock birth. Several years ago, my wife Ann volunteered to teach one day a week at the Mother Caroline Academy, an inner-city school for at-risk girls in Boston. The school was founded by two dynamic nuns who were intent on providing not just a good education but also good values. One day, in Ann's class of about twenty fifth graders, Ann asked how many of them wanted to go to college. Almost every girl raised her hand. Then she asked,

"How many of you want to have a baby before you graduate from high school?" And again, almost every hand went up. She was stunned, as was I when she related the experience to me. But then we realized that we should not have been so surprised; because virtually every one of the girls came from a single-parent home, they didn't know anything else. They had never learned that attempting to combine college with teenage motherhood would be all but impossible, or that marriage would provide an enormous advantage for them and their children. Ann and the other teachers at the academy sought to teach those lessons and reinforce those crucial messages, but for millions of girls and boys, that message is never received, because it is never even taught.

In fact, today, our government's policies often send the opposite message. If a girl and boy with no income fall in love and have a baby, they receive significantly more money from the government if they *do not* marry than if they do. Our safety-net programs inexplicably have been designed to penalize marriage, and as a result, for low-income parents, getting married typically means receiving fewer or no food stamps, welfare, subsidized housing, or Medicaid benefits. These benefits are linked to household income, and if the mother and father marry, they must report their combined level of income, which often disqualifies them from benefits. Think of the message that gives to a young mom: If she marries, she and her child will have less on which to live. What a terrible choice.

Most out-of-wedlock births are not accidental. By a wide percentage, the mothers are intent on having a child, so increasing the availability of birth control does not even remotely address the issue. In fact, only 1 percent of low-income single mothers report that they did not have adequate access to contraceptives. We are simply failing to help prospective parents make the best decision—to marry first, establish a household, and begin a family thereafter.

Given the dire consequences for the nation and the heart-wrenching implications for children, why has no alarm been sounded and no emergency measures enacted to staunch this grave crisis? To some degree, it results from our entirely appropriate reluctance to censure single parents and their children or to be indifferent to the burdens they are carrying. Most often, these are wonderful, even heroic people. Many single moms made the choice to bring their child into the world rather than to abort it. Many make enormous personal sacrifices to provide for their children. And it is true, of course, that many single parents are extremely successful providers and examples for their children, and that their children have achieved great things. Almost all of us know more than a few of such people. My sister Jane was left alone to raise her four children, and they are all now happily married with accomplished children of their own. But such successes, while they can inspire us and encourage other single parents, should not mask the tragic implications for so many others. The societal and human toll is too high to pretend that it doesn't matter if a child has a mom and a dad in stable marriage. Some single moms are the most adamant about this—they know how hard it has been for them and they do not tolerate those who minimize the hardship they and their children have borne.

I believe there is another reason we have failed to act. The disparagement of out-of-wedlock birth is often perceived as racist. But remember, there are more out-of-wedlock births to Anglo mothers than to African American moms. During my campaign for the presidency, every time I drafted a speech that drew attention to out-of-wedlock births, and particularly if I cited ethnic and racial statistics, some of my advisers were concerned that my comments would be taken out of context, twisted, or used to mischaracterize my views. My remarks seldom attracted the criticism my staff feared, but neither did they motivate the change I had hoped for. Author and commentator Hugh Hewitt observed that "many of our media elites are petrified by the subject of the impacts of single parenting on children, a discussion that triggers all sorts of emotions and touches not just a third rail, but often a fourth, fifth, and sixth rail, involving as it does race, gender, sexual orientation, and religion."

The Heritage Foundation concluded in its open letter to Barack Obama, "You now have a unique opportunity and ability to halt this destructive trend and to take the first decisive steps to restore marriage in our society." President Obama is to be commended every time he raises and takes action to remedy this critical challenge. His visible involvement in the lives of his daughters is a quiet affirmation of the role of fathers in the lives of their children.

To reclaim marriage and family, we must begin by telling children and young adults the truth. Strong voices of concern and redirection must come from the president, governors, legislators, community leaders, pastors, and teachers. The issue should be discussed openly and at length in our public schools, and preferably, it should be a part of the standard curriculum. We also should require government-funded birth-control clinics to inform their clients of the advantages of marriage.

We must absolutely remove the marriage penalties from our social safety-net programs. My personal preference would be to include the income of both parents in the calculation of eligibility for government benefits, regardless of whether they are married or living together or not. Under this approach, every father would also be required to help support his child, regardless of his marital status. Requiring fathers to behave responsibly would encourage marriage and sharply reduce out-of-wedlock births, and at least partly, it would curb some predatory behavior by men and young men. Single men might not attempt so many sexual conquests if they knew that the government would require them to pay support for any child that their exploits brought into the world.

Due to the decisions of a few state courts and legislatures over the past few years, the discussion of marriage in America has tended to focus on same-sex relationships. Proponents of same-sex marriage have attempted to characterize its opponents as being universally antigay. That has sometimes been an effective campaign tactic, but it is untrue. And because most Americans know it is untrue, same-sex marriage has repeatedly been rejected by voters. For me and for many others, opposition to same-sex marriage stems from the strong conviction that the ideal setting in which to raise a child is in a home with both a mother and a father. Regardless of whether one's opposition to same-sex marriage is rooted in religious beliefs, moral convictions, or societal considerations, the marriage relationship has been the cornerstone of the institution of family since the beginning of time. Marriage is not just a quaint social custom. It is critical for the well-being of our children and therefore fundamental to the future strength of the nation. It's time for us to recognize its critical role and finally act to preserve it as the institution that nurtures and protects our next generations.

Honor, Law, and Constitution

A brilliant scholar and university professor told me that from his studies, he had concluded that differences in economic success between countries resulted from the willingness of their citizens to honor their word. From a very young age, we are taught that "your word is your bond." Family honor and the value of a good name are among our highest possessions. When my father left Utah to head east to marry and to begin his career, he took his own father to the cemetery where his mother was buried. "Dad," he said, "this is as close as I can get to you and Mom in mortality. I want you to know that I will never do anything that would dishonor your name."

Our estimation of personal honor extends to our respect for the law. Adherence to the law transcends our passions, even when they flow from our sense of justice and right. Despite the public clamor and outrage, the British soldiers who fired on Americans in the Boston Massacre of 1770 were freed by an American court of law.

At the commencement of the Revolution, the Founding Fathers labored to set forth its legal foundation. The declaration was a good deal more than a notice of intent—it was a rigorously reasoned justification for revolution. The culmination of the Founders' work was the Constitution and Bill of Rights. These set the bounds of conduct upon which the entire society of Americans would establish life and livelihood. And just as with the law at the trial of the Boston Massacre soldiers, the constitution would rise above the passions of the people.

There is a strain of thought among some liberals, however, that advocates lowering the bounds of law and the Constitution in order to accommodate the sentiment and sensibilities about right and wrong held by the elite and wise. They favor justices who will do "what they think is *right*" rather than what they know the law and the Constitution demand. This explains incongruous rulings on abortion and same-sex marriage—they are clearly beyond the contemplation of the Constitution, but well within the sensibilities of select society. This also explains the attempt by some to substitute their preferences for those constitutional guarantees they would rather ignore, as with the Second Amendment right to bear arms. This amendment, like all the others, preserves a principle that is fundamental to the American experience: The individual is sovereign, not the rulers.

Respect for the law will continue as part of our culture only so long as it extends to the entire Constitution. When justices breach the bounds of the

Constitution and law, society may choose to follow them, with untold consequences for the national character.

The Demands of Citizenship

At the core of our system of government is an informed, involved, and responsible citizenry. The real peril to the nation if its citizenry fails to meet its duties was recognized by the Founders. John Adams was fearful of pure democracy, in which citizens could direct the affairs of the nation without the participation of office-holders who were elected to promote the public's best interests. In his 1814 letter to John Taylor of Virginia, thirteen years after he left the presidency, Adams wrote:

> Remember, democracy never lasts long. It soon wastes, exhausts, and murders itself. There never was a democracy yet that did not commit suicide. . . . When clear prospects are opened before vanity, pride, avarice, or ambition, for their easy gratification, it is hard for the most considerate philosophers and the most conscientious moralists to resist the temptation. Individuals have conquered themselves. Nations and large bodies of men, never.

Adams believed that history proved that such human frailty was a constant, and the shared fear of direct democracy led the Founders to establish a republic. Representatives stood between the people—who could be "hurried away by the torrent of contagious enthusiasm"—and the state. Electors, not the voters themselves, chose the president. Senators were not originally elected by popular vote, but selected by state legislatures. Two conditions were essential for the new Republic to succeed: voters who were informed and responsible in choosing their representatives, and representatives who were committed to rising above the immediate "passions" of the people and to acting in the interest of the entire nation. Failure of the citizens to take their role seriously and elect responsible representatives, or the representatives' willful refusal to seek the good of the nation on the greatest issues, they feared, would result in the democratic suicide of which Adams wrote.

There are places today where voters are probably as well informed and involved as they were in our nation's past. The first two presidential nomination contests take place in Iowa and New Hampshire. During my 2008 campaign, I got to know those states' voters at close hand. One of the best by-products of a presidential campaign is close contact with an amazing variety of Americans—and it never gets closer than it does in Iowa and New Hampshire.

On a very hot weekday afternoon in 2007, I was scheduled to speak and take questions in the loft of a barn in rural central Iowa. When I arrived at the site, it appeared that there would be a lot more pumpkins in the garden than interested voters in the loft. But when I climbed the stairs, I found about two hundred people waiting patiently in the heat to hear my pitch. No one had paid them to come. No one had twisted arms. They came simply to get the measure of one of the ten Republicans running for president. A scene like this one took place several times almost every day during the primary season in both Iowa and New Hampshire.

Candidates are peppered with pointed, no-nonsense questions about matters of policy. I'm asked whether the crowds are tougher in Iowa or in New Hampshire. Both, is my answer. The folks in both states don't put up with wandering or evasive answers. And they have given a good deal of thought to the issues and to the construction of their questions.

On the other end of the spectrum are questions of the zany variety that put me back on my heels, at least for a moment. I remember being asked: "Why don't you just leave Massachusetts and move to New Hampshire like the rest of us?" "Do you believe in UFOs?" "Do you support the secret government plan to unite the United States and Mexico in a single country called 'Americo'?" And, "Has your wife always been that beautiful?" Ann won't forget that one any time soon.

We Bay Staters joke that politics is a blood sport in Massachusetts. Outside Faneuil Hall in Boston prior to my 1994 debate with Ted Kennedy, my vehicle had to be escorted to the building by a phalanx of police motorcycles. As Kennedy signs pummeled my car and the patrolmen did their best to push back the aggressors, my friend Bob White and I broke into laughter. Bob chuckled, "Hey, Mitt, this makes the whole thing worth it!"

Perhaps not everyone is as engaged in politics as the folks in New Hampshire, Iowa, and Massachusetts, but wherever the presidential campaign took me, I found people who cared deeply about the country and its future. It's important that Americans retain their interest and involvement with the electoral process. For the Republic to function as it must, I believe voters must continually renew their understanding of the critical role they play, take the time to learn about pressing issues, and judge candidates based on their character, intelligence, relevant experience, and positions on issues. Parents need to instill in their children a sense of civic responsibility, to discuss political questions at the dinner table, and to make sure that their children see them taking the time to inform themselves and to vote. I was always pleased to see young adults and children at my campaign events; if they are introduced to political issues at an early age, they are more likely to be involved and active throughout their lives.

There have, of course, been too many instances where our elected representatives have let us down. Some do so in flagrant and shocking ways—sex scandals, cash in the freezer, or the Massachusetts state senator who was filmed stuffing cash into her underwear.

Others succumb to less obvious failings. One of those is policy making by poll. In a republic, we count on our leaders to represent the best interests of the people, not to count noses. When that is what they do, they subject the republic to the hazard of a government driven by the fleeting passions of a majority, as John Adams foresaw.

Soon after I became governor, I realized that a politician who seeks popularity and high approval ratings can achieve them by slavishly agreeing with public opinion and by actually *doing* very little. In my case, politics was a departure from my career, not a continuation of it. My reading of history had given me a profound appreciation for the sacrifices made by the Founders. I felt then as I do now that it is an enormous challenge to live up to their example. That challenge is also a useful guide for conduct in office, particularly as a defense against the temptation to take the easy, popular path when short-term political advantage may be gained by doing so. I have tried always to be more interested in making a difference than in making a hit in the polls. Beth Myers, my chief of staff while I was governor and still a trusted adviser, joked that sometimes it seemed as if we did unpopular things on purpose. In my first months on the job, as the state faced a multi-billion dollar crisis, I sought and obtained emergency power to cut the amount of state aid given to localities. Cutting funding to 351 cities and towns guaranteed outrage from mayors as well as local newspapers. Any cut at any school—whether in music, football, or art—was attributed to me rather than to the ruinous fiscal policies of the past. That's just the price of admission to leadership.

At the national level, politicians occasionally succumb to the temptations of populism, especially when the economy is troubled and people are understandably fearful, hurting, and angry. The shouts for action come from both the left and the right—calls to protect jobs from foreign goods, claims that immigrants are taking away our jobs, and charges that our problems are the fault of the rich and powerful. When President Franklin Roosevelt failed to restore the national economy during his first term in office, his reelection campaign asserted that the problems were caused by the wealthy and by the corporations. In the wake of the 2008 financial collapse, anti-CEO sentiment in America grew extraordinarily high. President Obama added fuel to that fire by castigating companies for holding sales and management meetings in resorts and high-end hotels. His rhetoric certainly scored points, but it also pushed hundreds of companies to cancel meetings, costing the jobs or incomes of thousands of hotel, airline, and hospitality employees. The human consequences of playing to the crowd can be high.

Policy by polls is one problem, but policy by campaign contributions is an even bigger one. Campaigns have become enormously expensive. Barack Obama's presidential campaign spent at least $750 million in securing his victory. When candidate Obama broke his pledge to abide by the post-Watergate practice of accepting public funding and spending limits, he effectively ended that practice for all future presidential campaigns. The media, enamored with Barack Obama, barely blinked. But his abandonment of his promise now means that money and campaign contributions will have a far greater role in national politics.

When I ran for the U.S. Senate in 1994, I worked hard to raise the millions I would need. My father spent six months at our Massachusetts home, helping on the campaign. Recall that my dad was one of the most successful politicians of his era; he was a realist about the need to raise money to fund campaigns. But after seeing how much time I had to spend fund-raising, he was convinced that the system made no sense at all. In his race for governor of Michigan in 1962, he explained, his finance chairman, Max Fisher, raised all the money they would need in a single night. Fifteen or twenty people were invited to an event, Max made his pitch, and no one left the room until the campaign had what it needed—each check probably totaling $25,000 or more. Dad was then able to campaign across Michigan, from the Upper Peninsula to the border with Ohio, without having to be holed up in hotel rooms dialing for dollars.

I asked Dad whether accepting large contributions encouraged corruption; surely the contributors wanted something in return. He replied that not once during his three terms in office did one of his contributors ask for a favor. They were some of Michigan's most prominent and successful citizens, and instead of favors, they were looking for good government. I'm not defending the old system; I'm sure it had its share of abuses. But so does the current one.

Although the amount an individual can contribute in federal and many state races is now limited, contributions do in fact play an even greater role in influencing policy than they did in the past. Today the people who can raise money are even more important to a politician than the people who once could write big checks. And because campaign budgets are far bigger, the obligations are bigger as well.

In the post McCain-Feingold world of campaign finance, union CEOs have become the 800-pound gorillas. They can amass funds from the dues of their members—who number in the millions, in some cases—and then spend the money on the candidates or cause of their choice. In some Democratic Party primaries, it's virtually impossible to defeat a candidate who is backed by organized labor. No other type of organization I know of is allowed to collect political funds in the way that unions do.

Unions have an important role to play. They must defend the interests of their members. But the political power of organized labor has gone beyond the bounds of responsible measurement. The costs to the country are large. Union pension obligations will bankrupt states and cities. The demands of teachers' unions block essential education reforms. And the sway of private sector unions causes political leaders to sacrifice the interests of the nation for the interests of the few, as with the president's decision to restrict foreign tires and to deny Colombia favored trade status.

Our current campaign finance laws let politicians off the hook. In the past, campaigns themselves received and spent the lion's share of the contributions made on their behalf. But under campaign finance reform, contributors are limited to $2,400 to an individual campaign, while they are permitted to donate unlimited amounts to so-called independent expenditure committees. What this means is that the big money now isn't controlled by an individual campaign or candidate, but rather by an "independent" group. Ugly attack ads can readily be launched by the independent committee and the candidate can wash his hands of any responsibility. Campaign finance reform didn't get money out of politics. It simply made that money less transparent and more difficult to trace, strengthened the hand of union bosses, and put financiers and ideologues like George Soros in the driver's seat of many contests.

I wish there were a good, workable way to utterly remove the influence of money from politics. Instead of the current laws on the books, I'd much rather let people contribute the full amount they choose to whomever they want and simply require those contributions to be posted on the Internet for everyone to see. No organization—unions included—should be allowed to assess its members or collect dues for political campaigns or causes. Period.

We need a renewed commitment to the First Amendment guarantee of political free speech. When I went to law school more than three decades ago, we didn't discuss campaign finance law; it would have struck everyone as extremely improbable that the incumbents in Washington could write laws that would limit the ability of others to criticize the job they were doing or campaign to replace them. But that is what they have done. The Supreme Court should revisit this ill-advised course.

John Adams and his fellow Founders foresaw the fragility of democracies, and their fears were not unfounded. They had considered the universal experience of people who had ruled themselves throughout history. Today, the failure of some voters to become informed and involved is worrisome. So, too, is the rise of populism and the sway of campaign fund-raisers. Because office-holders are unlikely to vote for an end to the finance system that helps them get reelected, statutes, and regulations are unlikely to remedy the problems. The answer is to promote a strong and renewed commitment to the entirety of America's culture of citizenship. In other words, the best way to encourage voter involvement and political statesmanship is to take steps to encourage hard work, risk-taking, love of country, sacrifice, integrity, and education—the foundation of American culture. The more our fellow citizens work, invest, sacrifice, and devote themselves to their families and their country, the more they will inherently care about who they elect to office and the laws and programs their representatives formulate while they are in office.

The best way to heal our politics is to strengthen our commitment to bedrock American values and to defend those values every day in the public square.

American Destiny

There is a current of opinion flowing among some of our elected leaders and popular icons that seeks to diminish the accomplishments and greatness of our collective culture. It is manifest in legislation that would reduce our work ethic by removing work requirements from welfare. It threatens risk-taking and opportunity with confiscatory taxes and income redistribution. Our love of family and our appreciation of its central role in society are worn down by the blithe acceptance of out-of-wedlock births. Expressions of patriotism and national pride take a backseat to incessant national fault-finding, and rather than recognize our national morality and goodness, some are inclined to apologize for America. I do not see this as a vast left-wing conspiracy, but I do see this as ominous and potentially ruinous if allowed to course unchecked. The danger of national demoralization and consequent decline is why we must mount a bold and effective plan to protect and strengthen our culture of citizenship—with no apology to those who deride our mission.

Despite the attack on our values, I am optimistic about America's future because I've seen the heart of the American people. It's easy to become pessimistic when we're bombarded with media reports of the aberrant and the abhorrent, but we can learn more about our fellow citizens on the street than on the screen. My decades in business, charitable, religious, and public life—and my visits to every state but one—have convinced me that the American people are inherently good, and that America is destined to remain great.

In May 2006, I was invited by the Department of Defense to go to Iraq and Afghanistan to visit the members of the Massachusetts National Guard who were stationed there. I made the trip with Governor Matt Blunt of Missouri and Governor Brian Schweitzer of Montana. We departed from Washington, D.C., refueled in Iceland, and landed in Kuwait, where men and women of the Massachusetts National Guard were stationed at an airbase, flying and maintaining a fleet of helicopters—one of which had been hit by small arms fire on a mission a few days before. The temperature on the tarmac was over 110 degrees—and we were assured that the *hot* summer weather was still to come.

We flew on to Baghdad aboard a Hercules C-130, wearing protective vests and sitting knee to knee with soldiers on their way to combat duty. The airplane's crew kept a constant lookout for incoming missiles, making a trip that was just another day at the office for them but that was eye-opening for a first-time visitor to the theater like me. From Baghdad, we flew by helicopter to a number of different bases, and at every stop, each governor met with guard members from his state. We repeated similar stops in Afghanistan a few days later.

Along the way, I asked the Massachusetts guard members if any of them wanted me to call their spouse or family when I got home. I knew they could call or e-mail themselves, but I thought perhaps they might want me to report home that they looked fine and were faring well. I asked those who wanted me to place a call on their behalf to write their name and home number on a piece of paper; by the time we departed, I had collected sixty-three phone numbers. My plan was to make a few calls every day over the next couple of weeks.

I returned home on Memorial Day, which I had planned to spend with Ann and our kids and grandkids at Lake Winnipesaukee in New Hampshire. But first I decided to make just a few of those calls. After I'd placed only two or three, a guardsman's wife answered and said, "Oh, Governor Romney, I thought it might be you calling." She explained that after I had contacted the first of the wives on my list, she had e-mailed her husband about it, and he in turn had e-mailed his buddies in Iraq and Afghanistan, telling them to let their wives know to expect my call. The dynamic of instant communication combined with extraordinary closeness of military families with deployed loved ones had kicked in.

So I realized that sixty-three spouses and families would be waiting, so I placed sixty-three calls to Massachusetts homes that Memorial Day.

I was deeply moved by what people said to me. Remember, May 2006 was a bleak time in the Iraq War. We were suffering a terrible number of casualties. The Iraqis appeared unwilling to come together as a nation. And the "surge" that would ultimately prove so successful had not yet been implemented. At home, many pundits and politicians alike had thrown in the towel. These people with whom I spoke weren't likely to be hearing congratulations and words of thanks from their neighbors. And I presumed that almost all of them would ask me why their soldier couldn't come home—*now*.

Yet in sixty-three calls, I did not hear a single complaint. Not one. And each time I expressed gratitude on behalf of our nation for the service and sacrifice of their family member and themselves, virtually everyone told me that it was an honor to be able to sacrifice for America and to serve the nation that is the hope of the earth. Many calls left me with tears in my eyes. It was, without question, the most memorable Memorial Day I have ever spent.

There is nobility in the hearts of Americans like these—and in all Americans. What makes this nation great is her people—not our government, not even our "spacious skies" and "amber waves of grain." I suggest without apology that if we strengthen the American people, America will meet its destiny for greatness for centuries to come.

11

America the Beautiful

When John Adams doggedly worked his way through the grand capitals of Europe in pursuit of loans for our fledgling republic, he could not have imagined that in only a few generations, it would be America that would rescue Europe. In some ways, our nation's ascent has been wholly improbable: our founding was based on a war nearly lost, a set of Articles of Confederation that failed, a Constitution that was barely ratified, and a second war with Great Britain that went badly. Less than a century later, we succumbed to a "great civil war, testing whether that nation, or any nation so conceived and so dedicated, can long endure." The war claimed more than 600,000 lives.

But endure we did. And not merely endure but rise to a greatness and goodness never before seen in human history. Our beneficent geography and natural resources deserve a share of the credit, but it was the geography of the American heart that brought us to the heights to which we have risen.

In times of turmoil, anxiety often clouds the larger view. The current recession's agonizing unemployment and its destruction of great amounts of our wealth and savings have blinded some to our great achievements and to our unquestioned ability to rise again to even greater heights of prosperity, leading the world to the same end. Our standard of living still exceeds that of almost every developed nation. Our individual ability to rise above humble beginnings and make what we want of our lives causes people around the globe to marvel. Our innovative spirit has again transformed the world's largest economy, permitting America to excel in almost every emerging technology. All of these things can and will continue far into the future if we preserve the conditions that nurtured them in the first place.

More important than a clear view of the past is our vision for the future. Conspiring rivals gather economic and military might, hoping to surpass us as the world's most powerful nation and to limit our ability to preserve prosperity and promote freedom. Even as other nations pursue their ambitions to narrow America's lead, some voices both here and abroad welcome the potential for greater balance of international power. If they seek balance with the other liberal democracies like Japan, India, or the European Union, then I stand with them, for the rising strength of all free nations strengthens America. But with few exceptions, the gap in power between the United States and these other democracies is widening, not narrowing. Europe faces debt and entitlement liabilities far greater than our own. Its militaries have been decimated. And with a precipitous drop in population, they are confronted with a demographic night.

China's economy will almost certainly grow larger than ours by the middle of this century. By that time, its military capabilities in the Asian Pacific may exceed all others nations in the region, but they must not exceed ours. Everything the Chinese leadership tells us now is meant to assuage our fears about their ambitions. Their leaders assure us of their desire for a partnership with us that will create world stability and peace. They remind us of our current economic and military lead. And they recount their dependence on our consumer market for their growing employment. Everything points to their intent to be a responsible, unaggressive world player—except their actions.

If those in the world who look forward to greater balance with the United States hope it will come from Russia or the jihadists, they will surely regret it if they get their wish. Russia's paranoia, autocracy, and repression of civil liberties do not mix with liberty and democracy—it endeavors, in fact, to eliminate them. And the jihadists seek to kill us, to enslave us, or to consign us to a twenty-first-century Dark Ages. North Korea and Iran also rush to narrow our military lead. By devoting a massive share of their economic wealth toward the development of nuclear weaponry, they aspire to hold a nuclear knife to our throat.

Before any of us extols the approach of an era of decay of America's relative power, as President Obama did at the United Nations in September 2009, we must consider what our strength has meant to the world, and what its decline would presage.

In 1975, only a quarter of all countries were electoral democracies in which their citizens were guaranteed civil liberties. Today, almost half the nations in the world are free. Billions of people have been lifted from poverty thanks to the defeat of totalitarianism, to the promulgation of the principles of freedom and free enterprise we pioneered, and to the growing access to free markets. In all these arenas, America's leadership has been indispensable.

"We are well advanced into an unformed era in which new and unfamiliar enemies are gathering forces," counseled the late congressman Henry Hyde, "where a phalanx of aspiring competitors must inevitably constrain and focus our options. In a world where the ratios of strength narrow, the consequences of miscalculation will become progressively more debilitating." Yet, as we have seen, miscalculations abound: too much spending and debt; too little investment in our defense; too little support for our friends and allies; too much foreign oil; too large a burden of entitlements and health care; too easy an acceptance of failure in our homes and schools. The miscalculations persist, in part, because we don't add them up and weigh their collective toll, and because there is passing political advantage in minimizing them or discounting them completely.

Forecasting America's Strength

During the 1930s, economists began compiling a series of figures they hoped would predict the future direction of the American economy. Today, the Composite Index of Leading Indicators is composed of ten components, from weekly jobless claims to building permits to consumer sentiment. Particularly when several indicators move in the same direction as the overall index, it provides "useful signals about the likely direction of the economy," according to the Conference Board's 2004 report, *Using Cyclical Indicators*. However, the predictive value of the index can be trusted only for the very short term—a period of months or a couple of years at the most.

I believe that we could also identify useful signals that would inform us of conditions that are likely to exist over a much longer time horizon, from twenty-five to fifty years. Specifically, these markers would help us gauge the extent of America's economic and military lead in the more distant future, thereby shedding light as well on the prospects for world peace, prosperity, and freedom. We might call it the Index of *Leading* Leading Indicators, and it would forecast America's strength and thus the prospects of global progress. Such an index ought to include the following indicators, described below in the order in which I've presented them in this book:

1. *The Prevalence of Freedom.* What proportion of the world's nations, population, and GDP are in countries that maintain electoral democracy and civil liberties? The global reach of freedom clearly has an impact on our nation's security and safety, but it also affects our and the world's economy: the more freedom, the more the opportunity for trade and productivity, and the more we and others prosper. Over the past fifty years, the number of free countries has more than doubled, but recently the trend has reversed. Freedom House reports that from 2007 to 2009, four times as many nations have experienced reductions in their freedoms as those countries that saw advances.

2. *National Security Assessment.* How do America's military capabilities compare with those of other military-minded nations and with threat groups like the jihadists? Is *accurately calculated* U.S. defense spending at least twice that of either China or Russia? What is the extent of our nuclear vulnerability to North Korea, Iran, and other rogue nations or entities, and are we capable of keeping ourselves safe from their deep malevolence? How militarily capable are democracies like Japan, the countries of the European Union, India, and Canada? While America maintains a significant military lead, the Obama administration's planned spending reductions—despite ever greater threats from abroad—suggest that we are becoming less secure. In fact, the retreat from missile defense by the president is sufficient reason to conclude that this indicator is falling.

3. *Relative Productivity.* What is America's productivity relative to major economies like those of China, Japan, Korea, Germany, and France? Because our productivity is currently the highest among our rivals, our average income, standard of living, and GDP are also the highest. But political forces are at work that could sharply affect our productivity, including protectionism, expansion of union demands and power, the rising taxation of capital, and the growing disfavor of free enterprise. A 2009 Rasmussen poll found that 33 percent of Americans under thirty prefer socialism to capitalism. If our economic competitors continue to move to the right and we move to the left, our productivity advantage will decline.

4. *Relative GDP and Growth Rate.* Our economy is still the largest in the world; China's population and growth rate, however, mean that it will pass us by the middle of this century.

5. *Trade Share of the GDP.* How large a share of our economy is represented by exports, and how much by imports? Which of the two is growing the fastest and how large is the trade gap between them? High levels of trade represent opportunity for American businesses and entrepreneurs, more plentiful jobs for American workers, and better value for consumers.

6. *Relative Market Shares in Growing, Traded-Product Industries.* Are American companies the leaders in the fastest-growing and emerging fields, particularly in products and services that are exported and traded around the world? And, are these companies gaining or losing market share relative to their international competitors? Sadly, American companies have lost their competitive advantage in a number of industries: aircraft, semiconductors, mobile phones, consumer electronics, copiers, cameras, musical instruments, marine products, shipbuilding, textiles—and the list goes on. Fortunately, we lead in some of the fastest-growing industries like biotech and pharmaceuticals, software, data storage, defense products, entertainment, and financial services.

7. *Innovation Index.* How many Ph.D.s currently graduate in math, science, and other growth-sector disciplines compared with our economic rivals? Once the leader, we now follow in this area. How many Ph.D. immigrants are we attracting to the United States each

year? What is the extent of private and public investment in basic science and research? Here, too, we have pulled back. What is the level of taxation on innovation relative to other nations? Unfortunately, U.S. capital gains taxes are slated to rise.

8. *National Debt and Liabilities.* Our national debt is projected to grow by $9 trillion over the next decade—more in ten years than in the last two hundred years. According to *USA Today,* in 2008 alone, the federal government added $6.8 trillion to the total of our national liabilities, bringing the year-end figure to $63.8 trillion— almost five times as large as the national economy. This federal obligation represents $546,688 "owed" by each American household. Unless entitlements are reformed and the federal budget reined in, these obligations will continue to sharply expand, absolutely and as a percentage of the GDP.

9. *Tax Bite.* What is the level of federal, state, and local taxes as a percentage of the GDP? Historically, the federal burden has ranged between 18 percent and 20 percent of the GDP, but spending plans, entitlement growth, and resistance to U.S. borrowing levels may lead Washington to break through this level, creating an even greater tax burden with all its attendant repercussions.

10. *Health-care Funding Gap.* We spend about 6 percent of the GDP more on health care than other developed countries: 7.4 percent more than the United Kingdom, 7.2 percent more than Japan, 5.3 percent more than Canada, 6.8 percent more than Italy, and 4.8 percent more than France—and *that 6 percent gap alone* represents an annual amount that is greater than the 3.8 percent of the GDP that we spend each year on national defense. Given that our health and mortality rates are comparable with these nations, this funding gap represents a very large burden on the economy, and President Obama's government takeover of health care will cause this figure to rise.

11. *Energy Burden.* What percentage of total energy consumption and percentage of the GDP are our energy imports? Both figures have risen sharply over the last two decades

12. *Children Born Out of Wedlock.* This is perhaps the most reliable predictor of the future education level of the population, as well as

an indicator of future social ills. The number of children born out of wedlock continues to climb alarmingly.

13. *Relative Educational Attainment.* What is the quality of the education that American students receive in comparison with those of other countries? What is the extent of the achievement gap for minorities? What proportion of our immigrants have attained high school, college, or advanced degrees?

14. *Citizen Engagement.* What percentage of eligible voters actually vote? How many minutes or hours per day do people spend reading the news and informing themselves about important issues, as measured by Nielsen ratings, Internet hits, and newspaper and magazine circulation? What is the level of our citizens' patriotism, respect for human life, work ethic, obedience to law, and willingness to sacrifice?.

My index is pretty easy to criticize, of course. It takes no obvious account of a host of important additional factors that will have an impact on America's future strength—but that's in the nature of indices. This particular index is simply meant to help us anticipate the future level of America's prosperity and security. It doesn't necessarily tell us much about the income gap between the wealthiest and the poor among us. It doesn't predict the level of racial, ethnic, gender, or religious discrimination in our country. And it doesn't say much about the health of our environment. These are important topics in their own right. But our national strength is vital to our ability to continue to address and make progress in each of those areas. The disparity between poor and rich and between the weak and the powerful is greatest in poor nations, where discrimination can become genocidal, and where the environment is not given even a passing thought. Real progress is more possible in strong nations with growing vibrant economies and in nations protected by strong friends. That's one reason why a strong America deserves our applause, not our apology.

The results from this index are cause for real concern. When you examine each of its components, you see that almost every one is trending in the wrong direction. Concern, in fact, is too soft a word; *alarm* is more apt—the trends are so alarming that we must take action. Now. Yet Washington appears not only to be sanguine about our decline, it actually is pursuing policies that would make matters even worse. Each policy decision has its rationale, of course, but consider the effects of bigger deficits, new entitlements, increasing the power of union CEOs, raising taxes, shrinking military spending, enabling out-of-wedlock births, promoting pseudo-reforms in education, and restraining free trade. If we continue down the current path by enacting policies that further weaken us, the very real prospect is that America will be surpassed by another nation or nations. The consequences of inaction are dangerous to the country and especially to its next generation, our children and grandchildren. Fortunately, there is time for us to take corrective action.

A Conversation with a Friend

Despite my affiliation with the Republican Party, I don't think of myself as highly partisan. Neither party can claim 100 percent of the good ideas. As governor, I worked with a number of thoughtful and capable Democrats, and appointed a few to positions of significance in my administration. All that said, I am having a more and more difficult time understanding how so many people who basically agree with views such as those I have expressed in this book nevertheless choose to be Democrats. I know that neither party has all the answers, that both parties have their share of bad actors, and that each has been known to fall short of its principles. But in light of the challenges faced by the country, I am puzzled by those who align themselves with a political agenda that may be well intentioned, but that weakens the country and hazards our freedom.

First, however, there are people who correctly presume that they will get more money from government if it is run by Democrats. I understand these kinds of Democrats very well. Adam Lerrick of the American Enterprise Institute calculated for *The Wall Street Journal* that under candidate Obama's tax plan, 49 percent of all Americans will pay *no* income tax. Added to that number are another 11 percent who would pay federal income tax of less than 5 percent of their income. So for 60 percent of Americans, spending restraint and lower taxes championed by Republicans may not mean a great deal to them personally—at least in the short term, even though lower taxes promote economic growth, good jobs and higher incomes in the long term.

I also understand the position of Democrats who feel that the Republican Party has dragged its feet on civil rights or on social issues they feel are critically important. However, I believe that my party long ago caught up on civil rights, and many Republicans like my dad were never behind to begin with. And on certain social issues, such as the importance of life and marriage, we'll just have to agree to disagree.

The Democratic voters I have a hard time understanding are those who don't have a personal financial interest at stake or who don't vote solely on the basis of a social issue.

Just a few days ago, I sat down with a good friend who happens to be a Democrat. He's highly educated, reasonably well informed, and financially secure. I asked him why he's not a Republican—not to debate him, but to try to better understand him. Abortion came up. So did gun rights—he's never owned a gun and really hasn't given much thought to the Second Amendment. And he said that he doesn't like the "influence" of religious conservatives in my party. But he said these issues were mostly about image and cosmetics.

His comment reminded me of a lunch I had in 2006 with a famous Hollywood actor who will remain nameless. He admitted that it would be devastating to his image if he were seen as anything other than a liberal Democrat. Then, he added with a smile, "but no one knows how I vote." I wonder how many people choose to be Democrats, as he does, because it's a better fit in their social circle? Of course, something similar also happens on our side of the aisle. But given everything that is at stake, it's past the time for choosing parties and candidates based on image.

As my friend and I continued our discussion, he mentioned the environment, and it turned out that we largely agree on environmental issues. He doesn't like cap-and-trade any more than I do, and he acknowledged that he lines up with so-called green Republicans, who are really just Teddy Roosevelt conservationists, more than with the extreme environmentalists in his own party. He isn't in favor of higher taxes, but he believes Republicans make taxes too big an issue. "Raising capital gains from 15 percent to 20 percent," he argued, "isn't as big a deal as you make it out to be." But he agreed with my opposition to the death tax, calling it "clearly unfair." As we ran through the issues, we found ourselves more and more in agreement, especially on the threats to America from our rivals and enemies. When my friend had run out of explanations for why he's not a Republican, I took the opportunity to explain to him why I am.

I began with my observations about the importance of America remaining the strong and leading nation in the world—and he agreed with them. Then I noted each of the major positions of the Democratic Party, pointing out the weakening effect I believe each of them would have on our future. In education, the Democratic Party is so allied with the teachers' unions that it cannot adopt the reforms that would close the achievement gap and elevate our student performance; instead, it simply endeavors to send more money to the same schools to do the same things that have failed in the past.

We agreed on the need to increase productivity to strengthen the economy and raise incomes. With that, I noted that the Democratic Party is so beholden to labor union leaders that it is advancing productivity suicide by promoting a plan to remove a worker's right to a secret ballot, virtually paving the way for worker intimidation and the imposition of unions throughout big and small business. The impact of such a measure on small business and on entrepreneurship would be catastrophic. He couldn't argue with that, or with the fact that productivity is also burdened by the Democrats' obligations to trial lawyers, some of whom prey on employers with frivolous, megamillion-dollar lawsuits, which provide little benefit to the aggrieved plaintiffs but millions in fees for the lawyers.

I acknowledged that each party has special interests. For many Republicans, for example, nothing is more important than preserving the constitutional guarantee of the right to bear arms or than protecting unborn life. I support both of these "special interests" and pointed out to my friend that even though he disagreed with both of them, they do not weaken the economy or put our nation's future in jeopardy. His party's special interests, on the other hand, would do just that.

The Democratic Party is obsessed with spending more, borrowing more, and taxing more, all of which sap our national strength, I contended. But my friend pointed out that the Republican Party wasn't much better when we held the reins in Washington. I had to agree, at least with respect to spending and borrowing. But we also count among our ranks a good number of spending hawks. They are on the ascendancy in my party, in fact, and are in line with long-standing Republican philosophy. The party is returning to its roots as the party of fiscal discipline. My friend acknowledged that there are many more spending hawks in the GOP than have ever existed or will exist in the Democratic Party.

My friend's party inaugurated and still defends, against all evidence and experience, the welfare policies that created a culture of poverty, diminished our work ethic, and promoted out-of-wedlock births. These effects continue when Democrats resist welfare work requirements or safety-net reforms that would compel unwed fathers to care for their children.

I ran through the undeniable litany of Democratic mistakes since sweeping to power in the elections of 2008. The party leadership is apparently convinced that government knows best. Rather than reform health care by making it more consumer-oriented, it seeks to make ours a single-payer system. Rather than distribute shares in General Motors to the public, it prefers the idea of guiding the company from Washington. And rather than adopt a stimulus bill that would create new jobs in the private sector, it has funded the largest increase in government programs and government jobs in memory. Free enterprise strengthens America, freewheeling government does not, but the Democrats seem almost to fear and distrust markets and free enterprise.

I pointed out that his party has retreated from support of missile defense, perhaps our single most effective protection from rogue nations such as North Korea. Democrats are cutting military spending to make way for domestic priorities and social programs.

I concluded with the observation that on almost every policy issue that would have an impact on our nation's strength, his party chooses the course of weakness. It justifies the choice by insisting that it is attempting to help the disadvantaged, but in reality, surely the most important thing we can do for the disadvantaged is to sustain a strong, prosperous, and safe America. Too often, I fear, the Democratic Party is focused less on the disadvantaged than on union bosses, trial lawyers, environment extremists, and the self-interested who want higher government benefits for themselves paid for by higher taxes on others.

I didn't convert my longtime friend. I didn't really expect to, at least not that day. Arguments have to be advanced day in and day out to make progress in this media-charged world. Over and over again we have to make the central point that I made with my friend: If the special interests that control the Democratic Party have their way, they will make America less strong, less secure, less able to generate the highest standard of living for all our citizens, and less able to protect our freedom. The Republicans aren't perfect—far from it, of course—but ours is a party committed to strength and prosperity for all Americans.

A Force for Good

There is good and evil in the world. Many do not agree; they dismiss such a claim as simplistic and moralistic. From their point of view, people and nations do not act from altruistic empathy, sacrificing self for others. They believe humankind is incapable of choosing anything but self-interest. As they see it, there is no good per se, only selfish acts with beneficent by-products.

Rather than recognize inherent evil, they ascribe aberrant and destructive behavior to the influence of a warped society. Change the society, they maintain, and people will behave. They ascribe the conduct of rogue nations to the distortions brought about by past imperialism and exploitation. For such nations, they withhold judgment. For their own United States, on the other hand, they often have little good to say.

In a world with neither good nor evil, no one needs to account for his actions or acknowledge heroism in another. There is no place in their worldview for self-assessment, judgment, or aspiration. They insist that the people I would label evil are simply misunderstood. Everyone, they believe, shares "common interests"; everyone is just as good as everyone else. This is the perspective of many of those in power in Washington today. It underpins a foreign policy that draws us closer to accommodation and appeasement of the world's worst actors.

As this worldview has developed and spread, it has sapped our collective judgment and our willingness to speak candidly about the world in which we live. The label "evil" sends many into outbursts of indignation on behalf of the "simply misunderstood," who, they believe, are fully capable of joining the community of human kindness and acting responsibly, if only we would use "carrots instead of sticks."

I don't think so. From the beginning of recorded history, we have seen too much evil to be persuaded by sophistry of the sort that dominates much of the Beltway conversation these days. The most influential book in history recounts events that are intended to teach about the harsh realities of the world:

Cain killed Abel, not because of a broken home but because of evil jealousy. Pharaoh brutally repressed the Jews, and centuries later, Herod would kill their firstborn sons. These two rulers were not twisted by circumstance, but by their evil lust for power. The same kind of lust has driven murderous tyrants from Stalin to Saddam, leaving literally millions of their own countrymen in their wake. Only the notion of evil can explain Hitler. And during my lifetime alone, I have witnessed Idi Amin, Milošević, al Bashir, Hussein, Mao, Pol Pot, and bin Laden, who have collectively been responsible for the death of millions. Like author John Steinbeck, "I believe there are monsters born in the world to human parents. . . . The face and the body may be perfect, but if a twisted gene or a malformed egg can produce physical monsters, may not the same process produce a malformed soul?"

Evil has been with us from the beginning of time, and it is not going away. Indeed, technology means it is very close. Today, the available means of creating horror are even more deadly than ever before.

I submit that it is vital to believe in evil—it is neither confused nor deterred by vacuous introspection. We should study what is said and written by evil men, and take them at their word. Adolf Hitler told the world exactly what his aspirations were in *Mein Kampf* and in his speeches, but at first the world dismissed his claims as political bluster. Osama bin Laden's declarations of war against the United States didn't make the news until he had killed thousands of our fellow citizens. Today, Kim Jong-il and Mahmoud Ahmadinejad hurl bellicose rants—Kim threatening to use nuclear weapons offensively, and Ahmadinejad denying the awful reality of the Holocaust even as he opens the door to a new one and uses Western confusion about his motives to make possible his murderous ambition. "Our dear Imam [Ayatollah Khomeini] said that the occupying regime [in Israel] must be wiped off the map and this was a very wise statement," Ahmadinejad exhorted at the 2005 World Without Zionism conference. "I have no doubt that the new wave that has started in Palestine, and we witness it in the Islamic world too, will eliminate this disgraceful stain from the Islamic world."

Wall Street Journal contributor Michael Ledeen has warned that "the world is simmering in the familiar rhetoric and actions of movements and regimes—from Hezbollah and al Qaeda to the Iranian Khomeinists and the Saudi Wahhabis—who swear to destroy us and others like us." I agree.

These are evil men and they have made it very clear what they intend to do to us and to our allies. The challenge of our time is not to deny the threat, but to soberly and swiftly pursue the policies that will defeat it.

American Greatness

There are also good people and good nations. At great risk to themselves, many Danes valiantly helped Jews escape from the Nazis who occupied their country. The Australians, Canadians, British, Poles, Czechs, and many others engage wherever freedom needs defenders. And then there are our fellow Americans.

It is not uncommon to hear an American claim that the United States is the greatest nation on earth and the hope of the world. My European friends have confessed that they find this sentiment both naive and offensive, and when a Canadian colleague chided me for making the statement, I said that I was sorry he had been offended. But I did not say I was sorry for having said it—because I believe it. Given all that I have witnessed in my lifetime, and all the history I have read, I cannot *not* say it. I am proud to be an American. It is long past the time to begin again to proclaim the absolute truth of American greatness and its singular purpose and calling in the world as the protector and defender of human freedom and human dignity.

Most of us presume that modern history begins at the time of our own birth. I was born in March of 1947. The Second World War had recently ended, but it remained a major presence in many people's lives, including those of every member of my family. During the war, my father had been charged with coordinating wartime production in Detroit's auto factories, and many of my friends' fathers had served in the armed forces in Europe or the Pacific. Ann's father and my sister Lynn's husband had been in the navy. Throughout the 1950s, World War II was regularly the subject of Hollywood movies and radio and television documentaries. The details of that epic struggle made up the conversations around my family's dining room table. Mom and Dad talked often about the war, about FDR and Churchill and about our generals Ike and Douglas MacArthur, about Pearl Harbor, D-Day, and the battles of the Pacific and the surge toward Berlin.

To most Americans today, I suppose, that war is ancient history. But not to me. I can still hear those conversations.

When I served my church in France during my college years, I made a trip to Normandy to see the beaches where our soldiers had come ashore to begin the liberation of Europe. It was a gray and windy day, and looking out from Utah Beach toward the English Channel, I felt waves of melancholy, but little grief. Then I saw the cemetery—acre on acre of perfectly aligned rows of crosses and stars of David. I was overwhelmed with a consuming sorrow for the young and promising lives that were so quickly extinguished, and I felt enormous gratitude for the goodness and the sacrifice of these men. As I walked among the graves, I experienced alternating waves of sadness and thankfulness.

The valor of America's men and women in uniform did not end with that war. They have served the cause of freedom in Korea, Vietnam, the Persian Gulf, Afghanistan, and Iraq, as well as in Lebanon, the Dominican Republic, Grenada, Panama, Somalia, the Philippines, Liberia, Kosovo, and many unnamed places around the globe where we have sent our men and women to serve freedom's cause in complete anonymity. During these conflicts, critics have always trumpeted charges that America had sinister motives. China accused the United States of intervening in Kosovo as a colonial effort to control Europe. Critics at home and abroad claimed that we entered Kuwait and then Iraq to secure oil for ourselves, yet we left after the first Gulf War and we still buy oil like every other country, even after we were obliged to return and topple Saddam for good. For the trillions of dollars those conflicts cost, we could have bought a lot more oil than either country will ever send us.

The critics may bellow, but "facts are stubborn things." During my lifetime, America has paid very dearly in blood and treasure to secure freedom for ourselves and to win freedom for others. We have taken no colonies, only cemeteries where we have buried our dead.

The greatness of America lies not simply in what we have done with our power; it is also informed by what we have *not* done with our power. For more than a quarter century, America's military prowess has dwarfed that of any other nation. We could have crushed nations that posed future threats or seized control of the Persian Gulf's oil. These and scores of other actions we neither did nor even considered doing. So deep is restraint and goodness etched in our collective character that the abuse of our power is never even on the table or in the back of our minds. To those who are sanguine about the "decline of America and the West," ask how many other nations or world actors would have exercised such restraint had they enjoyed such power.

My appreciation for America flows in part from our national sacrifice and forbearance. And it also comes from individual Americans, men and women whose humanity is as inspiring as our history. The first summer my family and I spent at Lake Winnipesaukee in New Hampshire is one I still remember well. We attended church in Wolfeboro on the first Sunday after our arrival, and halfway through the service, an elderly woman in the row in front of us began to tremble, slowly at first and then violently. She was quite crippled, and as her elderly husband helped her stand to leave, I asked if they needed help. When he turned to decline my offer, I saw he was blind. He simply smiled and said, "We'll do fine by ourselves: she's the eyes and I'm the legs."

Robert Sterling lost his eyes in World War II, as well as a good deal of his hearing. Over the course of our summers in New Hampshire, I have watched him with interest and with reverence. He has memorized the 169-word sacrament prayers so he can take his turn administering it to the congregation. He makes comments from time to time in Sunday school and he acknowledges those who take his hand to say hello. I have never witnessed any bitterness, never heard a word of self-pity. He feels fortunate, he says, because he had many friends who never came home from the war that cost him so much. And the things he has lived for since the war have filled his life: his wife, his faith, and his country. His has been the face of service and sacrifice from that war, multiplied more than a million times. Like so many others of the greatest generation, he has now passed on.

As governor, I asked Tom Kelley to head the Massachusetts Department of Veterans Affairs. At sixty-four, he was the oldest member of my cabinet, and he was also the first Congressional Medal of Honor recipient I had come to know personally. One afternoon in June 1969, Lieutenant Kelley led eight river assault craft in a mission to rescue a company of soldiers pinned down against the bank of a canal in Vietnam. In the process of landing, one of the boats became disabled. Tom directed the remaining craft to circle the crippled boat, placing his own in the direct line of enemy fire. When a rocket hit his boat, shrapnel tore away a portion of his face and skull, and he lost an eye. He could no longer speak well enough to issue radio commands, but lying on the deck, he whispered his directions to one of his sailors, who in turn broadcast them to the others until at last the enemy was silenced and the boats and soldiers were safely evacuated. Like every other Medal of Honor recipient I have since met, Tom is humble and service-oriented, an example of how to live, given by someone willing to lose his life for others. Since the battle in which he was wounded, Tom has had many surgeries, but the injuries he suffered will never be completely disguised. I have not seen him wear his Congressional Medal, but his face is a profound emblem of honor.

> *O beautiful for heroes proved*
> *In liberating strife.*
> *Who more than self their country loved*
> *And mercy more than life!*

The American spirit is just as evident at home as it has been on the battlefield. From time to time in the weeks leading up to the 2002 Winter Olympics, I caught up with the Olympic torch as it made its way across the country. In New York City, the torch sailed on a ferry to the base of the Statue of Liberty. On board were families of police and firefighters, each of whom had lost loved ones in the World Trade Center attack. They gathered at the bow of the boat, taking turns holding the torch high, just as Lady Liberty did, silhouetted behind them. As they hugged and cried and sang "God Bless America," I remember thinking to myself, yes, He does bless America—with noble and courageous souls like those we had gathered to honor. These were the families of those who had rushed *into* the towers, who had *mounted* the stairs in hopes of rescuing those who had been left behind.

In May 1999, a devastating tornado hit Oklahoma City. A friend was watching the news. He turned to his wife and announced, "I am going to do something for those people—it will take days for FEMA to get there." His wife reminded him that they lived a thousand miles from Oklahoma City, that they didn't have anything those people needed, and that they didn't have enough money to buy those things. Undaunted, he went out to his van and drove it to a nearby bakery, where a sympathetic owner and employees helped him pack the van with donated bread that he was determined to drive to Oklahoma. When a local radio station broadcast the story, people began to arrive with more food, clothing, and plastic tarps for him to take as well. A semitrailer truck arrived, and *it* was filled to the brim before his little caravan got under way. When they arrived unannounced at barricades outside the city, police simply waved them through.

Ann's brother Jim lives in San Diego, and among his friends at church are Gary and Valerie Sabin, parents of five children, three of whom they discovered were born with cystic fibrosis. Their eldest son passed away when he was just nineteen, and not long thereafter, Jim heard that their daughter Jennifer was doing very poorly. She wouldn't live much longer unless a lung donor was found who matched her tissue type. Jim volunteered to be tested, and he was a match. Within days, two-thirds of his left lung had been successfully transplanted into Jennifer's body. She has since married and is doing well, although she will always struggle with her disease.

> *And crown thy good with brotherhood*
> *From sea to shining sea!*

Given the challenges that America faces and the fact that so few of our leaders recognize them and are committed to doing something about them, it's understandable that some of us become discouraged—and fearful. But I am not. I have seen the greatness of the American spirit time and again. We can be counted on to rise to the occasion. We are willing to sacrifice ease and comfort to help others, defend the nation, advance learning, and provide a bright legacy for those who follow us.

Some years ago, I traveled to Weston, Massachusetts, to attend a Boy Scout Court of Honor, the ceremony at which scouts receive Eagle awards and other honors. Because I was serving a lay leadership assignment for my church, I was invited to sit at the end of the head table, next to the flag stand. The speaker was a scoutmaster from Monument, Colorado, who described how his troop had purchased an American flag that they hoped they could make especially meaningful. First, they succeeded in having it flown above the U.S. Capitol, and then they petitioned NASA to see if it could be taken aboard the space shuttle. Astronauts can hardly fill the shuttle with souvenirs, but NASA officials said they would be happy to take the flag onboard the shuttle's next mission. The speaker described how excited and proud his scouts were as they watched on television as the shuttle lifted into the sky with their flag. And then *Challenger* exploded.

The scoutmaster grieved with his scouts and with his country. He explained to us that he telephoned NASA a few weeks later, asking if any remnant of the flag had been found. He had hoped to honor the astronauts who had been lost by honoring that remnant. No trace of the flag had been found, his NASA contacts told him. He called every week from February until May, always receiving the same answer. Then in September he read an article listing the debris that had ultimately been found from the *Challenger* disaster, which included a flag. He called NASA once more and officials confirmed that the scout troop's flag had been recovered, and arrangements were made to return it to Colorado.

The flag had been carried next to a number of souvenir medallions from other service groups like the scouts; when recovered, these had melted into a single lump of metal.

At the ceremony, the troop was presented with a container—a plastic bag in which the flag had been carried. When they opened it, they found their flag inside, entirely intact, free of any damage whatsoever.

"And that's the flag on the flagpole at the end of the table," the scoutmaster said.

With no small emotion, I grasped the corner of the flag and held it out so everyone present could see it. I suddenly felt as if electricity was coursing through my arm. I thought of the lives risked and lost, of the courage of the *Challenger* crew, and of the grief of their families. I thought of the pioneering spirit of astronauts, willing to explore new frontiers of knowledge and to further the lead of the United States. Along the border of the flag, the scouts had embroidered, *CHALLENGER,* JANUARY 28, 1986.

It is America's abundance of people of character, goodness, and sacrifice that merit the protection of Providence and that preserve America's greatness.

> *America! America!*
> *God shed His grace on thee . . .*

Epilogue

W hen Ann finished reading the manuscript for this book, she insisted that I gather the primary recommendations from each chapter and restate them as plainly as I could. These include only those subjects considered in the book, and as such, do not include every important policy. Many critical areas are not addressed here, including Homeland Security, conservation, intelligence policies, agriculture, national infrastructure, and communications policy.

There are three pillars that sustain a free and strong America:

1. A Strong Economy
2. A Strong Military
3. A Free and Strong People

The action steps to secure each of these include those noted in the Agenda, below.

AGENDA FOR A FREE AND STRONG AMERICA

1. Promote small business and entrepreneurship (with lower taxes, especially where there is "double taxation," by eliminating outdated

and burdensome regulations, by refusing to impose unions on employees, and by enacting tort reform)

2. Stop the trillion-dollar deficits, and spend only what we have. No more borrowing for unnecessary "nice to have" government programs.

3. Publish an annual balance sheet for the country

4. Adopt dynamic regulations

5. Reduce and simplify taxes, especially double taxes that depress job creation. Do not allow taxes to be raised.

6. Adopt a "strong dollar" strategy, including spending restraint and entitlement sustainability reforms

7. Reform entitlements to make them sustainable in the long term and to honor all the promises that have been made to our seniors

8. Adopt an annual budget process for entitlements

9. Reform tort liability to reduce the burden of frivolous lawsuits

10. Stop any new "government-growing" stimulus program

11. Get the government out of General Motors—and other private companies

12. Increase our investment in science and basic research

13. Promote trade and American goods and services, insisting on intellectual property protection

14. Protect the right of workers to vote by secret ballot

15. Establish incentive and employer-based job-training programs to help people find new and sustainable employment

16. Reform immigration to attract and retain talent, simplify the legal processes, and end illegal immigration

17. Encourage shareholders and boards of directors to adopt reasonable compensation and long-term incentives for CEOs and executives

18. Encourage the measurement of corporate CEOs and union CEOs on the basis of teamwork, productivity, and long-term success of the enterprise

19. Test and enact consumer-market-like incentives in health care, at the state and federal level, including HSAs, co-insurance options, single-fee structures, etc.

20. Let states craft their own programs to insure the uninsured, providing flexibility in the use of federal funds that already go to the states

21. Enable insurers to establish incentives for healthy living and preventative care

22. Reform medical malpractice

23. Reform nuclear regulations to provide safety, not to block nuclear plants

24. Build new nuclear power plants

25. Promote coal and coal CO_2 sequestration technology

26. Promote natural gas and establish the infrastructure for it to fuel power plants and transportation fleets—immediately

27. Explore and develop new oil and gas wells, off and onshore

28. Develop, test, and promote incentives to encourage energy efficiency investments by private and public users

29. Establish a comprehensive energy security plan—a "no-regrets plan"—that frees us from dependence on oil oligopolists and that reduces our emissions of greenhouse gases

30. Endeavor to establish global international energy and greenhouse gas policies that reduce both greenhouse gas emissions and global dependence on oil

31. Establish an Index of Leading Leading Indicators to measure America's long-term strength

32. Stand by our allies and friends including Colombia, Israel, Poland, the Czech Republic, Georgia, Ukraine, etc.

33. Fast-track NATO admission of our friends

34. Promote and defend democracy and Western values around the world, including in Honduras and Iran

35. Deploy far-greater soft-power resources, with accountability, budgets, and regional envoys

36. End the practice of pursuing meaningless agreements that will not be honored by others

37. Establish a forum for democracies to collaborate and promote freedom, using NATO as a foundation

38. Maintain a defense budget of at least 4 percent of our GDP, and at

least twice the *actual and comparable* military spending of either Russia or China

39. Add at least 100,000 troops to our ground forces; provide top quality care and benefits to our veterans

40. Immediately replace and repair essential equipment and armament that has been lost in conflicts

41. Update our nuclear deterrent

42. Do not agree to reduce our nuclear capabilities such that we fall behind Russia; consider their "tactical" nukes

43. Expand our commitment to missile defense

44. Return our navy and air force to the levels needed to meet their respective missions

45. Increase our commitment to defend against discontinuities, cyber-attack and space attack.

46. Establish Special Partnership Forces to aid in removing insurgencies

47. Push our allies to carry their fair share of the military requirements

48. Attract top students to become teachers, with higher starting salaries

49. Open pathways into teaching for individuals who have excelled in other fields

50. Pay teachers like the professionals they are, and provide opportunities for advancement and mentoring

51. Promote the use of student-performance measures, and do not prevent the use of these in the evaluation of teacher effectiveness

52. Promote school choice, with vouchers, charter schools, etc.

53. Promote cyber-learning, at school and at home

54. Do not allow teachers' unions to prevent the few ineffective teachers from being removed from the classroom

55. Do not allow teachers' unions to prevent higher pay for better teachers and for those with skills in short supply

56. Encourage states to develop programs that prepare parents of at-risk children for education

57. Promote state and local programs to keep kids in school—teacher bonuses, mentors, curriculum matching, etc.

58. Endeavor to provide the dignity of work in every safety-net pro-

gram where that is possible, even if it costs the government more money to do so

59. Teach our children to love America by teaching our history, by describing our patriots, and by extolling America's greatness as the defender of liberty

60. Teach our children the benefits to them and to their children of getting married before they have babies

61. Remove the marriage penalties from safety-net programs

62. Provide for a father's financial responsibility in the care of his child, even if not married or in the household

63. Reform campaign finance laws to remove the inordinate power of donation gatherers and to prohibit any organization from assessing individuals for political funds

64. Appoint judges that follow the Constitution rather than invent a new one

Acknowledgments

Several people helped me a great deal in preparing this book. A number read the entire book and provided advice, additions, and comment. Ann and my family always began conversations about the book by saying that they really enjoyed it, but then suggested some important revisions—they have learned that "a spoonful of sugar helps the medicine go down." Kerry Healey, my former partner as lieutenant governor, provided her characteristic expert corrections and improvements. Bob White, my career-long wingman, sent me several pages of notes, all designed to help keep me from flying into a mountain. Hugh Hewitt, whom I had met when he interviewed me about my 2008 prospects, offered helpful language, edits, and perspective, undoubtedly gleaned from his listening experiences as a prominent talk-show host. The aptly named Jim Talent, former U.S. senator from Missouri, kindly contributed policy thinking and insights, as he has done for me many times before. Eric Fehrnstrom, my press and communications professional for seven years, made sure that what I wrote accurately reflected what I actually wanted to say. And Beth Myers, my chief of staff when I served as governor and my campaign manager in 2008, read and reread what I wrote, reminding me of relevant experiences to relate, tightening my writing, and providing key insights. She made the book happen.

Kelli Harrison, who has worked with me and with my PAC since its inception, kept the writing, logistics, and research processes on track. She also came up with the title after I had spent at least six months trying.

A number of other people read and helped with select chapters and subject areas. Patrick Connelly, Robert Joseph, and Dave Johnson shared a great deal of their brilliant understanding of military matters. Dr. Walid Phares added and corrected portions related to jihadism, a subject about which he is a widely read and respected author. Mark DeMoss and Peter Flaherty shared with me their perspectives and introduced me to great Evangelical thinkers, who expressed a number of helpful views and thoughts. Greg Mankiw not only sent me a copy of his bestselling economics textbook and introduced me to his blog (gregmankiw.blogspot.com), he also volunteered helpful corrections and supplements. Glenn Hubbard, dean of the Columbia Business School, added a number of thoughtful perspectives, particularly regarding the human impact of productivity and economic vitality. I learned a great deal from Robert Kagan, Fred Kagan, and Kim Kagan, each of whom is a vital national resource in matters relating to foreign and military policy. Tim Murphy, my former secretary of health and human services, and Cindy Gillespie, my former state director of policy and legislative affairs, provided their unique expertise on health-care policies. Paul Stringer added his perspective from years as a health-care industry analyst. Risa Kaplan led my research on education, and Bob Costrell and David Porreca helped with materials and perspectives. Matthew Faraci was kind enough to help with research on competitiveness. L. E. Simmons helped bring me up-to-date on the developments in the world of energy. Muneer Satter, an accomplished business leader himself, focused attention on global economic and productivity measures and their impact on consumers. Dan Senor and Pete Wehner sharpened my appreciation of the dangers presented by the shift in our foreign policy. Ambassador Mitchell Reiss has exposed me to foreign policy leaders, thinkers, and players and offered his own expert views of events and dynamics. David Weinstein, formerly of Fidelity Investments, helped organize my treatment of the national economy.

Peter Matson's expertise as an agent served me particularly well, as did the support of his assistant, Rebecca Friedman. Russell Martin, the accomplished author of several books, edited my writing from the beginning of the project, and St. Martin's George Witte, with help from copy editor Helen Chin, edited it one more time at the end. Sarah Lenti, a policy fixture in D.C., was my lead researcher over the entire period. Risa Kaplan, Ted Newton, and Chris McInerney were so kind to take time off so that they could do the critical work of fact-checking, as well as corrections and edits.

To all of these friends, I owe a great deal.

I also owe a great deal to the scholarship of the many others on whose work I relied upon for facts and figures. In some cases, their names and work were cited in my text. In particular, I am appreciative of the material and perspectives of the scholars at research centers such as the Heritage Foundation, the American Enterprise Institute, the Hoover Institution, the Pioneer Institute, the Cato Institute, and the Brookings Institute. From time to time, on this book's Web site, NoApology.com, I plan to update figures and materials from these and other sources.

Index